CONOR CRUISE O'BRIEN

CONOR CRUISE O'BRIEN
Violent Notions

DIARMUID WHELAN
University College Cork

IRISH ACADEMIC PRESS
DUBLIN • PORTLAND, OR

First published in 2009 by Irish Academic Press

2 Brookside,
Dundrum Road,
Dublin 14,
Ireland

920 NE 58th Avenue, Suite 300
Portland, Oregon,
97213-3786
USA

www.iap.ie

British Library Cataloguing in Publication Data
An entry can be found on request

ISBN 978 0 7165 2865 4 (cloth)

Library of Congress Cataloging-in-Publication Data
An entry can be found on request

Printed by CPI Antony Rowe, Chippenham, Wiltshire

Contents

Acknowledgements   vii

Introduction   ix

PART I: CONOR CRUISE O'BRIEN: THE MAN

1. Dispossession: O'Brien's Family and the Irish Revolution   3
2. Father   17
3. Mother   31
4. Owen: the Sheehy Skeffington Influence   47
5. Seán O'Faoláin   57
6. Camus   67

PART II: THE MIND OF CONOR CRUISE O'BRIEN

7. Overview   81
8. The Siege   86
9. Religion: Church and State in Ireland   96
10. Histories   109
11. Legitimacy: Violence and Irish History   128
12. O'Brien and Nationalism   152
13. Conclusion: 'Our Greatness with our Violence?'   173

Select Bibliography   185
Index   200

Dedicated with gratitude and love to my mum
Kay Whelan

Acknowledgements

I would like to acknowledge the assistance of the Irish Research Council for Humanities and the Social Sciences for providing me with a post-doctoral fellowship which enabled me to compose a great deal of this book. The College of Arts, Celtic Studies and Social Sciences, UCC also provided funds which assisted in the finalization of the book. I would like to offer thanks also to the many individuals who talked to me about O'Brien and especially to those who allowed me to interview them. Sincere thanks to Mrs Christine Hetherington, Dr Garret FitzGerald, Mr Justin Keating, Justice David Sheehy (Snr), Mr David Sheehy, Mr James Kirwan, Dr David Caute.

I am grateful to the staff at the National Library of Ireland, National Archives, Boole Library UCC, UCD archives, Trinity Archives, Cork City library, the British Library, and especially my colleagues in Manuscripts in the NLI, Gerry Lyne, Peter Kenny, Jenny Doyle and Ciara Kerrigan. A special word of thanks to all in the History Department in UCC, but especially Dermot Keogh, David Ryan, Donal Ó Drisceoil, Hiram Morgan, Gabriel Doherty, Geoff Roberts, Charlotte Holland, Geraldine McAllister, Déirdre O'Sullivan and Dawn French. A word of thanks also to our Head of College, Professor David Cox and to two friends in UCC, Pat Crowley and Eibhear Walshe. Professor David Gwynn Morgan shared some of his insights into O'Brien and kindly commented on an early version of this text. Several individuals through the years – Michele Dowling, Liz Mullins and John Paul McCarthy – also offered advice and observations, while others provided illuminating material, notably Daire Keogh, Felix Larkin and Joe Skelly. Throughout the many years I have had O'Brien on my desk many friends enriched the experience: a collective thank you to Billy, Tina, Labhrás, Padraig, and Elaine Whelan, Pat, Frank, Teddy, Ken and Aiveen Daly, Lorraine Singleton, Benny McCabe, Tom Bradley, Gary O'Flynn, Ronan O'Farrell and David Dillon. I am grateful to Richard

English, Eunan O'Halpin, John Logan, Deirdre McMahon and Michael Kennedy for assistance, advice and a forum. A special thanks also to my editor Lisa Hyde, for her warm attention and impeccable professionalism throughout this entire project, as well as Heather Marchant

I owe a profound debt to Professor Joe Lee who assisted me in so many ways with the original preparation of this work. His insistence on its worth, his energy and his tremendous insights went a long way to formulating all that is valuable in this book.

He won't thank me for singling him out but one friend in particular has been a constant source of insight, stimulus and assistance; he has immeasurably improved a whole host of drafts and closely proofread what must have seemed like endless pages; a very sincere thank you to my good friend (and one of Ireland's brightest) – Ciarán Madden.

To my wife Alex, I offer apologies for bringing this book with me through all the years I've been fortunate to be with you, along with a hope for many, many more together. And finally, as I close the door on O'Brien (maybe), I am overjoyed to turn my attention to a far more perplexing character – my newly arrived son Gabriel!

Diarmuid Whelan
Cork
March 2009

Introduction

Contrary to the view that O'Brien was an 'unimportant, expendable man' (Harold Macmillan), recent obituaries referred to his passing as 'the closing of a chapter in history'.[1] 'Ireland's restless conscience' was gone, and with it Ireland 'lost its greatest 20th-century public intellectual'.[2] Perhaps a little less overdone was the view of Roy Foster that O'Brien was 'the pre-eminent Irish intellectual of his generation',[3] an estimate echoed by *The Telegraph*'s obituary that O'Brien was 'the leading Irish intellectual of his time' (although to say that 'he was revered' in this role misses the majority view on O'Brien).[4] Even a far from uncritical observer remarked that while he was the author of 'just two competent stage plays, Conor Cruise O'Brien was the most important public man of letters Ireland witnessed since W.B. Yeats died in 1939'.[5] Possibly the view that best captures both his stature and mode was Brian Fallon's in *The Guardian*: 'probably the most pugnacious Irish intellectual since George Bernard Shaw'.[6]

While most obituaries passed over the less digestible aspects of his career – the uncritical alliance with Israel and the UKUP – on the whole most of the obituaries were not just appropriately laudatory, but both well considered and informed. However, if there was one issue which might raise a flag, it was the uniformity of approach that explained his life. It went something along the lines of: crash comes the Congo, bang goes the North, and wallop went his political career. The complicated and distinctive background, brilliant academic trajectory, stormy diplomatic career and angry old man of politics, all took a brief bow also. What is unsettling about this is their similarity with O'Brien's self-portrait. All the well chosen anecdotes, jokes, family tableaux and character pieces, as told by O'Brien for the past thirty or so years, were given an airing. It seems as though our appreciation of the keynotes of his career are to a large part generated by O'Brien's own decades long tending of just such a moment when his posterity would make its debut.

What needs to happen now is to begin a new attempt to understand Ireland's foremost intellectual of the past half century. Fundamentally this means that we must come to terms with O'Brien's ideas about Ireland's ideas – the dangerous dynamic between thought and deed – the violent notions of idea and context. To attempt this we must begin with a historical recreation of his life's influences. Enamoured of the view that his thinking is what made him worthy of study, I have attempted to recreate the original context which gave rise to the worldview and series of ideas that now appear inescapably O'Brienish. The approach of this book – to discover rather than re-tell – will attempt to synthesize what O'Brien's private papers, his unpublished writings, his correspondence, his drafts of articles and speeches tell us. All of this material is fused with original portraits of his parents and his immediate family based on their own words and recorded deeds, as well as interviews with a range of contemporaries. An example of what I mean can be seen in the discovery of O'Brien's 'lost book' – *The Story of Ireland*.[7] This was a potted history of Ireland which he penned in the late 1940s as part of the anti-partition propaganda drive of that era. O'Brien would come to disavow this work and the entire approach of anti-partition. However, as one commentator charitably put it, 'for all his later protestations, there is no evidence that he was other than enthusiastic about the policies he helped to propound'.[8]

What is perhaps most interesting about this one-eyed history of Ireland from St Patrick to Seán MacBride is how it forms an almost exact mirror-narrative to his later historical works of the 1990s, when O'Brien was a committed Unionist. While the crusty unionist foil to his nationalist green shoots suggests an obvious conversion, what is worth exploring is a *noticeable similarity in his extremes*. Now this might be hard to discern in the case of a man who excoriated Albert Schweitzer and took a Professorship endowed by Schweitzer a year later. Or there is the uncomfortable case of ripping the 'dismal poltroons' of the Labour party before running as one himself a few years later. More seriously there are quite a few examples thrown up by his intellectual progression from the late 1960s to the 1980s: for example, he once castigated Enoch Powell for his 'sophisticated and modern bigotry'[9] and would go on to share a platform with Powell against the Anglo-Irish agreement of

1985. What one might view as simple wrongheadedness or a change in circumstances, others might castigate as a baseless conversion. Nonetheless, without too much special pleading on his behalf we can divine a fundamental consistency within him. The second part of the book is devoted to critically exploring this possibility.

Perhaps what obscures such an appreciation at the moment is a host of complexities in O'Brien's personality. In one view O'Brien was 'an inveterate controversialist'. 'Rather than search for common ground, he preferred to focus on points of disagreement. It was always an imperative to spell out his views to the full, however impolitic that might be.'[10] In the view of another, 'O'Brien was a maverick, both as a writer and politician ... a fine intellectual led astray into public life by ambition and the desire to prove himself a man of action ... a courageous radical nonconformist who ... ended up as almost a reactionary'.[11] However, a closer inspection of O'Brien reveals another aspect of his character that again is at odds with the image of a lifelong iconoclast.

> One of Conor's most striking characteristics was his deep respect for the mainstream tradition of Irish politics. He had a highly acute sense of what has become so dangerously depreciated in Ireland in the course of the last two decades: the continuities of Irish politics antedating the state, the absolute dependence of the Irish State on the integrity and independence of its political leaders and public servants, and the necessity for intellectual rigour in a parliamentary democracy.[12]

The man who recruited him into the Labour Party, Brendan Halligan, offered a similar appraisal.[13] Halligan spoke not just of O'Brien's loyalty to Brendan Corish, but O'Brien's almost reverential deference for the office of the Taoiseach. Liam Cosgrave was not the leader of a rival political party, but was now the holder of the highest office in the land, and therefore deserving of O'Brien's unswerving loyalty. It was a reverence for the office of Taoiseach which was impressed upon them by Eamon de Valera, and a duty of collective responsibility which O'Brien took very seriously. This is not to say that O'Brien was not also the man who left the UN and who wrote one of the most memorable kick and tells of his generation (*To Katanga and Back*). What it intimates is that he straddles both these opposites – he is as comfortable with hierarchy as he can be anarchical at heart. That understanding – an avoidance of an either/or scenario with O'Brien – is the engine of this book.

When asked what his favourite poem was O'Brien immediately quoted the gloomy prognosis of Yeats's 'Meditations in Time of Civil War':

> We are closed in, and the key is turned
> On our uncertainty; somewhere a man is killed, or a house burned,
> Yet no clear fact to be discerned:
> Come build in the empty house of the stare.[14]

Because of the presence of Yeats in all O'Brien's works I had for some time felt that a link with Yeats's epitaph – 'cast a cold eye' – with an overview of O'Brien's approach would be appropriate. That Yeats is present in all his works is only part of the story. To view O'Brien's contribution as casting 'a cold eye' is central to both his metier and his outlook. To many who have read his writings, watched his public utterances, seen him excoriate enemy and colleague, rail against the IRA or the peace process, the adjective 'cold' allied with his undoubted critical approach probably seems apt. But to those who know him or to those who have read his writings on non-political subjects, or indeed his correspondence, to describe O'Brien as cold is to miss the man entirely. It was a complete (and pleasant) surprise to discover his personal papers having turned over his books and essays for a number of years. While his published material was beautifully written, energetic, splenetic, serious, urgent and challenging, to immerse oneself in his papers was to discover an entirely different individual: warm, engaging, irreverent, assiduous and immensely caring to friends and family. It was hard to suppress the laughter in the small archives room in University College Dublin, and after a while I gave up library norms and caved in to the man's abundant and effortless sense of humour.

Yet it would be a lapse on my part if I plumped entirely for the warm, private individual over the austere public persona. Ultimately it would be a disservice to O'Brien to ignore what he has laboured so long at and the impact of those writings. And while it would be a mistake to try to dissociate the soft family man from the acerbic public one, perhaps the greatest mistake would be to miss not just the combination of these two parts of O'Brien, but to ignore the actual cause of the sundered self that presents itself in both his essays and letters. And at the bottom of his personality fount there lurks a steely intensity that lapses into humour only in respite; that returns again and again to drive an immensely prolific career, or to re-kindle an enmity, to spit out another coruscating

piece to an editor with a barely controlled anger. It is that fundamental
core of O'Brien that we will attempt to gauge here.

Any picture of O'Brien will lend credibility to this. The many images
of him through the years display a far off gaze that is not lost in some
fog, but has fixed on some person, object or thought. It is seen in pic-
tures of him again and again: a slightly uncomfortable individual who,
no matter what the angle, is caught staring rather than seeing. Many of
his friends, like Darcy O'Brien who penned a very warm tribute to him
in O'Brien's *festschrift*,[15] describe a man 'whose conversation is usually
pitched at the exalted, rarely descending to the personal'. On separate
occasions he refers to O'Brien's eyes and his gaze: 'with Conor's bright
unblinking eyes' and later, 'his unblinking and direct gaze'.[16] A less than
adulatory account of O'Brien, this time by Richard Murphy in his memoir *The Kick*, recalls meeting O'Brien with Murphy's wife in the Red
Bank restaurant in the winter of 1956.

> Raising a glass of wine to her, [O'Brien] quipped, *le sang du pauvre*, and
> his eyes turned up as if inside his head, showing their whites. Then he
> seemed to recognise and smile at a friend at the far end of the bar. Again
> and again he did this, usually after a witticism in French. I wondered
> whether we might ask the friend to join us, another sophisticate who
> might have amused Patricia. But in a quick glance over my shoulder I
> caught sight of Conor in a mirror on the far wall of the bar, smiling at
> himself.[17]

The pen-picture captures the arrogance and superiority that many have
railed at in their dealings with O'Brien. But it also concentrates on the
same far off smile, of a pair of eyes smiling and regarding their self if
only to point home their disdain for his company. Bizarrely, Murphy's
companion on that evening, his wife Patricia Avis, fell madly in love
with O'Brien at that same encounter and the two had a brief ill-fated
affair. Many years later in her *roman-à-clef – Playing the Harlot*[18] – she
recalls the scene after they first made love. O'Brien is at the wash-basin
shaving, lost in reverie. She recalls how he looked into the mirror, and
how, if he glared any more intensely, 'it might possibly splinter all over
if he stared hard enough'.

At a more abstract level this bleak vision of his led to portents of
an imminent civil war. O'Brien is synonymous with a whole range of
Cassandra-like prophecies on Irish politics that became clichéd to the

point of parody (there was for a time a regular column in the *Phoenix*
magazine spoofing his latest dire warnings). Yet on a biographical level
there is no doubt that the fearful impulse within him predated the North
or even the Congo. That impulse was demonstrably there from the beginning and lasted right until the end. His doomsday seer incarnation of
the 1970s and beyond seems to be a genuine reflection of his temperament, which is much in evidence in his teenage years. This particular
apocalyptic quality of O'Brien's is mistakenly ascribed to his fondness
for Edmund Burke, who is seen as the father-figure in his intellectual
recoil from the front line of the revolution. As this book will hopefully
demonstrate, this fascination with Burke comes late and does not fully explain his true intellectual foundations. A whole host of other individuals
– his father and mother, his clan: the Sheehys and Sheehy Skeffingtons,
Camus, Seán O'Faoláin, Jules Michelet and others – had a far greater
impact than Burke on his upbringing and intellectual development.
More so than Burke, the fear of civil war and the realization of man's
dark capabilities stem from an internal honesty: a view that comes
across in O'Brien's reading of Hobbes.

> Thomas Hobbes based his philosophy on fear. All of us experience fear;
> most of us are ashamed of it and try to hide it. Hobbes did not. Of his
> share in the English civil war he wrote with simplicity: 'I was the first of
> them that fled'. He ran and he thought. He thought about civil war, and
> how to avoid it.[19]

There is no doubt that O'Brien too felt the same impulse. His public
writings were to ensure that others did not have to experience the
reality of what he imagined so keenly.

Another idea behind this work is that when O'Brien entered public life
in Ireland he was in his 50s. He had a wealth of mishaps and brilliant
turns that schooled him in the ways of politics, international relations
and journalism. By the time he was elected in 1969 to Dáil Éireann his
mind was, to an extent, set. It then encountered a seismic occurrence
(the Troubles) which caused it to both change and develop once more.
What is important to understand is that as much as he cut ties with his
previous incarnation, events caused him to return to his intellectual
roots. The merit of this work then, it is hoped, will be to try to present
the complexities of his intellectual experiences as he wrote and thought
through these years.

While we need the space of time to accurately judge O'Brien's place in the annals of history, I fear that when we come to ruminate on his stature in the future we might miss the reactions his persona induced. To my mind the one outstanding feature of O'Brien is his ability to polarize opinion. And it is precisely this ability to both alienate and to inspire admiration that makes O'Brien worthy of study. If the reactions are frequently unthinking, they merely serve to demonstrate that O'Brien is important because he represents a challenge to what Irish people were at that time. It is necessary then to recall the fervour, energy and possibility his persona evoked in the late 1960s when he entered Irish politics:

> When Ireland elects a Labour government and Dr Conor Cruise O'Brien is Minister for External Affairs, the country will be strictly neutral in thought, deed and omission. In thought it will re-build Irish socialism based on the theories of James Connolly; in word it will emphasise at the United Nations Assembly its concern for peace with justice; in deed it will act with regard to its diplomatic relations as other neutral countries have done; and in omission it will include military alliances with NATO out. Not intent due to apathy.[20]

He was, as one critic observed, the 'golden calf of the Irish left'. The same critic wryly added that this 'would be less disturbing if they did not simultaneously try to portray him as its Moses'.[21]

Within a decade the contradictions of his character and the tempest that the Troubles created in southern politics had left him with the so-briquet of 'the fascist of the left'.[22] In an interview which became quite tetchy, the interviewer quoted Mary Holland's view that as a result of O'Brien's influence upon RTÉ in the mid-1970s, 'people were quite simply frightened out of their minds … Self-censorship had been raised to the level of an art and caution lay like a thick cloud over everything'.[23] In reply O'Brien denied the charge and implied that only Holland and her republican sympathizers would agree. However there are other examples from this time that tend to underscore the point that O'Brien took his responsibilities too far.

The academic and press ombudsman, John Horgan, re-tells a story from the early 1970s when the then head of Current Affairs in RTÉ, Desmond Fisher, encountered an irate O'Brien at a Labour Party conference. According to Fisher, O'Brien remonstrated with him for the content of a programme on internment with the words of warning: 'Just one more programme like last night's: just one more', while waving a finger under Fisher's nose. When Fisher tried to defend himself, O'Brien added, 'And it's the last of its kind you'll do.'[24] Incidents of this kind piled up over the subsequent years to the point that he was described by one Fianna Fáil minister as 'an intellectual terrorist'.[25]

Whatever, then, about the clarity of his own writings, O'Brien, it is fair to say, generated more heat than light. This passion, the ability to polarize an entire population as to his merits or otherwise, seems to stem from something within his psyche. As Richard Kearney put it in a prescient evaluation of O'Brien, 'the passion works both ways'. The gentleness toward friends and family is mirrored in a hatred of his enemies.[26] Another commentator echoed this view when he remarked how O'Brien's 'attitude seemed not only anti-republican' but something bordering on hatred, something 'which considering his essentially home rule background, was to be expected'.[27] Because he had close acquaintance with the 'seductive power of its myths' 'he understood Ireland's "ancestral voices" intimately'.[28] This particular irony points to the source of the strength of O'Brien's perceptions. His best books, *Parnell and his Party*, *States of Ireland*, some would argue *The Great Melody*, but above all *Camus*, are so powerful precisely because he applies to them the lesson that his own life taught him – we cannot escape what we have come from.

This focus on O'Brien's social reality explains who he is. But we also need to engage with O'Brien on the level that he wrote about: the key battlefield of the mind, the violent notions about our past and present. This points to another irony in O'Brien, one which was brought across in an interview with Garret FitzGerald. Trying to sum up O'Brien's contribution, FitzGerald suggested that O'Brien was 'more of a literary intellectual than a political philosopher'. However, it was O'Brien's 'uniqueness really to be a political philosopher in Ireland when all our intellectuals are literary ones'.[29] As the obituary of O'Brien in *The Irish Times* reminded us, while his political career 'looms largest in recent Irish memory, his critical, cultural and historical activities form part of a lasting legacy'.[30]

Much as O'Brien's own 'intellectual career' 'fell into two distinct halves, divided by the upsurge of the Northern Irish "Troubles"', this book also looks at a split O'Brien. First there is the man – or rather the personal influences that mentored his intellectual development and trajectory. Then when his arc crossed that of 1970s Ireland, I analyse the main themes and problems thrown up by O'Brien's writings in this decade. As a student of O'Brien since the 1990s I took the view that he had made his bed by the late 1980s (if not much earlier). Any commentary written after that had no more than curiosity value.[31] It is also worth pointing out that he was neither ignored nor isolated in his final years, he was simply viewed as irrelevant. The more the North edged toward a resolution, the more O'Brien banked all his chips onto the increasingly implausible outcome. In a way Irish society's greatest compliment to him was to have been able to brush past him in its hurry to its new debt nexus destiny. That it could afford the political luxury of not having to worry about either its stability or its security is in part a tribute to a man who fixated on these points when they were most in doubt. As one obituary put it: 'It was in the 1970s that Conor's influence on contemporary Ireland was greatest and most enduring.'[32]

Accordingly, this book looks at what he wrote when he was most relevant. To try and understand O'Brien's writings from the 1970s is the pathway to his political philosophy. The second part of the book devotes considerable space to trying to piece together broad ideas that enable us to make sense of O'Brien. That attempt leads to a number of chapters which focus on the main themes which present themselves in his writings in this decade. The chapter 'The Siege' examines what is widely regarded as O'Brien's most influential work, *States of Ireland*. In a recent examination of his life, the broadcaster Olivia O'Leary referred to it as 'a brilliant book' and 'the most important thing he'd done in his whole life'. The significance for her was that it illustrated to her generation that 'militant republicanism was fascist and anti-democratic'.[33] This suggests that *States of Ireland* had a critical role in moving a core group of opinion formers – exemplified by O'Leary – toward a negative view of not just the IRA but Irish nationalism. While there is a great deal of truth to this, O'Brien also relayed a positive narrative in *States of Ireland*. While attempting to tease out the motif of *States of Ireland*, the chapter on 'The Siege' suggests that what is even more lasting is the way O'Brien forces us to internalize both the fears and aspirations of the unionist community.

Another aspect of O'Brien's legacy which is partially obscured by Northern Ireland and the whole focus on conflict is the way O'Brien affected attitudes in Ireland toward religion. He persistently criticised the excessively authoritarian quality of the Irish Catholic Church. He challenged the way the Church expected its flock to accept 'guidance' in an unquestioning manner. I suspect that this path-breaking persona is what attracted many to him in the 1960s and led a few to forgive what appeared to be his Northern-related excesses. It is interesting to ponder what our view of O'Brien would now be if he had kept his contribution to domestic social issues within the Republic. It is quite likely that the implosion of the Church's authority from the late 1980s on would result in O'Brien receiving a far less mixed report card. Regardless of whether one agrees with this counterfactual or not, we must recognize the importance and persistent centrality of secularism in O'Brien's mental scheme of the world. The chapter 'Religion' is an essay on both O'Brien's view of religion's role in Irish politics as well as his attempts to draw a clearer distinction between Church and State.

A constant refrain of many of O'Brien's critics is that while they disagree with his views, be it on the North, the Irish language, church-state relations etc., his status as a historian of the first rank is unquestioned. While as he said himself, he 'found no welcome' in academic life after his stellar undergraduate days,[34] many 'still believe that O'Brien was at his best as an academic historian and that the book *Parnell and his Party* ... is his most valuable work'. The chapter 'Histories' takes a critical look at the notion that O'Brien can be described as a historian for the simple reason that while 'his interventions curbed the indulgence of militant radicalism in Ireland ... at the same time, he mythologized the very militancy he opposed.'[35] At the risk of seeming like some fusty gatekeeper at the historian's union, this practice of mythologizing (some would say demonizing) in his histories of Ireland and beyond (Israel and *The Siege* is a good example) might preclude him from being described as a historian at all.

Perhaps this is too strong and reflects a set of academic mores which don't belong in the harsh light of reality that O'Brien both lived in and wrote about. A recognition of O'Brien's street-fighting role, that he fought fire with fire so to speak, lies at the heart of the chapter 'Legitimacy' which investigates the enabling power of myths in our society or what we might call 'history writ large'. The chapter endeavours to describe how our understanding of history is tied to our own present self-conception: how loosely defined or understood convictions underlie a national appreciation of legacy, orthodoxy and progress. Through the contest of various historical camps an individual or group of writers can redefine the conceptual structure of state, society or situation. The effect of this leads to an altering of our thoughts and actions concerning the past, the present and the future. In short, it looks at the way history alters the fundamentals of our polity.

The hope of these chapters is twofold: firstly to sketch the intellectual flux in O'Brien's political odyssey, and secondly to determine what didn't change: what is left by the time he left office is the distilled O'Brien – his political core.

NOTES

1. Jenny McCartney, 'Farewell to Ireland's Restless Conscience'. *The Telegraph*, 20 December 2008.
2. Frank Callanan, *Sunday Independent*, 21 December 2008.
3. Roy Foster, 'The Cruiser', *Standpoint Magazine*, 1 February 2009. http://www.standpoint-mag.co.uk/the-cruiser-february-09-text-conor-cruise-obrien-roy-foster [accessed 20 March 2009].
4. 'Irish Intellectual of his Time'. *The Daily Telegraph*, 19 December 2008.
5. W.J. McCormack, 'Conor Cruise O'Brien: Irish Intellectual with a Long Career as Journalist, Politician, Literary Critic and Public Servant'. *The Independent*, 20 December 2008.
6. Brian Fallon, 'Conor Cruise O'Brien'. *The Guardian*, 19 December 2008.
7. The 'lost book' phrase was coined by O'Brien's biographer, Don Akenson. The title 'The Story of Ireland' is what O'Brien called his brief history of Ireland. For a discussion of this text and excerpts please see the chapter 'Histories' and pp.110–12 in particular.
8. 'Conor Cruise O'Brien: Diplomat, Politician, Historian, Journalist'. *The Times*, 20 December 2008.
9. Conor Cruise O'Brien, 'Introduction', in *Conor Cruise O'Brien Introduces Ireland* (London, 1969), p.16.
10. 'Master of Culture and Controversy: Obituary'. *The Irish Times*, 19 December 2008.
11. Brian Fallon, 'Conor Cruise O'Brien'. *The Guardian*, 19 December 2008.
12. Frank Callanan, *Sunday Independent*, 21 December 2008.
13. Interview with Brendan Halligan, RTÉ Radio, 19 December 2008.
14. W.B. Yeats, 'Meditations in Time of Civil War', in Norman Jeffares (ed.), *Yeats's Poems* (Dublin, 1989), p.312.
15. Richard English and Joseph Morrison Skelly (eds), *Ideas Matter: Essays in Honour of Conor Cruise O'Brien* (Dublin, 1998).
16. Darcy O'Brien, 'Conor Cruise O'Brien and *La Politesse de L'Espirit*', in ibid., pp.63–76.
17. Richard Murphy, *The Kick* (London, 2002), p.177.
18. Patricia Avis, *Playing the Harlot* (London, 1996), p.176.
19. Conor Cruise O'Brien, 'Nationalism, Democracy and the European Idea'. O'Brien papers, University College Dublin, P82/837 (9–10).
20. Interview with Conor Cruise O'Brien by Liam MacGabhann, *This Week in Ireland*, 1, 10 (12 December 1969), pp.82/256.
21. D.R. O'Connor Lysaght, *The Lace Curtain: A Magazine of Poetry and Criticism* (1969), p.61.

22. 'You are known in some circles as the fascist of the left'. Interview with Conor Cruise O'Brien in Naim Atallah, *Of a Certain Age: Interviews* (London, 1991), p.216.
23. Ibid., pp.206–27. See also Mary Holland, 'Conor Cruise O'Brien and the Church', *New Statesman*, 30 April 1976.
24. John Horgan, *Broadcasting and Public Life: RTÉ News and Current Affairs 1925–1997* (Dublin, 2004), p.134.
25. Brian Lenihan, *The Irish Times*, 11 October 1991.
26. Richard Kearney, 'Ulysses returns to Ithaca'. Review of *Memoir*, *Times Literary Supplement*, 15 January 1996, p.6.
27. Brian Fallon, 'Conor Cruise O'Brien', *The Guardian*, 19 December 2008.
28. Jenny McCartney, 'Farewell to Ireland's Restless Conscience', *The Telegraph*, 20 December 2008.
29. Author's interview with Dr Garret FitzGerald, Ranelagh Dublin, 12 November 2003.
30. *The Irish Times* obituary of Conor Cruise O'Brien, 19 December 2008.
31. For a considered view on the development of O'Brien's thinking in this period as a development of earlier themes on nationalism and the role of religion, see Richard Bourke's article, 'Violence and Conor Cruise O'Brien'. *Times Literary Supplement*, 11 March 2009.
32. Frank Callanan, *Sunday Independent*, 21 December 2008.
33. Olivia O'Leary as quoted in an interview on the RTÉ programme on O'Brien *Cloch le Carn*, broadcast 30 March 2009. http://www.rte.ie/tv/clochlecarn/prog2.htm.
34. Geoffrey Wheatcroft, 'Conor Cruise O'Brien, 1917–2008', *New York Review of Books*, 56, 5 (26 March 2009).
35. Richard Bourke, 'Violence & Conor Cruise O'Brien'. *Times Literary Supplement*, 11 March 2009.

PART I

Conor Cruise O'Brien: The Man

Dispossession: O'Brien's Family and the Irish Revolution

S peaking three years before the publication of O'Brien's *Memoir*, Geoffrey Wheatcroft made an acute observation in the essay, 'The Most Hated Man in Ireland'. O'Brien, he pointed out, 'has not written his memoirs'. Or rather, he added, 'not officially'. He went on to say that when O'Brien

> wrote in the preface to his idiosyncratic book on Israel and Zionism, *The Siege*, that 'this is a highly personal book' he was not guilty of overstatement. Almost all his books have been highly personal, and keen students of his oeuvre will sometimes recall what Balfour said about Churchill's *World Crisis*, 'a brilliant autobiography disguised as a history of the universe'.[1]

When O'Brien did actually write his *Memoir* this idiosyncratic blend of personal anecdote and world history was much in evidence. A classic example of this is the snippet of Cruise O'Brien driving up to Howth Head to listen to the announcement of the outbreak of the Second World War on the car radio. The overall picture is a powerful one. A young man with enormous promise, with his mind firmly trained beyond Ireland's petty troubles, contemplating the impending devastation of the continent that was his intellectual home. His actual entry into his college diary a few months later when France surrendered reinforces the image of someone with their mind on far-away lands. As he said at the time, 'our intellectual compass is revolving wildly from Moscow to New York. England's defeat was imminent and Ireland's fate beckoned: Surrender of France. Invasion of Ireland seems certain now .... We can only wait until we become a battleground.' A few other lines in the same entry question the image of O'Brien as a young Olympian on the head of Howth, with a flurry of ill-judged, almost

juvenile rants, about wanting to get to Moscow, and being worried
about several works by French authors that he was to take delivery of,
but which now seemed in jeopardy. And then at the end of this typically
self-involved (for a 22-year-old college student) entry we have a curious statement where he says, 'I am ready now to take up my place in a
liberal democracy.' To which he adds: 'Too late again.'[2]

That he considered himself a God-given bounty to liberal society and
its government, observers of O'Brien will understand only too well. But
that tail of an entry, 'Too late again', is perplexing. Or at least it is difficult to make sense of unless one takes these ideas of O'Brien as Fran-
cophone, Europhile, post-nationalist cosmopolitan and toss them for the
ill-fitting garb that they are on the young man. The thing about O'Brien
is that he can only be understood first and foremost in relation to what
went before him. His own description of his aunt Mary Kettle, 'proud as
Lucifer', could just as well be taken for himself. He was very conscious
of his forebears, their worth and their contribution to Irish politics. Mary
Kettle was a councillor, his aunt Hanna a member of the original Sinn
Féin executive. His uncle, Tom Kettle, husband of Mary, was an MP. His
grandfather David Sheehy was both an MP and one of the grandees of
the Irish parliamentary party. Several other members of his immediate
kin were well-known writers and journalists. Far more so than any European destiny, it was this intense clannish call that he felt he had been
born for. Rather than looking to far off horizons, or a fine future, the
young O'Brien focused his undoubted abilities upon the past. And that
is why he felt that he was 'Too late again'. An Irish disaster was the main
player in his young life's work. Too late to arrest the fall of his family,
what we might call 'the house of Sheehy', O'Brien would dedicate himself not to running away from this disaster, but to reversing it.

His political family is a theme of his writings from the 1970s and
increasingly becomes a pronounced tic of his newspaper columns in
The Observer and *The Irish Times* of the 1980s and 1990s. It is part
of a steadily accelerating tendency of his to enmesh public fact and
personal memory. This receives its most extensive and eccentric treatment in *The Great Melody* and *Ancestral Voices*. Its apogee is probably
the argument that he is in some way related to Edmund Burke and his
statement, in conversation to a friend, that his relationship with Burke
went far beyond an intellectual affinity: '[Burke] is in the room. He is
here. Now.'[3]

Looking back over the biographical events that populate his earlier writings reinforces this. The first sound he ever heard was the Free State Army bombing the republican forces in the Four Courts. To put it another way, his first sound heralded the civil war that fractured his country. Likewise, the position of his father as an increasingly isolated agnostic indicates the creeping confessional character of the new Free State. O'Brien's oft-repeated tale of his uncle Tom Kettle's children running away from their father because of his British uniform, signals the dramatic political change in allegiance after 1916. All these vignettes, and many more, fuse to create a particularly personal history of Independent Ireland. A good example of how O'Brien's family and history are intertwined is provided by the background to *Ancestral Voices*. He explained how the book arose from a request by his daughter, Kate Cruise O'Brien, at the time editor of Poolbeg Press, to develop the theme of 'GodLand' (O'Brien's view that all nationalism has a religious basis) in the Irish context. This would involve a history of Ireland from the Penal Laws up to the present. He was happy to do so and 'willingly because my interest in the general subject matter has derived mainly from my family's share in the specific Irish experiences of the workings of these formidable world-historical forces'.[4]

While he clearly goes too close to what Balfour said about Churchill here (autobiography dressed up as world history), there is an inkling of truth in it, but not the one he himself has in mind. By engaging in this process – the personal swept along by great historical change – O'Brien is placing himself in the stream of one of the outstanding features in twentieth-century history and literature. This is probably best described as the sense of alienation experienced by a great number of people who have been touched by the tumultuous forces of that 'age of extremes'. A large part of this stems from an almost reflexive impulse against fascism and Nazis. Likewise the virulent anti-Semitism from that era has also left its mark on the geography and the mind of the world with the creation of a potent intellectual impulse and awareness that is directed against anti-Semitism. Another example would be the flood of Russian émigrés escaping across Europe in the face of the Bolshevik Revolution. Out of this reaction against the communist interloper in their ancestral home came an entire political corpus. Vladimir Nabokov, one of those who fled, illustrates this view by referring to all the ideological émigrés of that century as 'Displaced

Persons'.[5] He, like many others of these 'Displaced Persons', has responded to these ruptures by taking this trauma as the motif of his life's work.

To map this onto Ireland and label O'Brien's dominant socio-political motive as attempting to end a perceived 'dispossession' might be seen as taking this too far. But there is an inherent truth in it that is worth exploring. We should acknowledge though that O'Brien never fled; in fact he was for many years an outstanding apparatchik of the state. To describe O'Brien as dispossessed or displaced (disgruntled might be more appropriate) by the drift of his country, is an attempt to reflect more than just his own personal resentment, but the deep mark it left on his historical understanding and indeed his entire way of viewing Irish history.

Within this nexus of dispossession, or social dislocation, there is a feeling of alienation. O'Brien clearly felt that the Sheehys were stigmatized as political pariahs. When we read *States of Ireland*, his apocalyptic vision, a fear of a recurrence of what happened to his family arising from the Irish revolution is quite pronounced. A partial explanation of this lies in *States of Ireland* being written at a time of a particular type of social stress, in which more than once 'a terrible beauty' came to many people's minds. It is significant that *States of Ireland* envisages two 'models', or outlooks on the future, in which the malign model is a parallel of a 'Greece of the colonels'. In this he fears for 'everything I love going under'.[6] At this stage we can see the relevance of that 'Too late again' from his college diary. O'Brien was born too late to avert his family's disaster. He was too late to be in the thick of the Second World War.

In the 1970s, however, he was in position. Reading his writings around this time, one should bear in mind these perceptions. Just as much as he was committed to undoing the wrong ('Too late again'), people of this tradition are almost congenitally attuned to spotting future troublemakers. In O'Brien's case, it isn't too much to say that having his family upended by Sinn Féin once, O'Brien approached politics with the mindset of expunging threats rather than leave anything to chance. As well as being an entirely human characteristic which O'Brien could do little about, it explains much of his judgement when dealing with a whole cast of individuals, be they Hume, Adams or indeed fellow party members such as David Thornley.

A classic case has been his dealings with Charles Haughey. Even though their relationship was muddied by the fact that they were constituency competitors and that O'Brien thought Haughey a 'crook' from the start,[7] it was in relation to his role in the Arms Trial in 1970 that O'Brien pursued Haughey with a savage intensity until his retirement from politics. In a private letter to a political reporter in *The Irish Times* he upbraided the media for their indulgent approach to a person who, to his eyes, was clearly a danger to the life of the country.

> The media including yourself have been remarkably tolerant of this person's return to the front of the stage in political life – something that would not have been permitted to anyone with anything like his record in any other democratic country. When I use the word fear I am not speaking metaphorically. I sincerely believe that a government which included him would be dangerous to security and even to democracy.[8]

While fear has a part to play in how his view of the past affects his political views and sharpens his political enmities, there is no doubt that a keen sense of *amour propre* enters into it as well. As mentioned, in his later works he uses biography at will. Yet there are traces of it in his earliest works which indicate that this is more than a voice acquired; it is more than egocentricity. An example of this is the manner in which he opens one of his earliest essays 'The parnellism of Seán O'Faoláin' – his first stab at tackling the interaction between politics and the Irish mind:

> There is for all of us a twilit zone of time, stretching back for a generation or two before we were born, which never quite belongs to the rest of history. Our elders have talked their memories into our memories until we possess some sense of continuity traversing and exceeding our own individual being.[9]

While apparently talking about O'Faoláin, it is clear that O'Brien got this from his own experiences and applied it to O'Faoláin. O'Brien chooses certain themes or events for their relevance to his sense of familial dispossession. As a result of this dispossession the various 'facts' of Irish history are chosen in light of this traumatic event. Behind his treatment of historical subject matter, a treatment that often leaves his countrymen perplexed, there lies a simple primal hurt. And the cause of the injury is his family's fall from grace.

Nothing demonstrates this more than an overheard conversation between O'Brien and his then father-in-law, Seán MacEntee.

> Conor Cruise O'Brien, as is his wont, provoked McEntee [*sic*] with a
> sweeping statement: '1916 was a mistake'. Séan McEntee replied, 'Maybe
> it was, but I am glad I was part of it.' McEntee's daughter, Maureen [*sic*]
> added with superb clear-sightedness, 'Conor, your grandfather was a
> member of the Irish Parliamentary Party. You were part of the elite. My
> father was the son of a publican. He would never have become minister
> without 1916. We would never have had a fine house, his children would
> never have been to the best schools.' Ruefully, Conor Cruise O'Brien
> answered, 'Exactly, your people pushed mine aside.'[10]

Throughout *States of Ireland*, his best known work, O'Brien subtly
points out that he finds himself explaining to the plain people of
Ireland that the world did not begin in 1916. Stemming from this
perspective is the insight that Irish Independence came at a certain cost.
1916 must be balanced against a War of Independence, a Civil War,
and a surfeit of violent ideologues amidst a malcontent citizenry. What
makes him acutely aware of the plusses and minuses of 1916 is that just
as some won in 1916, some also lost. His aunt, the proud Mary Kettle,
was human enough to reveal that, for her, 1916 simply meant that the
family had come down in the world.

Another example of this is the way in which Parnell features in
O'Brien's life. His work on Parnell carried out in the late 1940s and
early 1950s was one of the benchmark texts for a new professionalism
in Irish history.[11] It established him as one of the foremost historians
of his generation and a good deal of his authority and stature in later
life was in part attributable to his unquestioned scholarship and
apparent detachment. As one critic in the *Journal of Modern History*
put it:

> This is one of the many good books published during the last few years
> by what may be called a new school of Irish historians. It has in marked
> degree the qualities which distinguish earlier books by these men: exact
> scholarship, close attention to detail, a good narrative style, and above
> all, an entire absence of the tedious partisanship that has marred so many
> books on this, as on most subjects in recent Anglo-Irish history.[12]

The thing about O'Brien's *Parnell* is that while it might not be marred by 'tedious partisanship' there is undoubtedly something personal about both his treatment of, and fascination with, Parnell.

For O'Brien, Parnell was the decisive moment in Irish history, 'the great primal and puzzling event was the fall of Parnell'.[13] The depth of this is indicated by the concentration upon this one era, most notably his choice to do his doctorate on the Parnell era which led to *Parnell and his Party*. Similarly the earliest essays, such as 'The parnellism of Seán O'Faoláin', or indeed his editorship of the collection *The Shaping of Modern Ireland 1890–1916*, suggest that Ireland's artistic and social dilemmas sprang from Parnell's fall. But behind these high-brow notions of scholarly disinterest and big thesis questions there lies the simple fact that he under-took his work on Parnell in order to allow himself to study his own family history. In an interview O'Brien admits that 'the Sheehy family record of betrayal of Parnell ... weighed heavily' on his mind as a youth.[14] A letter to his aunt Mary quite baldly outlines his motives:

> I am not ashamed, however, to admit to you at least that in deciding to undertake the task certain motives of a lowly order from a historian's point of view, but valuable incentives, entered in: family piety and family pride.[15]

Even if in this context O'Brien is speaking about undertaking a bi-ography of Tom Kettle, the object was to have been what he called a 'Trojan horse' for a book on Dublin and the personalities of Kettle's time. Like his doctorate on Parnell and the Irish Parliamentary Party, this new book was to be about the milieu in which O'Brien's family – the Sheehys – held sway. What ostensibly was a 'sequel' to his doctor-ate was a 'prequel' of his own life and family. This glimpse of that 'twilit zone of time' was what attracted him to a study which, as he outlined to his aunt, would look at the career of his grandfather and grand-uncle, his two uncles, his two 'courtesy' uncles, and the role of his father in that sphere. It would have examined the 'proper relation' of O'Brien's ancestors to other less important figures who have subse-quently risen in stature because of the way Ireland's political trajectory went. The point is thinly veiled in the same letter to his aunt:

> Hitherto the period has been written about almost exclusively in relation to the biographies of people, who great as they were, were exceptional, and in some degree peripheral to the social and political life of the time – Joyce, Yeats, O'Casey.

O'Brien's new history was to be a riposte to the literary and political forces that cast a shadow over the Sheehys.

O'Brien's portrait of his grandmother, Bessie Sheehy, is an acute example of the family's high regard for itself. She is credited with having injected the driving ambition to be found in the Sheehy genes. Her rationale for producing academically successful daughters had a brilliant simplicity about it: servants were cheap, scholarships brought in more money than servants cost! Therefore, there was no point in having the girls wash dishes. As told by O'Brien, her softly demonic pursuit of Ireland's future leadership cadre (she thought of Tom Kettle as prime minister material), is one of his most unforgettable barbed tributes.

> Bessie did not know words like 'upward social mobility' and 'rising national bourgeoisie', but she had the idea … My grandmother intended, quite consciously I believe, to preside over the birth of a new ruling class: those who would run the country when Home Rule was won.

'It was not', O'Brien tells us, 'a fanciful ambition'.[16]

'Fanciful' or not, it seems a little too convenient to assume that it was 1916 that killed the Sheehy 'dynasty'. Correctly speaking, it was 1918 that shunted the Sheehys off the stage as the patriarch, David Sheehy MP, lost power in that year's General Election. But even this is to buy into the notion of a transfer of power from one Sheehy generation to the next. The problem with this perspective is that by 1916 there were no other candidates to replace David Sheehy, either from Bessie's loins, or through marriage or connection. 1916 was indeed responsible for killing Tom Kettle, albeit not in Dublin but at the Somme – following his decision to seek active duty in the British Army in apparent frustration at the Easter Rising.

But there is an argument that this is wishful thinking on O'Brien's part. Tom Kettle was not going to be in the shake up to be a future prime minister as he had resigned his seat in parliament in 1913. By all accounts it seems that the party leadership were not too sad at his departure, as his sobriquet 'poor Tom Kettle' and known propensity for drinking indicate. There is little to suggest that a combination of drinking and retirement from politics in 1913 was really going to enable him to pole-vault over Dillon, Redmond, Healy or, as it turned out, Griffith, Collins, de Valera or McNeill. Kettle might well have been

the jewel in the Sheehy crown, but if so then it must be said that it was an increasingly tawdry tiara.

Another contention made by O'Brien in his portrayal of a dynasty 'done in' by 1916 was the stain on his family name to have been associated with the Irish Parliamentary party.

> If Home Rule had been achieved by the parliamentary route, David Sheehy would certainly have had a seat in the Irish cabinet. Our whole family would have been part of the establishment of the new Home Rule Ireland. As it was we were out in the cold, superseded by a new republican elite. To be connected with the Irish Parliamentary Party had been an asset; now it was a liability.[17]

Maybe O'Brien wishes his family had been on 'the right side of history', much like he regretted that they were on the wrong side with Parnell. But to say the Sheehys became political pariahs is simply not true. Many members of the family prospered in the new political order – none more so than his aunt Hanna, who was for a time on the Sinn Féin executive. All the obituaries of David Sheehy when he died in 1932 describe him as steeped in the national cause.[18] Even many years later when O'Brien quit the UN and the Department of External Affairs, *The Irish Times* described his family as 'strongly nationalist'.

When he says that in 1918 'my grandfather ceased to represent Ireland at Westminster, and our family came down in the world' what O'Brien is really engaging in is a bit of special pleading. What actually happened is that in 1914 his grandfather, in spite of a salary of £600 per annum, went bankrupt through gambling.[19] The reality is that Sheehy was not defeated or beaten in the 1918 election, but had the decision made for him not to stand for election in 1918 by virtue both of his bankruptcy and his age. Another way of looking at it is to see how the remaining relatives, Eugene and Hanna, progressed in the new state. Far from being ostracized, they were in their own way scions of the new regime. In fact they were emblematic of the split and sundered regime. Hanna served in the Dáil courts, and was one of the foremost figures in both Sinn Féin and Fianna Fáil. Only when the oath was taken did she in August 1927 publicly resign, and with Lemass's 1934 *Conditions of Employment Act* did she leave Fianna Fáil altogether. However, it cannot be stated that she lost her place at power's table because the country took too Republican a course after 1916. On the contrary it was because it was a rather conservative and increasingly staid society that she felt it was betraying its republican 'roots' and egalitarian 'promise'. Eugene, on the other hand, was a bastion of the judiciary, being for a time an advocate general and later a circuit court judge. To elide all these factors – such as Tom Kettle's early retirement, his grandfather's bankruptcy, and Hanna being in the thick of it and on the rise in Sinn Féin[20] – and to blame it all on 1916 is more than just sour grapes. It is evidence of a deeply lodged hurt, something that needs a proper investigation of the Sheehys to understand.

To view his family with the knowledge that they once fell and are now gone misses the intrigue of Cruise O'Brien's parents first coming together, their personal vibrancy and the battles they fought against the Sheehys to get married. It misses a true sense of the justifiable self-regard that the Sheehys had for themselves, an opinion that fascinated a regular visitor to their home, James Joyce. Joyce's sketch of the Sheehys centres around their home, No.2 Belvedere Place, and the salon they held there known as 'second Sundays'.[21] In it we see David Sheehy MP and his brother Eugene, one half deaf, the other half blind, repeating and highlighting the missed expressions and utterances of their guests, in a fond and approving way. It gives a fascinating insight into the atmosphere that O'Brien's mother and aunts grew up in, and that they in turn passed on to him. It was, according to Joyce, a nationalist Catholic household, which is to say that the Sheehy family were as Catholic as they were undoubtedly nationalist. This is plain from a letter to Hanna Sheehy from O'Brien's mother in 1903:

> Dearest Joan,
> Hurra for Ireland! Not one of the Sheehy family went to see the King and so we can all safely say we are well in mind and body. Our blinds are all down since the Pope died and Mags, Mary and I wear black badges with pendants of the Pope, at which the wearers of 'Red, white and blue' scowl most beautifully.[22]

The recitations on offer at the Sheehy salon, Joyce tells us, were all historical and nationalist. The gossip was mainly political, but always entirely proper. After charades – a game Joyce took part in with great success – he describes David Sheehy's habit of adjudicating between various debaters, who held forth in the stilted pompous style favoured by parliamentarians. In the end, after much cajoling, he himself would give a sample of the real thing. Joyce leads us to believe that it was all slightly cringeworthy, and certainly that is the feeling *Stephen Hero* leaves us with. Perhaps O'Brien was entitled to feel that Joyce was a touch 'mean' in his portrayal of the Sheehys. After all, he returned on many occasions. The participants themselves all recall the 'second Sundays' with universal fondness. What Joyce and O'Brien do both seem to agree on was the class element to the occasions. Joyce portrays the old man Sheehy as intent on matching off his four marriageable daughters to suitably fine young men of the correct background, ability and prospects. Someone who was perceived to be in the way of such ambitions was the suitor to the Sheehy's youngest daughter Kathleen: Francis Cruise O'Brien.

Cruise O'Brien was 'merely' the son of a law clerk, of no noted genealogy, and of middling prospects. He had recently emerged from a 'brilliant academic career',[23] and as O'Brien notes, had been the auditor of the Literary and Historical Society in the Royal or the Sheehys 'wouldn't have let him into the house'.[24] Although they did not overtly object to his suit on social grounds, the argument was that he was too small, too weakly. Even in this, they introduced a class argument, as Bessie feared he might possibly be tubercular. However, there were other factors at play which can only be understood if we look back at the milieu of Conor's mother, her older sisters and their respective husbands.

Conor's mother Kathleen was the youngest of the four Sheehy daughters. The eldest and the best known in our time, as then, was Hanna Sheehy, the suffragist and Republican. She married Frank Skeffington in 1903, and as a gesture of their equality they became the Sheehy Skeffingtons; in later years, Frank was sarcastically referred to as the 'hyphenated democrat'. The two of them gradually evolved to positions of pacifism, agnosticism, socialism and, above all, suffragism. The other sisters, while committed suffragists, were more straightforward in their politics ('Hurra for Ireland!'). The second eldest, Margaret, was an amateur playwright.[25] Kathleen's nearest sister, Mary, was responsible, as we have seen, for landing the 'greatest prize of the all', Tom Kettle. The son of Andrew Kettle, one of Parnell's faithful few, Tom was according to many accounts among the most brilliant of his generation.

Kettle, Sheehy Skeffington and Cruise O'Brien were involved in the

setting up of the Young Ireland Branch. This was a branch of the dominant political vehicle of its day in Ireland, the United Irish League, of
which David Sheehy was the organizing secretary. After his death in
1932 'An Irishman's Diary' in *The Irish Times* recalled:

> The passing of the veteran David Sheehy brings back many lively recol-
> lections of the days when his remarkable daughters and sons-in-law, Tom
> Kettle, Sheehy-Skeffington, and Cruise O'Brien, as the leading spirits of
> the Young Ireland Branch of the United Irish League were frequently in
> a state of war with the old man in his capacity as one of the chief engi-
> neers of the party machine. Representing the younger intelligentsia, they
> were the *bete-noir* of past politicians ... and were regarded with any-
> thing but favour by party mangers.[26]

This branch, in brief, represented the impatient young who had grown
dissatisfied with the prevarication and apparent lack of progress by the
old guard. The essence of their gripe was that Home Rule had not been
achieved; instead, a whole series of piecemeal concessions had been
wrung from the Government. What the branch advocated was a return
to Parnellite tactics: the subjugation of all other concerns to the single
goal of Home Rule.[27] Sheehy senior, as one who had become 'increasingly aware of his status in life and inclined to pomposity',[28] did not
take kindly to political instruction from the political neophyte Francis
Cruise O'Brien. In some cases Cruise O'Brien went so far in the national press as to portray David Sheehy as at odds with his own daughters over the question of suffragism. That there was truth to the
accusation misses the point. Cruise O'Brien not only had crossed a line,
but he had given them the cause they were looking for to close the door
on their daughter's suitor. The possibility of Conor Cruise O'Brien ever
being born was now thrown into serious doubt.

This is a good example of how the various individuals from O'Brien's
immediate family contributed to a tension that would persist throughout his life. It might be too much to say that he was split from the outset. But it is true that while he would come to take on board all the
rights and privileges of the Sheehys, he would also find himself ill at
ease with the Sheehy worldview that viewed his own father so nega-
tively. Whether there was any basis to this negative view of O'Brien's
father we will now attempt to uncover.

NOTES

1. Geoffrey Wheatcroft, 'The Most Hated Man in Ireland'. *The Spectator*, 7 January 1995.
2. *O'Brien's Commonplace Book*. Entry for 24 May 1940. O'Brien Papers, UCD, P82/328/48.
3. Quoted in D.H. Akenson, *Conor: A Biography of Conor Cruise O'Brien* (Montreal, 1994), p.486. Reported conversation between O'Brien and his friend, Brian Garrett.
4. Conor Cruise O'Brien, *Ancestral Voices* (Dublin, 1994), p.1.
5. Vladimir Nabokov, *The Gift* (London, 1963), p.8, adopting the officialese employed after the Second World War.
6. Conor Cruise O'Brien, *States of Ireland* (London, 1972), p.316.
7. See Akenson, *Conor*, p.340. For original statements by O'Brien see *The Irish Times*, 3 and 5 June 1969.
8. Letter from Conor Cruise O'Brien to Fergus Pyle, 3 June 1977. O'Brien papers, UCD, Folder VII Labour Party TD Dublin North East 1969–77, Section 1.
9. Donat O'Donnell, *Maria Cross: Imaginative Patterns on a Group of Modern Catholic Writers* (London, 1953), p.95.
10. Maurice Goldring, *Pleasant the Scholar's Life: Irish Intellectuals and the Construction of the Nation State* (London, 1993), p.14.
11. 'It was fourteen years in the making but worth waiting for' was how one critic put it. P.M. Williams, 'Review of Parnell and his Party 1880–1890', *Political Science Quarterly*, 73, 1 (March 1958), pp.146–48.
12. D.J. McDougal, review, *Journal of Modern History*, 30, 2 (June 1958), pp.147–8.
13. O'Brien, *States of Ireland*, p.21.
14. Anthony Jordan, *To Laugh or To Weep* (Dublin, 1994), p.iii.
15. O'Brien to Mary Kettle, early 1960s. Sheehy Skeffington papers (SSP) National Library of Ireland (NLI) MS 40,489 /8.
16. O'Brien, *States of Ireland*, p.62.
17. Conor Cruise O'Brien, *Memoir: My Life and Themes* (Dublin, 1998), p.21.
18. Obituaries of David Sheehy, *The Irish Times* and *Irish Independent*, 20 December 1932. Similar evidence can be seen from the attendees at David Sheehy's funeral which included Seán MacBride, Maude Gonne and representatives from Cumann na mBan, who were hardly likely to pay their respects if the elder Sheehy were a Castle Catholic.
19. 'In Bankruptcy – The Affairs of an Irish M.P. Re: Sheehy' describes his deposition to the court that 'To supplement his income in 1905 he began betting on horse races ... In the last three or four years his aggregate losses in betting had been about £400'. *The Times*, 24 February 1915.
20. Which only leaves the youngest Kathleen – Conor's mother, an Irish linguist of distinction, a 'redeemed' Catholic, and someone who reconciled herself to the new regime, having enthusiastically voted for de Valera in 1932. She in her own way, powerless, widowed, running from the bailiffs, would through her only son have a distinct bearing on how the new regime evolved.
21. The Sheehys were referred to in *A Portrait of the Artist*, briefly in *Ulysses*, and at greatest length in *Stephen Hero* where, as the Daniels family, they are clinically dissected.
22. Mags and Mary are O'Brien's two other aunts. It is also a neat little tribute to his case of *GodLand*. Kathleen Sheehy to Hanna Sheehy, July 1903. Sheehy Skeffington Papers, NLI. MS 41,176 /3.
23. Obituary of Francis Cruise O'Brien, *Irish Independent*, 27 December 1927.
24. O'Brien, *States of Ireland*, p.62.
25. In another Joycean encounter, she wrote the play *Cupid's Confidante*, in which Joyce played Geoffrey Fortescue.

26. 'An Irishman's Diary', *The Irish Times*, 21 December 1932.
27. Frank Sheehy Skeffington to Willie Moloney, 10 February 1911. Sheehy Skeffington Papers.
28. Margaret Ward, *Hanna Sheehy Skeffington: A Life* (Cork, 1997), p.4.

Father

In order to understand the fight over the marriage proposal, and the seriousness with which the Sheehys fought the idea that Francis Cruise O'Brien would marry their daughter Kathleen, we must first step back into the ethos of that bygone day. Unfashionable as it is to side with parents in such situations, you can, to an extent, see a basis for their feeling that Cruise O'Brien was not an ideal match. First, there was the question of his fortune. He was unquestionably penniless, and beyond a few occasional journalistic contributions, unemployed. Moreover, he wrote for *The Leader*, which they would have characterized as 'that awful paper', as it would have labelled the Sheehys 'shoneens' and would have made them feel guilty about their lack of Irish.[1] To make his conspicuous absence of wealth more odious, there was that 'grand English accent' of his, 'which he certainly didn't get at Synge St. Christian Brothers'.[2] You can almost hear the parents saying, 'He came from nowhere, and I wish he'd disappear back there as soon as possible'. He not only had the habit of talking down to David Sheehy, but he had publicly criticized him. He had set Sheehy at odds with his own daughters (in public also!), and then had the entire parliamentary party baying for his blood at one convention. Just as worryingly he gave the impression that he was not long for the world – 'He might even be tubercular'.[3] Finally, as if that were not enough, he was a self-proclaimed agnostic.[4] On grounds of religion, politics, employment, health and background, Cruise O'Brien gave the parents cause for concern to the extent that the parents did everything within their power to stop the wedding.[5] The entire episode is captured best by Frank Sheehy Skeffington:

> The great event of the last 6 months has been the 'affair' of Kathleen Sheehy and Cruise O'Brien. Between October and Christmas, Kathleen and Cruise came to a definite understanding; that is to say, they were secretly engaged, without the knowledge of any of the family. In January

the bomb burst … Kathleen was questioned, and admitted the engagement. 'Excursions and alarms!' Cruise O'Brien was declared to be 'delicate' he wouldn't live two years; out of consideration for Kathleen, she
couldn't be allowed to have anything to do with him! Cruise having burst
that bubble by offering to procure a doctor's certificate, – he is really a
man of great vitality, if he took the slightest pains to conserve it, – the
real objection was unmasked, – namely, Mammon. Cruise has no money,
no position, no prospect of having any. Against this the fact that he's
only 23 didn't count … David Sheehy, who to do him justice is not a
devotee of Mammon, was infuriated against Cruise because he led the
Young Ireland Branch attack on the Party! The family harmony of the
Sheehys is definitely broken up, and will never be re-established on the
old footing. Henceforward there are two camps.

Ultimately the two camps went to war. 'We've put our foot down.
I've explained to Kathleen that there's no question of her marrying
Cruise O'Brien.'[6] Furthermore the parents would not host the bridal
party, they would not hold a wedding breakfast, and they would offer
no blessing. As a final gambit to break her determination they announced that they would not attend the wedding. Hanna was her sister's sole support in this period. Realizing that her parents' steadfast
refusal was unlikely to change, she offered to host a wedding party. In
the days before the wedding: the acceptances and regrets came in. All
family members refused to attend: Tom and Mary were to be in London; Margaret's husband, Gary Culhane, had some business to attend
to; her brother Eugene was pleading a case, and so forth. As Kathleen
took to her bed, 'while waiting desperately for some telegram', all her
family wrote to say that they would be unable to attend. In the end,
they did not flinch: none but Hanna attended her wedding. The happy
closeness of the family was sundered and was to remain so for many
years. The schism with the family was to heal eventually, although
Conor relates that his father never really forgave the Sheehys for their
behaviour. O'Brien himself seems to have taken the incident to heart
and bore a grudge against Eugene and Mary in particular in later years.

When they ultimately married the newly wed couple trooped off to
Wexford town with their 'thirteen steamer trunks' full of all their pos-
sessions. Kathleen had found the house of her dreams on her first visit.
We have little insight into the couple's time in Wexford other than that
Cruise O'Brien was fired within a year of taking up the editorship of the

Wexford Free Press. O'Brien himself recounts that his father was summarily dismissed for refusing the orders of his publisher. Apparently Cruise O'Brien spiked a story which linked Masonic lodges with the devil. When Cruise O'Brien refused to print what he considered specious sectarianism he received his marching orders. However, this version is purely anecdotal.

There is some evidence that Cruise O'Brien behaved, as one socialist put it, 'honourably'.[7] In a generally hostile analysis of O'Brien's life, D.R. Lysaght O'Connor mentions that Francis Cruise O'Brien gave some assistance to the union movement in Wexford during his brief sojourn there.[8] A forerunner of Dublin's notorious 1913 lock-out took place in 1911 when two foundries in Wexford told their staffs, 'no workman is acceptable if a member of the ITGWU', Larkin's newly formed union. The lock-out lasted six months, saw the importation of 'scabs' from England, and violent clashes with police brought in from Dublin in which one worker was killed. The employers acceded to some of the workers' demands, though as a face-saving exercise they insisted that the strikers form a different union. This was the Irish Foundry Workers Union, which affiliated with the ITGWU and two years later dropped the pretence and became a regular branch. The papers of Frank Sheehy Skeffington relate how Cruise O'Brien on the employers side, and James Connolly on the workers side, negotiated a compromise to end the dispute. While Skeffington singles out Connolly's selflessness, he also praises Cruise O'Brien's role in bringing round the recalcitrant employers. By involving himself in so contentious an issue it is quite likely that he upset a good number of the main local employers.[9]

That all was not well when the Cruise O'Briens left Wexford is apparent from a letter between the Sheehy Skeffingtons over a year later.

> This morning, Countess Markievicz called ... she spoke of Cruise O'Brien, expressing her opinion that he is a dangerous man to have on the Executive of the Civic League. She had heard from a number of people in Wexford ... that he was head and ears in debt, lived altogether beyond his means, and was very unpopular in Wexford; was thought to be trying to be in with all sides in politics! Not far from the truth, though I defended him as far as possible.[10]

This piece of reported conversation confirms what other fragments of evidence only hint at about Francis and Kathleen. Firstly there is the reference to debt, the beginning of a pattern that plagued their years together. Insufficient money coming in and expensive tastes meant that what little they had was never going to be enough. Whether their unpopularity in Wexford was solely due to debt is unclear. But it would seem that combined with the divisive issue of the 'lock-out', and a tendency to allow debts to accumulate, there is more to the Cruise O'Briens leaving Wexford than a story about cloven hooves.[11] The second thing it tells us is that both close friends, such as the Skeffingtons, and others less fond of him, such as Markievicz, were inclined to the view that 'he was trying to be in with all sides in politics'. The point is worth making because an attempt to tie down Cruise O'Brien's politics is somewhat difficult. By the time Markievicz made her opinions known at the end of 1913, Cruise O'Brien had already racked up several positions that are difficult to reconcile.

If Cruise O'Brien's political views are difficult to actually pinpoint, they can in a sense be triangulated. If we take his estimate of Arthur Griffith in 1910 we can see that Cruise O'Brien, although a leader of the Young Ireland Branch with its focus on Home Rule, was not overly enamoured with the objective of total independence. He seemed content to accept that he could lullaby it into its grave. He reckoned Griffith was:

> the last of the extremists, the prophet of the old dream of armed conflict with the English, of the old ideal of a sovereign Irish nation. And there was no man among the constitutionalists who did not respect Mr. Griffith for upholding that dream and that ideal, so full of the appeal to the imagination and to the heart. There was no man of those who held the dream to be a vain one, and the ideal to be an unattainable one, but felt it good to be preached were it never so impossible; but felt inspired and uplifted by the thought that Ireland had the right to sovereign nationhood, even if never again she might attain it.[12]

But on the other hand he was a member of the Young Ireland Branch that was so impatient for self-government that it openly castigated the Irish Parliamentary Party leadership for failing to demand Home Rule *à la* Parnell. In order to drive this forward, Francis Cruise O'Brien penned a moderate sized introduction to a re-publication of a series of essays by the historian Lecky which was to be a contribution to building bridges in Ireland. Again, this particular effort was an example of his trying to be in with all sides, as another letter from Skeffington makes plain:

> Did I tell you of the new Self-government alliance that has been started, to keep the idea of autonomy in the foreground? – the YIB policy, but so worded as to get in a lot of Imperial Home Rulers and Sinn Féiners who wouldn't join the YIB. It is to make its debut in public next week by publishing a forgotten essay of Lecky's on Clerical Influences, with an introduction by Cruise O'Brien and Lloyd, bringing the argument up to date. The book should go well, and do a great deal of good in the Home Rule campaign in England.[13]

The object of Francis Cruise O'Brien's introduction was to disabuse 'The many who find in the existence, or the fear of, sectarianism in Ireland, their strongest argument against the establishment of a national Government in Ireland'.[14] The editors maintain that the situation in the Ireland of 1911, fifty years after Lecky first published this work, was, according to the logic of the republication, similar. The basis for this impression is that there was still some substance to Lecky's synopsis that there was no public opinion in Ireland, just perpetual vacillation on all points, but one: antipathy to the present situation. For Cruise O'Brien this was the challenge: the removal of sectarianism, the achievement of self-government, and the establishment of a truly worthwhile national life.

A clear parallel between Conor Cruise O'Brien and his father can be seen in a number of ways. Firstly, there is their propensity to establish an argument from a historical basis. Francis Cruise O'Brien, adapting Lecky, takes for his starting point the Act of Union. The editors disagree with Lecky when he asserts that sectarianism was the result of clerical influences solely. Rather, they felt that sectarianism arose from:

> The democratic tendencies of the O'Connell movement, and the linking together of the Catholic agitation for emancipation and the national movement for repeal of the Union, had no doubt their effect in alienating the feelings of the Protestant gentry, and that alienation reacted upon the National party who were Catholics, and who more and more identified the Protestant religion with the anti-national party, and directed their resentment against the Protestantism as well as the Unionism of their opponents.[15]

In addition to a historical approach, there are fundamental affinities of temperament between father and son. Having traced the 'undoubted decay of sectarianism', Cruise O'Brien and Lloyd assert that it can hardly be denied that sectarianism still exists in Ireland. Consequently, they 'do not wish to emulate that unfortunately rather numerous class of people who, because they do not wish to face the disagreeable truths of life, have an ostrich-like habit of putting their heads in the sand'.[16]

Another instance of similar temperament can be seen in a disposition which tends to trepidation. The example of the growth in popularity of The Ancient Order of Hibemians is cited to demonstrate the blurring of religious and political criteria, and consequently 'the apprehension it creates of the establishment of a Catholic Ascendancy'.[17] Reasoning from the aphorism 'that there should be no politics in religion, and very little religion in politics', the existence of the Ancient Order of Hibemians is described as the 'evil of a purely sectarian society'.[18] This, on the evidence presented, scarcely seems proven. Nonetheless it appears to be taken as given.

As well as this re-issue of Lecky's essay, in 1917 Francis Cruise O'Brien drafted and published an alternative constitution to the one arising from the 1914 Home Rule Act. Speaking of this Act he offered that 'there are many apologists for the Act of 1914, but it ought definitely to be realised that the provisions of the Act make no appeal now to any except a very small section in the country'.[19] In arguing the case for Dominion status he felt that the overwhelming benefits of such an arrangement would be the maintenance of the unity of the country, and that the 'demand for safeguards made by the people of North Eastern Ulster could be satisfied'.[20] In his draft Bill there were three primary sections which would direct all subsequent articles. The first two are brief. Power would be constituted in an Irish parliament. This body would not have power to make peace or war, or be concerned with the defence of the realm; it would not have the right to make treaties, or to bestow titles of honour. In the third section, the absolutely secular nature of the state was asserted. Its length is striking in contrast to the first two sections. In the specific nature of its stipulations it spells out quite clearly what is meant by secular:

> In the exercise of their power to make laws under this Act the Irish parliament shall not make a law so as either directly or indirectly to establish or endow any religion, or prohibit or restrict the free exercise

thereof, or give a preference, privilege, or advantage, or impose any disability or disadvantage, on account of religious belief or religious or ecclesiastical status, or make any religious belief or ceremony a condition of the validity of any marriage, or affect prejudicially the right of any child to attend a school receiving public money without attending the religious instruction at that school, or alter the constitution of any religious body except where the alteration is approved on behalf of the religious body by the governing body thereof, or divert from any religious denomination the fabric of cathedral churches ... Any law that contravenes this section will be void.

Perhaps if there is any clear example of a resonating genetic echo between father and son it is here in this insistence on a secular approach to politics.

There are only three occasions when Francis Cruise O'Brien's actions get a mention in the London press. The first was a furore over the annual singing of God Save the King, which he prevented and was nearly thrown out of college for. The next related to a speech made at a United Irish Convention when his criticisms of the party were howled down in protest. The third occasion was when he came out in favour of the war and supported Redmond's call for Irishmen to join the British Army. To this day, hints of divisiveness remain in the debate about the Irish and the First World War. Amidst the memory of Irish nationalists of that generation, a certain tainted retrospect applied to those who enlisted, or who supported enlistment. Two individuals who were keen on the war effort were Tom Kettle and Cruise O'Brien.

On this occasion, the latter seems to have picked the 'right' side in terms of family politics. The Sheehys, with the exception of the pacifists Hanna and Frank, were in favour of the war and recruitment to army ranks. David's son Eugene joined up, as did Tom Kettle. The story goes that Cruise O'Brien would also have but for his physical demerits – the received opinion being that 'no recruitment officer would have looked at him twice'.[21] Deemed unfit for active service he wished to use his undoubted eloquence and 'name' to aid enlistment, just like Kettle.[22] However, his son reports that his mother on this occasion put her foot down, and forbade him to give pro-recruitment rallies when he himself was ineligible to serve.[23] Nonetheless, there is more than one reference to Cruise O'Brien dressed in British uniform.[24] It is testament to the whirligig nature of the politics of the time that when war broke out

Tom Kettle was in Belgium purchasing arms for the Irish Volunteers to head off the threat posed by the Loyalist volunteers.[25]

Apart from these rumblings, we know very little of Cruise O'Brien's movements during the war. Apparently he was employed as Sir Horace Plunkett's secretary and basically 'did what needed to be done'. We know however, that he was sufficiently well connected to be able to appeal for clemency for his brother-in-law Frank Sheehy Skeffington, who had been imprisoned for anti-recruitment speeches and had gone on a hunger and thirst strike in Mountjoy prison. He had been on the strike for six days when he was released and Cruise O'Brien was the first to bring the news of his impending release to Hanna who doubted if Frank could have lasted much longer.

Another instance of a similarity between father and son is evident in Cruise O'Brien's brief foray into drama. Towards the start of 1914 he was working on a play, *Candidates*, that resulted in a one night performance in the Abbey Theatre that won little critical approval.[26] While noting that there was an exceptionally large gathering, the critic began by saying that rather than calling it 'a new comedy', it would have been better if it was 'plainly entitled "a farce"'. There was to be no respite in the critic's appraisal:

> The idea that permeates it – the squalid rivalry between two local politi-
> cians for the filling of a 'job' by their respective sons, is so threadbare,
> in its treatment at least, that with every anxiety to say something in its
> favour, one has to pause and wonder how a clever and aspiring young
> writer could not have chosen something worthier of his gifts. The play
> is at best very immature, its humour leaves the impression of being
> greatly forced. The dialogue is poor, affected, and suggests the idea of
> one who wished to caricature, but had not the dramatic instincts to do
> it humorously. And were it not for the really earnest efforts of the ama-
> teurs who filled the parts even the greatly sympathetic audience would
> have wearied of it before the second act was accomplished. The play was
> much applauded and the author was called for at the end. [27]

We can console ourselves with the thought that not only was the play greatly appreciated by most of those present, but that Cruise O'Brien evidently had a good number of friends, who were happy to turn up and support him for such an occasion.

Perhaps the motivation behind the play was his own personal

circumstances. In the five years before and after Conor's birth (1917) Francis Cruise O'Brien was struggling. It was less a case of struggling for an income, although that was a consideration, but he was also struggling to influence events, something which someone of his talents and experience expected to be doing. The son's desire to portray his family in the post-1916 era as a dynasty 'done in' by the new radical politics of the day, while inaccurate, can at least be explained by his need to address his father's lack of success in the world. In O'Brien's case there seems to have been an acute perception that his father neither did enough nor produced enough to merit having fathered so obviously talented a young man as himself.[28] Even if his son's eyes had been a little more dewy, Francis Cruise O'Brien would have suffered by comparison with his Sheehy in-laws. In the years after the Easter Rising, both of David Sheehy's sons were gaining notice and traction in the law. Kathleen Sheehy's sister Hanna was thrusting ahead with both Sinn Féin and the lecturing circuit in the United States. Her other sister, Mary, went on to become a councillor in Dublin. Even O'Brien's mother had several short stories published in *The Irish Statesman*, and a play of hers, *Apartments*, was staged in the Abbey. The one family 'disgrace', Margaret, who had given birth to a son out of wedlock (the father of the child was her own godson), had decamped to Canada. How Conor's father arrived at this inglorious contrast with his in-laws repays a little investigation.

In the years immediately after the Rising Francis Cruise O'Brien was doing a good job of putting forward yesterday's politics. This was mainly because his prospects were attached to the trail of Sir Horace Plunkett's waning star. In the first two decades of twentieth-century Ireland, Plunkett had been one of Ireland's most influential figures. In the third decade he was without any. He is synonymous with the introduction of the cooperative movement into Ireland, and is credited with having had a profound modernizing effect on the country. As one of the most highly regarded figures of his day he spent much of the war as an unofficial envoy between Britain and the United States. The Easter Rising brought him into the thick of Irish politics, where he sought clemency for its leaders and relief for the working class from the worst privations of the day. Francis Cruise O'Brien was by his side for all this. In July 1917 Plunkett was elected chairman of the Irish Convention, an unsuccessful attempt to agree a settlement between the many political claims of the day. Francis Cruise O'Brien, who had for the previous four years in effect been Plunkett's factotum, worked daily on this Convention as one of its secretaries until May 1918. However, this coming together of nearly all of the Irish political parties (Sinn Féin did not attend) served only to make clear the irreconcilable convictions of the day.

> It did not represent popular sentiment in the South which was rapidly accepting the Sinn Féin demand for an independent Republic and it was hamstrung by the promise of partition already given to the North. The failure of the convention drove Plunkett to launch the Irish Dominion Party in 1919 and a new journal, *The Irish Statesman*.[29]

Cruise O'Brien was appointed sub-editor to this new venture, and was secretary to the Dominion Party as well. Neither succeeded.[30] As the final insult to Plunkett his house – 'Kilteragh' – was burned down in 1923: 'The healthiest house in the world and the meeting place of a splendid body of Irishmen and friends of Ireland was destroyed.'[31] Cruise O'Brien, one of those Irishmen, could only watch as his main employer retired to England in disgust and disillusion. 'The man of moderation' as O'Brien portrayed him some forty years later, was squeezed out by the extremes. With Plunkett's departure, Francis Cruise O'Brien became one of yesterday's men.

Cruise O'Brien's various positions in the post-Rising decade are emblematic of the blows fate dealt him. When Conor was born in 1917 his father's occupation was entered on his birth certificate as librarian.[32] During the war he published several economic pamphlets on food production and shortages.[33] He carried these out under the aegis of the Co-operative reference library. This served as a sort of base from which he undertook the various tasks assigned to him by Plunkett. However, this library closed down in the early 1920s when, as a result of a clerical row, its overseers, the Carnegie trust, moved it to Scotland. *The Irish Statesman*, of which Cruise O'Brien was briefly co-editor, was a failure in terms of circulation while being something of a literary success. Its main downfall was that it had no base as it was an extension of the Dominion League, a party of compromise without any real constituency in the extremist environment of the Anglo-Irish war. After losing the position as sub-editor, he joined *The Irish Independent*. It was a wise if unpalatable move. His previous paper the *Freeman's Journal* was destroyed through arson and one of Europe's oldest papers succumbed to the changed political landscape of civil war Ireland. His move to the *Irish Independent* involved a distasteful accommodation. The irony of it was that he ended up working for the paper that cared least for the labour movement, was fully signed up on the nationalist side, was happy to be shot of all of the Anglo-Irish (Plunkett and his ilk), and was staunchly clericalist in its tone and views. That there was little sympathy between the views of the two mattered little in the end: the *Irish Independent* did not really court O'Brien's undoubtedly forthright opinions. According to one view he 'was kept on a very short rein. He was told what to say in editorials, or to write the obituary of a bishop in so many words ... from a journalistic point of view, the rest of his life was one of frustration.'[34]

Socially speaking, O'Brien's father continued much as he had before 1918. He participated in, and occasionally chaired, the Abbey Theatre Lectures group with, amongst others, Æ, Lennox Robinson and W.B. Yeats. Increasingly one of his haunts was the United Arts Club – where he is mentioned in Yeats's diaries in relation to Club activities and various petitions. He was a noted mimic, whose best turn was an impression of Yeats from behind a screen. O'Brien's ex-wife, Christine Foster, had the impression that O'Brien's father's acid tongue, what his son referred to as, 'an ability to wound in a memorable way', led to a few unnecessary skirmishes.[35] Interestingly, when O'Brien came to evaluate some of his father's poetry, he commented that only the pungent satirical ones were of any value.[36] These reflections give the impression that, bar a few friends, his father was encircled by an unfriendly group. If his father was generally unpopular and, as previously mentioned, in debt, then this would go some way to explaining why O'Brien might be forgiven for seeing his father as encircled by a hostile nationalist-clerical nexus. Allied to this, O'Brien persistently blames Sinn Féin for undermining the financial basis of his father's employers. There is undoubtedly some truth to this. But it is also worth pointing out that in contrast with the Sheehys he was singularly unsuccessful in adapting to the new circumstances of independent Ireland. The words of O'Brien's aunt, Hanna, upon Yeats's death, that he was 'a link with the past', offer a good insight into how Cruise O'Brien's set appeared in the new republican scheme of things: otiose.[37]

By way of explanation for his father's situation, O'Brien is keen to stress the intolerance of the early years of the newly founded Irish Free State. In his autobiographical sketches, O'Brien alludes to a disparity between his father's 'spacious principles'[38] and the narrowing tolerance of his fellow countrymen; typified by the legislation that banned divorce and tightened censorship. There is no doubt that the introduction of these new laws gives some substance to O'Brien's charge. It should be noted, however, that the odious censorship legislation only came into effect in 1929, two years after Francis died. The irony is that the majority of the legislation that O'Brien as a young man felt was an encumbrance on the liberty of the individual was only introduced after his father's death. Few would argue against the perception of an increasingly Catholic ethos in the Free State, or the impression that its first years were unhappy ones. But it is also pertinent that during the five years that he experienced the newly independent Ireland, Cruise O'Brien was unsatisfactorily employed and of less and less significance. O'Brien's father's position in the fledgling state could go some way to explain his son's marked asperity toward the period in to which he was born.

However, behind all this social and political conjecture, one is left with the impression that Francis Cruise O'Brien could have done far more with his abundant talents if he were not dogged by ill health. Several letters from his wife in the war years and after refer to him as bed-ridden.[39] The Sheehys had repeatedly counselled Kathleen against marrying him on the grounds that he was so obviously weak. Frank Sheehy Skeffington reports that around the time of their engagement Cruise O'Brien had agreed to undergo a medical to try and convince them that he was physically well. O'Brien himself says that a recruiting sergeant would not have looked twice at his father. Whether Francis Cruise O'Brien would have remained forever marginalized by the inhospitable 'new' Irish society will remain unknown. He died from tuberculosis after a long illness on Christmas Day 1927.[40]

The legacy of the lost parent is something which would leave a lifelong mark on O'Brien. In his later years he would continually refer to his father's contribution to his own distinctiveness. There is no doubt a great deal of truth in this view. But it is also right to investigate what might be seen as an even greater contribution: the Sheehy legacy embodied in his complicated relationship with his mother.

NOTES

1. See Conor Cruise O'Brien, *States of Ireland* (London, 1972), p.62 for a brilliant analysis of the Sheehys' relation to the language.
2. Ibid.
3. Ibid.
4. According to Margaret Ward, *Hanna Sheehy Skeffington: A Life* (Cork, 1997), it was a religious issue. FCOB was an agnostic. She also mentions that at the time there were incessant family rows and that Tom and Mary were ganging up against Kathleen and Cruise O'Brien. Sheehy Skeffington papers (SSP), National Library of Ireland (NLI), MS 40,470/9.
5. Frank Sheehy Skeffington (FSS) to Willie Moloney, 5 July 1909. SSP, NLI, MS 40,470/9.
6. O'Brien, *States of Ireland*, p.83.
7. Author interviews with Justin Keating, Dublin, November 2003.
8. The Irish Transport and General Workers Union (ITGWU), Jim Larkin's newly founded union that would be central to the main lockout. D.R. Lysaght O'Connor, *End of a Liberal: The Literary Politics of Conor Cruise O'Brien* (Dublin, 1978).
9. Another view is that he left because of his agnosticism: Frank Sheehy Skeffington to Willie Moloney, 22 May 1911: 'I think he will be able to get along there for a time at any rate. Of course he will have to go to Mass and pay dues to the clergy! But he may be presumed to have accomplished his Easter Duty this year, so that difficulty won't crop up for a twelvemonth.' SSP, NLI, MS 40,470/9.
10. FSS to Hanna Sheehy Skeffington (HSS), 20 December 1913, SSP, NLI, MS 40,463/4. Markievicz added: 'When he came back to Dublin, Mrs. Duncan gave him credit for dinners at the Arts Club, and he accordingly owes Mrs. D. £36; which Madame M thinks a shame, as Mrs. D is very poor and hardly able to get along! She is afraid of Cruise being made Treasurer of the Civic League, and getting moneys carelessly mixed up; but there is no danger of that. She apparently came to me as a warning not to run him for any post – which needless to say I had no intention of doing! But its quite on the cards that he may become one of the secretaries. No one has mentioned such a thing yet, but I feel it is in the air … and there appears no-one else to be competent.'
11. I am using the plural throughout, because Conor's mother had noticeably spendthrift ways as well.
12. Frank Cruise O'Brien, 'Contemporary Irishmen – Arthur Griffith', *The Leader*, 10 May 1910.
13. FSS to Willie Moloney, 10 February 1911. SSP, NLI, MS 40,470/9.
14. W.E.G. Lloyd and F.C. O'Brien, 'Introduction', in W.E.H. Lecky, *Clerical Influences: An Essay on Irish Sectarianism and English Government* (Dublin, 1911), p.1.
15. Ibid., p.10.
16. Ibid.
17. Ibid., p.13.
18. Ibid.
19. Diarmuid Coffey and Francis Cruise O'Brien, *Proposals for an Irish Settlement. Being a Draft Bill for the Government of Ireland* (Dublin, 1917).
20. Ibid.
21. O'Brien, *States of Ireland*, p.84.
22. Mary Kettle, in a tribute to the subsequent stigmatization of enlistees as much as how Kettle perceived his actions at the time, describes him some fifty years later as: 'a great Irishman fighting in the allied ranks, not as a British soldier but as an Irishman in a European Army fighting to establish the rights of the small nations in Europe'. Mary Kettle to Conor Cruise O'Brien, 22 February 1965. SSP, NLI, MS 40,489/8.
23. Another concern for Kathleen was the possibility of a serious breach with Hanna.
24. Ward, *Hanna Sheehy Skeffington*. Also Leah Levenson, *With Wooden Sword: A Portrait of Francis Sheehy-Skeffington, Militant Pacifist* (Dublin, 1983).
25. Alvin Jackson's book on Home Rule states that Francis Cruise O'Brien, Diarmuid Coffey and Erskine Childers were 'all gun runners for the Irish Volunteers before the War'. Alvin Jackson, *Home Rule: An Irish History* (Oxford, 2003), p.179.

26. One of 'Three New Plays'. *A Game For Two* by Ernest Tunbridge, *A New Question of Honour* by Annie Lloyd, and *Candidates: a New Comedy in 3 Acts* by Cruise O'Brien. The play was on Friday 27 March 1914.
27. 'Review of Candidates', *Freeman's Journal*, 28 March 1914.
28. When reading his parent's notebook, he came across the words 'failed to set a single straw ablaze', and felt that this accurately summed up his father's lack of achievement. College Notebook, Monday February 1939. O'Brien papers, UCD, P82/328.
29. J.J. Byrne, 'Æ and Sir Horace Plunkett', in Conor Cruise O'Brien (ed.), *The Shaping of Modern Ireland* (London, 1960), p.130.
30. A re-launched *Irish Statesman* (incorporating *The Irish Homestead*) under the editorship of Æ was, however, very successful.
31. Byrne, 'Æ and Sir Horace Plunkett', p.135.
32. 'Permission to travel card'. 1918 permit to FCOB to return to Ireland for one month. '32 years old, slight build, dark hair, 5'5' tall. Profession: librarian.' O'Brien Papers, UCD, P82/653.
33. Lionel Smith-Gordon and Francis Cruise O'Brien, *Co-operation in Denmark*, *Co-operation in Many Lands*, *Co-operation in Ireland* (Manchester: The Co-operative Union Movement, 1919–21).
34. D.H. Akenson, *Conor: A Biography of Conor Cruise O'Brien* (Montreal, 1994), p.68.
35. O'Brien, *States of Ireland*; O'Brien, *Memoir*. O'Brien's ex-wife also mentioned that she had met O'Brien's aunt, his father's sister, who worked in the Embassy in London, and her son. 'They both had pretty acid tongues, which I think is characteristic of the O'Brien's.' Interview with Christine Foster in Anthony Jordan, *To Laugh or To Weep* (Dublin, 1994), p.19.
36. Conor Cruise O'Brien, Diary, February 1939. O'Brien Papers, UCD, P82/328.
37. Quoted in Conor Cruise O'Brien, 'Passion and Cunning: An Essay on the Politics of W.B. Yeats', in A.N. Jeffares and K.M. Cross (eds), *In Excited Reverie* (London, 1965).
38. W.E.H. Lecky's phrase, which is often quoted with approbation by O'Brien's father in his reprint of Lecky's essay on religious tolerance. Lloyd and Cruise O'Brien, *Clerical Influences*.
39. In 1915 Francis Cruise O'Brien was reported to be recuperating in Limerick on holiday with the Monteagles: 'Cruise is getting on nicely. He has to take it very quietly, any exercise makes his head dizzy still so he mostly basks in the sun and argues.' Another letter chips in, 'he is cheery and argumentative as ever when not headachey'. Or on another occasion Kathleen reports that, 'The sight of a doctor would end him. Having no ambitions in the widow line, I declined to call one.' Kathleen Cruise O'Brien to Hanna Sheehy. SSP, NLI MS 41,476/4.
40. Francis Cruise O'Brien, Obituaries. *The Irish Times* and *Irish Independent*. 27 December 1927.

3

Mother

Before we can first speak of legacies, maternal love and O'Brien's intellectual formation, it is important to discover who O'Brien's mother was. Physically, if Francis was short, light and wiry, Kathleen by all accounts was altogether more substantial. She was not too bothered by her weight: in one of her articles she allowed her size to be a light-hearted punch line (everybody was laughing because she was handing out leaflets in front of a Guinness sign which read 'Extra Stout'). She was happy to describe herself as 'as large a person as you can comfortably think of'.[1] She was, nonetheless, an active lady who ultimately was more industrious than her husband.[2] In letters to her family there are frequent references to various short-term projects undertaken and yet another mounting pile of scripts to be corrected. She was seen as the most pliable of the Sheehys: 'I hate refusing to do things you ask me – that's my confounded amiability I suppose.'[3] In a similar vein O'Brien has said that she was regarded as the 'nicest of the Sheehys, in favourable contrast to her formidable sisters, Hanna and Mary'.[4] Outwardly, she could be a vivacious woman. Even if she seemed 'quiet', she was, after all, a Sheehy, which meant that she was hardwired for a comic turn or a charade or an evening of lively banter. In the weeks after her death, many of the friends who commiserated with her sister Hanna remarked on her good nature and excellent company. An earlier letter from her nephew Owen to Hanna reported that her fellow guests on a holiday in Glencormac were 'asking for Aunt K and Conor. Says Aunt K was life and soul of party here.'[5]

She was similar to Hanna in that she was highly intelligent and was an academic overachiever. Like Hanna she went on to pursue a master's degree after her BA at the Royal University. She lived abroad for a year in France and became fluent in French. In later life she had a marked propensity for interspersing her utterances with Gallicisms, a trait that she passed on to Conor. What marked her out most from her siblings was that she also studied Irish and spent much of her time in the Aran Islands. A family legend, albeit one initiated by Richard Ellmann in his landmark biography of James Joyce,[6] has it that she was the original of Miss Ivors in Joyce's 'The Dead'. However, it is highly unlikely that she was a model for Miss Ivors as Kathleen was at least five years younger than Joyce, and Miss Ivors was a fellow university instructor with Gabriel Conroy in the story. Even if 'The Dead' need not be taken so literally, it would be unusual if O'Brien's mother made that much of an impression on Joyce. At the time he was attending the Sheehy family salons she would have been 13 years old. Furthermore her time in the Aran Islands and her proficiency in Irish would have come well after Joyce left Dublin.[7] Finally, the accusation Miss Ivors whispered at Gabriel, that he was a 'West Briton', would to an extent have fitted onto anyone of the Sheehy family, as they had all allowed the Gaelic revival to pass them by, and were quite vehement in their refusal to learn Irish. O'Brien himself was initially unimpressed by the evidence and quite honestly stated that the possibility that his mother was the original of Miss Ivors only became 'apparent' when Richard Ellmann suggested it in his book.[8]

Whatever about her near Joycean immortalization, she could have been Miss Ivors as she was a committed Irish language revivalist who made teaching Irish her career. After Francis died she was a full-time teacher of Irish in Rathmines Technical Institute. In the 1920s she went so far as to write the textbook introduction to standardized Irish for Irish language students, and an Irish version of Gregg shorthand.[9] She was also an inspector and examiner of some sort, as there are references to her travelling from school to school around the country, and awaiting cheques from the 'N.U.I.'[10] Possibly as significant is that a play of hers, *Apartments*, was good enough to merit a production at the Abbey Theatre in Dublin in 1925.[11] Although it received little critical acclaim, it did manage to avoid being panned. It must have made something of a good impression, as there were several attempts to re-stage it and to bring it on tour to Manchester.[12] She also wrote several short stories that were published in *The Irish Statesman*. If her play *Apartments* is light, bantering and tongue in cheek, these earlier stories are examples of a dark and more brooding character, which according to O'Brien could be solemn and introspective. An extract from one of these stories two years after he was born betrays what the editor describes as 'the true note, the note of passionate gloom'.[13]

She walks as in a dream, a cruel tearless dream in which she must play her hard part to the end. Her happiness has fallen in pieces around her. The last link with life has snapped. Her heart grows cold and numb.[14]

Although it might not be evident from this piece, she was, much more so than her husband, a gifted and natural writer. The best examples of it come across in beautifully concise and well-crafted letters, which was perhaps her true metier. These letters convey an unmistakeable voice of infectious glee and a warm and disarming wit; half the fun of her wit was in how it was mischievously, if charmingly, employed. It was a gift that she passed on to Conor, whose personal correspondence is totally at variance with his sombre public articles. As his ex-wife Christine later commented, O'Brien 'was incapable of writing a bad sentence'.[15] One could go further and point out that, in the eyes of one critic, he was once described with Gore Vidal, as 'the best living essayist'.[16] He can be grateful to his mother for this.

In religion Kathleen Cruise O'Brien was undoubtedly a practising Catholic. In later years O'Brien was anxious to portray her as merely lurching back into the faith after the trauma of her husband's death. There is undoubtedly a good deal of truth in this; for a time she was grieving manically. Nonetheless, while Francis was still alive, she carried out all the Catholic sacraments with his full knowledge, despite his apparently strongly held views on agnosticism. Thus, she not only made sure that Conor was baptised, but she brought him up to be fully Catholic: he attended Mass weekly, and she went to considerable lengths and personal trouble to see that he made his Holy Communion and Confirmation.[17]

His mother clearly doted on Conor; if others thought he was a reasonably good-looking baby, then she knew him to be 'a distinct success'. While not even a year old, she helplessly reports that 'Conor has developed a certain strength of will – in other children it might be known as obstinacy or "divilment" but of course in him it is just "Mrs. Skeffington's spirit" and therefore to be encouraged rather than blamed.'[18] Nonetheless, the fallout from the spotlight of his mother's love can be seen a decade later. Writing from a convent in Athlone, where Kathleen was superintending Irish, she wrote:

Conor and I are being very well treated here. Conor of course made himself at home from the start and has all the nuns fluttering about him,

giving him drinks, rides and chasing him up trees, till he's quite convinced that that's what they're there for.[19]

If the image of nuns fluttering about him didn't quite mark out his life
course, another report, this time to her nephew, creates a charming
image of the mother and very young son, side by side writing to the
same person:

> While Conor is painstakingly hammering out his thoughts on the corona
> [typewriter] I take refuge in pen, ink and paper of a past age and enter
> the race ... Your mother took Conor to Dalkey Island yesterday. I gather
> he is telling you of it. The young runt refuses all assistance with his
> labours, so I hope it will make a good impression. I am not to see it till
> it is a fait accompli.

While Conor's father began reading Latin to him, and taught him chess,
it was his mother who made writing fun, and brought in to the young
boy's mind the strange wonder of writing to an audience. From the
letter itself we can see that she was providing all the conditions
necessary for the development of the future journalist who, after the
family excursion, painstakingly re-crafted it on the typewriter, the
apprentice sorcerer's new toy.[20]

On the other hand, the young boy who was utterly doted on by both
parents was unquestionably spoilt. If anything, when his father died,
his mother tried to compensate by spoiling him more; thus the new
typewriter, or camera, or giving him a great big bedroom, or a brand
new bike or table tennis table, or the setting up of a little museum and
library within his room. All of this was done to the highest and best of
standards. The family tradition of spending fast and big, regardless of
income, became a trademark. In the aftermath of her husband's death
she is reported to be taking a much needed holiday with some of the in-
surance money.[21] A few years later her nephew could still marvel at her
extravagance in the face of clearly straitened circumstances: 'Aunt K is
the limit: New eider-down, linoleum, ping-pong table (50/- !).'[22] It was
typical that the Cruise O'Briens who really had only a modest
income employed a housemaid and a nursemaid at the time of Conor's
birth. The indispensability of a maid to his mother is clear from the
following extract:

> Conor and I returned from Glencormac on the 30th, to find a maidless

house awaiting us, as Nora evidently made up her mind she couldn't stay idle any longer and had better get a place where she'd have some work to do ... I had to send an S.O.S. to Sadie to come a few hours a day till I got someone to take pity on me.[23]

The extent to which this was a genuine pickle or a penchant for drama is hard to gauge. Clearly, while she was no doubt a highly capable woman in many regards, she was, either by nature or choice, 'all thumbs' when it came to cooking and housework. This was something she also passed on to her young son, who apparently 'never so much as boiled an egg'.[24] Coming from a family who were more grand and voluble than actually rich, this pretence of a genteel existence, however parlous or shabby, was a central part of her upbringing and self-image. As one commentator remarked, 'she was very conscious of who she was'.[25] This social fiction and the necessary shabby genteel snobbery that came with it were 'mother's milk' to the young (and old) O'Brien.

The trait of wilfulness that had begun when the young Conor was not even one (the 'divilment' of 'Mrs. Skeffington's spirit'), is further enhanced by a bevy of retainers, and reinforced again and again by adoring parents, until it reached the stage where the very presence of grownups, or even nuns, could be construed as part of a grand design for his convenience and amusement. It is little wonder then that a certain egoism can be detected in a good part of his later actions and words when, according to one reviewer, the young O'Brien 'seemed to have been like the child Jesus in the Temple surrounded by adoring elders who listened to him spellbound'.[26] However, the relationship between the 'child Jesus' and his mother did not always run the way it might have in his ideal world. One or two incidents show that while his mother always adored him, she could on occasion be a stern woman. For instance she was capable of holding her own against the ranged forces of her entire family who attempted to block her marriage. She also intervened to curb one or two of her husband's exuberant political meanderings, such as pro-War recruitment speeches. Occasionally Conor was prevented from getting his way, as in the time when he was not allowed to choose Greek as a school subject. His mother insisted that he choose Irish, perhaps because it was very dear to her heart, and perhaps because it made a great deal more sense to his career. In any case Conor did Irish. However, one gets the impression from his latter day account of this 'choice' that her insistence continued to rankle with him. More darkly perhaps, his relationship with her, as portrayed in *Memoir*, is characterized by what he describes as a sense of 'faint mistrust'.[27] The reasons for this are linked to a few separate incidents, but the essentials in all cases are the same: his mother became angry with Conor for reasons he found hard to determine, and he never forgave her. On one evening, for example:

> I was in bed between my mother and father, something that had never happened before. I felt so happy and secure that I did a kind of somersault in the air. Unfortunately as I did so, my nightshirt fell over my head, exposing my naked body. Apparently my mother found this spectacle revolting. She spoke to me with sharp disgust, a tone she had never used to me before, telling me to cover myself immediately. I felt as if I had been hit by an icy blast in a moment of joy and security. I cowered under the sheets.[28]

Writing about the incident seventy years later, O'Brien said that although it 'had been a tiny incident lasting only a few seconds which seared me', nonetheless the memory of it 'occasionally returned to haunt me in my maturity'. Apparently it was not the first time that she lost her temper, either with Conor or Francis. As quick as she was to anger, her husband jokingly chided her for not being as scary as her sisters. She had the disagreeable tendency to merely 'go off the handle', which was but a pale imitation of their 'cold fury'.[29]

In religious terms O'Brien's father is described as what in the Jewish tradition would be called a *maskil*, 'that is to say that he was a person of the Enlightenment', an avowed agnostic.[30] In the parlance of Ireland this simply meant that he was 'a lapsed Catholic'. O'Brien's mother, on the other hand, did not lapse in her faith. Although not as demonstrably religious as her sister Mary, nor her father David who attended Mass six times daily, Catholicism was clearly a central part of her life, especially after her husband's death. Even when Francis Cruise O'Brien was alive, Conor underwent the full gamut of Catholic rituals. Not only was he baptised, but he also went to school in Muckross Convent to allow him to take part in his first Holy Communion. After his father's death, the difficult decision to send him to Sandford Park School, a largely Protestant institution, was made for what were largely financial reasons. A collection was got together to allow him to study there. This, as pointed out by O'Brien in his *Memoir*, constituted a sound financial reason to soften the blow of what would otherwise appear to be an openly 'heretical' decision in the eyes of the clergy. Nonetheless, that is not to say that this was an easy decision for his mother, nor was it a decision without emotional and spiritual sacrifice. There is a very moving passage in one of his later works, when he recalls how his mother had to beseech the local priest to allow Conor to make his confirmation, even though he was not attending a Catholic school at the time.

> I not merely stayed on at Sandford [after his father's death], but was allowed while there to be confirmed (in the Catholic church in Haddington Road), an unusual, though not unique concession at this time. The process of obtaining this concession was, however, distasteful. I remember standing with my mother one winter evening outside the front door of the Parish Priest of Rathmines, while that ecclesiastic – a purple, pear shaped person – spoke gruffly to my mother through a chink in the door.[31]

Even at a distance of fifty years, this incident recalls a certain bitterness, which led him to immediately launch into a barbed reflection on 'the oppressive pieties of the Catholic State'.[32]

To be put in this position would clearly have an effect on the young boy's attitude to all things clerical. Possibly, in trying to ensure that her son stayed within the Catholic fold his mother made his departure from it all the more likely. That he did turn his back on the church is evident, although it probably did not happen as quickly as one might suppose. As late as 1938 a friend of the family, Rosamund Jacob, wrote into her diary that his aunt was making the complaint that 'Conor was no longer a Catholic' as if it were a recent revelation. It would seem O'Brien's departure from Catholicism was a gradual distancing from the church, which was probably connected to his mother's death in 1938 and his entry into college, where he adopted the guise of a godless radical. The point is worth making though that it was in some ways a part of his inheritance to become an agnostic. As the characterization of his father as a *'maskil'* indicates, this was always going to be one half of his intellectual inheritance. Not only had his father been one, but Owen Sheehy Skeffington, in effect his older brother, was a very determined one and when O'Brien went to Trinity he was to an extent choosing this path.

However, to put forward an outright victor in some notional
battle between mother and father is a step too far. His biographer, Don
Akenson, characterizes it as a 'serious parental power struggle', which
focused on religion.[33] This posits a major cultural divergence between
the two with Francis looking to the world of Europe and Kathleen to
Ireland. Akenson reckons that on every issue Conor became his father's
son. This ultimately drew him toward 'the male, the non-Catholic, the
Enlightenment, and effervescence'.[34] This seems too strong. Perhaps
from a 1980s or 1990s perspective it would seem appropriate. But it is
wrong to map the political standpoint of a 70-year-old man onto his
embryonic teenage self. If we re-examine the interaction of the various
positions of his parents, the situation is a lot less clear-cut. On the question of religion, and from a typically Irish point of view, his mother was
perfectly in synch with the vast majority of the population. Conor's
father on the other hand was a professed agnostic, which in 1920s
Ireland was not quite the thing. His father's political point of view was
decidedly less in tune with the country's post-Independence anti-British
mood. It was not just his association with the now defunct Irish Party
that would have separated him from the 'madding crowd'; it was more
his active support of the war effort, his support for enlisting Irishmen
into the British Army, and latterly for the Irish Dominion League.
Whatever the merits of these positions at the time, when viewed
through a post Irish-revolution retrospect, all Francis Cruise O'Brien's
stances were seen as essentially 'colonial' or British.

Conor's mother Kathleen on the other hand came from 'good'
nationalist stock. While she too may have been comfortable in the
'colonial set', as it were, it was more of a question of social preference,
rather than political conviction. She could mix in these circles while
still being of the 'sitting down for God Save the King' variety. As her
suffragist background attests, she was inclined by natural persuasion to
a more radical outlook. On the question of the language there is a
similar division. If Conor's uncle, Judge Eugene Sheehy, was dismissing
the Irish language in 1932 as a 'useless cult',[35] Conor's father was not
too far behind as there is no record of him having ever engaged in any
revival activities. On this point the mature O'Brien regrets that Irish
and Greek clashed on the school curriculum. When it came to making
a decision, with his father now dead, he was alone in wanting to do
Greek. The unanimous decision of his family was that he should do

Irish as it was at the time viewed as the 'union card' for success in Irish public life. Thus, if he ever wished to join the public service, or have credibility in politics, he simply had to choose Irish. On this issue, whether he liked it or not, he ended up on his mother's side.

On matters of society, both parents were singing from the same hymn sheet. Amateur dramatists and actors, journalists and writers, sprinkled with colourful Anglo-Irish characters such as Lord Monteagle and Conor O'Brien (his godfather) were, typically, their set. There might have been some pressure on them to maintain social status in challenging financial times, but it was a task to which both parents were committed. When O'Brien in later life showed himself to be remarkably adept at keeping his head above the financial water, it was a trait learned early from the mistakes of both parents. So too his fondness for sharing elbow space in Fleet Street, or his comfort in anglophile establishments, be they in Ireland, England, the United States or colonial Africa.

It is an overstatement, then, to say that on every count his father won each of the important parental battles for Conor's future direction. In the immediate aftermath of his death, we will see that the concerns of his mother and his radical aunt and cousin were far more to the fore than the passé stances of his father. His father's voice might loom large in later life, but to the early outlook, and indeed the mature mind of the young O'Brien, that voice was far from compelling. To a large extent the tensions between the claims of the two parents were fought out in O'Brien's mind over the next eighty years. But for this 'battle of ideas', the competing claims of his Sheehy and Cruise O'Brien heritage, both his life and his mind would have been far less interesting.

All the charms and tensions between the two parents were sundered with the blow dealt to O'Brien on Christmas Day 1927 when his father died.

> The disaster began at mid-morning when I went to my father's bedroom – to which he was confined by his illness – to receive his present: a bow and arrow. He greeted me with his usual cheerfulness, and sat up to bend the bow. As he bent it he suddenly turned deadly pale and fell back on the pillow.[36]

Conor's mother immediately sent Conor away to get his aunt Mary. His father died shortly after. In his *Memoir* he does not tell us what he felt at the news of his father's death. Any trace of a wound is expunged. He seems to have come to terms with the death itself in that he manages to state what his father's loss would mean to him. He would miss his sense of fun, his lively good humour and 'his keen intelligence and loving attention to me'.[37]

What he does dwell on from that day are the details of what happened after the death. He was ignored. When he got back to the house with his aunt, he was told his father was dead. He was immediately sent away while his mother and aunt engaged in a fierce debate about whether a priest should be called. His mother stood her ground and respected her dead husband's wishes: no priest was called. His strongly Catholic Aunt Mary left with an aura of strong disapproval and 'without taking leave of me'. For the rest of the day he was left alone.

> My mother then retired to her room, roaring crying, and remained there for the rest of that terrible afternoon. During those hours, my grief-stricken mother seemed entirely to have forgotten my own existence. It was as if I had lost both parents, not just one.[38]

In his portrayal of the long emotionally torrid afternoon that followed, a rift in his relationship with his mother seems to have opened. The 10-year-old boy felt that he should not have been ignored and left alone to deal with the demons of loss. Many years later when O'Brien the octogenarian wrote his *Memoir*, it is remarkable to witness the still live feelings of hurt and bewilderment at having been 'abandoned' over seventy years ago. In those few hours he recalls being rooted at the end of their long mahogany table while staring transfixed at an enormous picture entitled 'The Polish Conscript'. It is a painting of a young man with his parents who are crying before he is sent off to a war they fear he will never return from. O'Brien's raw account of the day leaves a very clear image of him sitting at this table, brooding over a cruel world in a near empty house envisaging a perpetual winter, petrified with fear of a future without his parents. As he said of that time, the painting and its subject symbolized 'the gloomiest period of my life'. He also remarked of that day, that if he had not been rescued by his relatives, if 'the conditions of that terrible afternoon had lasted much longer, I believe I would have been psychologically impaired for life'.[39] He was 'rescued' by his cousin and aunt, Owen and Hanna

Sheehy Skeffington. In the immediate aftermath, they provided normalcy and consolation, and in the years that followed their guidance and political mores became central to his development, perhaps to an even greater extent than either his mother or father.

How his mother lost his trust is bound up with the year that followed his father's death, which was undoubtedly their worst time together. The first crisis they had to deal with was the financial impact of his father's death. While the Cruise O'Brien's were never wealthy, and had always lived beyond their means, with the loss of the main breadwinner the family finances took a serious dent. His mother now returned to work fulltime. Even so, given her extravagance and her need to maintain an appearance of wealth, she was increasingly forced to turn to moneylenders. Conor recalls that on one such occasion, 'she handed me a letter addressed in neat handwriting to 'The Sterling Finance Co.' ... my mother had been forced to borrow money from a firm of usurers at interest of 39 per cent'.[40] One commentator has it that 'the bailiffs were in and out of the house from Francis's death onwards. The public shame of these seizures of chattels must have been deeply humiliating, especially for a Sheehy.'[41] Strangely, the worst forebodings of Kathleen's parents had come to pass. Her husband had died young and she was flirting with a repeat of her own father's bankruptcy.

A knock-on effect of their financial troubles was an attendant emotional absence. She was now obliged to work full-time in order to try and keep the bodies and souls of what remained of their little 'trio' going. She was fortunate to get a full-time position in Rathmines Technical Institute teaching Irish. She was also able to supplement her income by supervising and invigilating. Naturally, she was present at home a good deal less. When she was actually at home she had a large workload of corrections and preparation. She also took upon herself the task of writing a book – the Gregg shorthand primer for Irish – at this time. All in all, it would have been a significant lifestyle change for her and for Conor. One gets the impression that he felt the lack of attention and intimacy keenly. It is unfair to her memory and her effort but all this reinforced his impression that he had lost both parents.

Another way in which Francis's death affected Conor was the strengthening of his mother's Catholic faith. In her loneliness and despair she turned to prayer. From his perspective this no doubt signalled yet another preoccupation with things other than himself. To the grown-up, decidedly agnostic O'Brien, this religious 'turn' encapsulated the gloominess and dreariness of those dark days. What signalled this change most clearly was the presence on his mother's bedside table of a book entitled *In Heaven We Know Our Own*, by the unfortunately named Father Blot, SJ. O'Brien connects this development with a general feeling of guilt towards the soul of her recently departed husband. He felt that guilt-ridden questions along the lines of, 'Should she have let him have the last rites?', 'Should she have brought him closer to God?', and the innumerable other questions which plague a Catholic grief-stricken widow, had a coruscating effect on her in the years after his father's death. A further pressure added to this mix, was the question of his indefinite time in purgatory. This flexible metaphysical conundrum was a form of psychological torture for the newly widowed Kathleen. It found its most concrete test in the question of whether to send Conor to Sandford Park. That she held her nerve, in the face of repeated provocation, amidst a sea of theological pressure and doubt, is tribute to a heroic attempt on her part to remain true to her husband's wishes.

One particular occasion served to demonstrate the pressure his mother was under when her financial position and the theological battlefield combined.

> After my father's death, my mother was desperately short of money and started to teach longer hours. This sometimes meant leaving me alone in the house, at night, when I was ten to eleven years old, and frightened of being left, perhaps, without any parent.

On one such occasion he did become frightened and seeing a light on in the house next door, made his way over to their neighbours, the Adams's, who brought him in and fed him. When his mother arrived home and he was not there, she became frantic. Eventually she called on her neighbours:

> She found me comfortably ensconced at the Adams's table, and she was furiously angry: angrier than I had ever seen her before or was ever to see her again ... When we got home my mother threatened me: something she had never done before, and was never to do again. She said that if I ever did something like that again she would have to send me 'to Cabra'.[42]

Conor understood Cabra to be an institution where 'people sent un-
wanted or unmanageable boys'. (Typically for the sharp-tongued
Sheehy sisters there was an added barb, as Cabra was typically reserved
for boys with mental difficulties!) He knew that she would not do such
a thing, but continued to be deeply hurt and perplexed by the outburst.
As he said himself, it was 'quite unlike her usual friendly, rather genial,
self'.[43] The only reason he could find was that the Adams were
Protestants. Knowing that his mother was no anti-Protestant bigot, and
that many of their friends were Protestants, only made it more
perplexing. But the reason he came up with was that there was
considerable pressure on her at the time to give him up for adoption to
a Lord Monteagle. Here he is referring to a claim that Lord Monteagle,
who was on friendly terms with the family, had offered to adopt the
young O'Brien. Unfortunately this would have meant that his mother
would have to give him up entirely and that he would be brought up a
Protestant and heir to the Monteagle seat. If the offer did genuinely
occur, then it is testament to the obvious financial and emotional
squeeze that Conor's mother was suffering at the time. It also suggests
that Conor came across as a bright and articulate young boy, who even
at so young an age was creating a strong impression. To Kathleen Cruise
O'Brien's credit she refused, and one of Ireland's most intriguing lives
was allowed to come into being.

While the Monteagle adoption story is one explanation for her
outburst, an equally plausible reason for his mother's fury presents itself, and this reason probably actually did have something to do with
'Cabra'. This was simply that in the 1930s, and before and beyond, it
would not have been unheard of for a cleric to petition a court to have
the child removed from the custody of an unfit mother. While not
suggesting that his mother was anything approaching unfit, it would
be entirely plausible for someone who resented or disliked her, or who
disapproved of his schooling, to put together the devilish equation of
a young Catholic boy alone and 'neglected' being taken into the
company of Protestants. Such things did happen to boys of that age,
even in Dublin, and even to middle-class families.[44] Whether it would
have happened or not, the possibility of it goes someway to explaining
the loneliness and difficulty of Kathleen Cruise O'Brien's position in
those days after her husband's death. What was worse was the effect it
began to take on her health, and the knock-on effect of this on him.

In her deep and multiple worries, my mother started smoking very heavily, around sixty cigarettes a day. Her health suffered and she was racked,
once a week or so, by violent disabling headaches. She knew that I was
emotionally dependent on her, and that I resented her frequent unavail-
ability and glum preoccupations. But those were the conditions of her life
with me.[45]

In this time of glumness, the only outlet was the surrounding family.
But in all three cases of the extended family, they too were widowed.
His Aunt Hanna's husband, Frank Sheehy Skeffington, his Aunt Mary
Kettle's husband, Tom Kettle, and his Aunt Margaret's husband, Frank
Culhane, had all passed away. Even more bizarrely they had all died in
1916. As if that were not bad enough, two other widows lived close
by, and were in some way connected to the family, Constance
Markievicz (although she herself died not long after) and Maud Gonne,
Yeats's muse. O'Brien paints a marvellous picture of the legendary
Maud Gonne, or 'Madame MacBride' as she styled herself in the
afterglow of the Easter 1916 Rising.

> When her husband, whom she loathed, was shot by a British firing squad
> after the Easter Rising, Madame MacBride – as she now came to be
> known – attired herself from head to toe in the most spectacular set of
> widow's weeds ever seen in Dublin, to which she returned from Paris in
> 1917 ... I still remember her as I first saw her in that garb, about ten
> years later in Leinster Road, Rathmines. With her great height and noble
> carriage, her pale beaked gaunt face, and large lustrous eyes, and gliding
> along in that great flapping cloud of black, she seemed like the Angel of
> Death: or more precisely like the crow-like bird, the Morrigu, that her-
> alds death in the Gaelic sagas.[46]

This is where his description (in one of his earliest diary entries) of his
upbringing as a 'walled-in city childhood' comes in. It is a rather
compelling picture of the year after his father's death, where it seemed
that he was 'walled-in' by widowhood. Even worse was the effect it all
seemed to have on his life. It is a sad image of the two of them within
the set-up of their large and frequently empty house: 'We loved each
other but were desperately lonely together.' This barren and oppressive
urban landscape with its mix of death and bereavement, of cigarettes
and ill health, of a renewed Catholic faith and its attendant morose
absorptions, formed 'the twisted dream' in the young boy's mind. If

this winter did not overwhelm him, he was not entirely successful in rejecting it either. Its effects were like a vague shadow that would threaten his happiness forever.

Something which snatched O'Brien from the threshold of gloom that enveloped his youth was the fraternity of another isolated and unusual individual – his cousin Owen Sheehy Skeffington. Their relationship offered a radical camaraderie and a common bond in dealing with the cloying atmosphere of their Sheehy mothers, the isolating ménage of widowhood and the oppressions of their family's historical legacy. How his cousin Owen shielded him from the effects of this ethos is worth exploring. Not only does it illustrate the tensions instilled by their similar upbringing, but it also suggests a departure from the warring camps of his youth, and a beginning of O'Brien's own unique voice.

NOTES

1. Katherine Cruise O'Brien, 'From Ireland'. No date, no publication details. A typescript for a memorial volume in memory of Frank Sheehy Skeffington. Sheehy Skeffington Papers (SSP), National Library of Ireland (NLI).
2. 'I am looking after 118 Upper Leeson Street, as an abode and as a dwelling.' Another letter goes: 'Tired! Taught all Saturday and Sunday.' Katherine Cruise O'Brien to Hanna Sheehy Skeffington. No date, c. 1913. SSP, NLI, MS 41,176/4.
3. Katherine Cruise O'Brien (KCO'B) to Hanna Sheehy Skeffington (HSS), from 'Arts Club' 1913, no other date. SSP, NLI, MS 41,176/4.
4. Conor Cruise O'Brien, *Memoir* (Dublin, 1998), p.13.
5. Owen Sheehy Skeffington (OSS) to HSS. No date (1933). SSP/NLI 82, MSS 41,176/5.
6. Richard Elmann, *James Joyce* (Oxford, 1959).
7. Peter Costelloe, *James Joyce the Years of Growth* (London, 1992) definitively rejects the notion that Mary Kettle could have provided the model for Emma Clery in 'Portrait'. He also states that Miss Ivors was most definitely the same Emma Clery.
8. However, in later years he swallows the legend whole and recycles it in his *Memoir*, pp.6–7.
9. Richard Hayes (ed.), *Manuscript Sources for the History of Irish Civilization* (Boston, 1970). Mrs Cruise O'Brien, *A First Irish Book* (London, 1924). Review of Caitlín Bean Chrúis Ó Brien's *Luathscríbhinn Greg* in *Irish Booklover*, XXVI (Jan.–Feb. 1929), p.92.
10. National University of Ireland, collective term for the universities in Cork, Galway and Dublin.
11. *Apartments*, 17 March 1925. Only extant version I can find is in Matthew O'Mahony papers in the National Library of Ireland. Ms 24,903. (Acc. 3844).
12. Ibid.
13. Fand O'Grady, 'The Burying of Seán Beag', *The Irish Statesman*, 19 December 1919, p.576 is a story set in Inishmaan, one of the Aran Islands. Another of her stories, 'Seán Dubh', is also set here. It too is concerned with loss, in this case Seán Dubh is 'caoining for his lost love Eibhlín'. *The Irish Statesman*, p.621.
14. 'Seán Dubh', *The Irish Statesman*, Volume I, p.621. Other stories by O'Brien's mother include: and 'Return of Sighle', 'Stranger at Peig's', p.83, 'Wooing of Maire Ruadh', 'How it Fell Out for Sadhbh', p.251, 'Cait of the Sea', p.371, all *The Irish Statesman*, Volume II.
15. Author's interview with his ex-wife, Mrs Christine Hetherington (née Foster), Dublin, 20

January 2004.

16. R.W. Johnson, 'Lordspeak', review of *Passion and Cunning* and *GodLand*, *London Review of Books*, 2 June 1988, pp.12–15.

17. 'The second school I attended was a Catholic convent school and I have unpleasant memories of the severities practiced there, not actually by the nuns, but by some of the lay teachers. My recollections of Catholic teaching are of being told, this is how it is, repeat after me; it was all authoritarian. Then I went to my main school, and found that I was invited to discuss, to question, and I liked the atmosphere. What appealed to me was not Protestantism, but enlightenment, and I have related to it ever since.' Stan Vrana, *Interviews with Conor Cruise O'Brien*.

18. We know she was not totally comfortable with this 'divilment', as she told the same 'Mrs. Skeffington', Hanna, that 'she had a lot to answer for'. KCO'B to HSS, 14 August 1918. SSP NLI.

19. KCO'B to HSS, from 'Our Lady's bower, Athlone, June 22nd (no year)'. SSP NLI MS 41,176/4.

20. KCO'B to OSS, 1925. SSP NLI MS 40,490 /1.

21. HSS to OSS, 1928. SSP NLI MS 40,484 /3.

22. OSS to HSS, 13 December 1933. SSP NLI MS 40,482 /6.

23. KCO'B to OSS, 15 September 1930. SSP NLI. MS 40,490 /1.

24. D.H. Akenson, *Conor: A Biography of Conor Cruise O'Brien* (Montreal, 1994), p.69.

25. Ibid.

26. Maurice Walsh, 'A Talent to Offend', *New Statesman*, 1 January 1999.

27. O'Brien, *Memoir*, pp.41–8.

28. Ibid., p.45. The year was 1924.

29. KCO'B to HSS, 14 August 1918. SSP NLI, MS 41,176 /4.

30. Conor Cruise O'Brien, *The Siege: The Saga of Israel and Zionism* (London, 1986), p.19–31. Conor Cruise O'Brien, *States of Ireland* (London, 1972), pp.109–10.

31. Conor Cruise O'Brien, *States of Ireland* (London, 1972), pp.109–10.

32. The bitterness and the difficulty of the situation were attested to by Eugene Sheehy, his younger cousin. Author's interview with Eugene Sheehy, Dublin, 25 November 2004.

33. Akenson, *Conor: A Biography*, p.69.

34. Ibid.

35. KCO'B to OSS, Summer 1934, SSP NLI MS 40,490 /1. As she reported in a letter, in her ideal world Irish would be made compulsory for judges, for she would love to 'be hammering it in to him'.

36. O'Brien, *Memoir*, p.41.

37. Ibid.

38. Ibid.

39. Ibid., p.42.

40. Ibid., p.47.

41. Akenson, *Conor: A Biography*, p.74.

42. O'Brien, *Memoir*, p.36.

43. Ibid., p.35.

44. An example of this can be seen in the autobiographical tale of a young boy taken to Artane in the 1950s because his widowed mother consorted with other men. Joe Dunne, *The Stolen Child* (Cork, 2003).

45. O'Brien, *Memoir*, p.47.

46. Ibid., p.35.

4

Owen: the Sheehy Skeffington Influence

In a penetrating study of O'Brien, the philosopher Richard Kearney talks about how O'Brien was split from the outset by the conditions of his upbringing. His mixed feelings toward his parents and his clan – the Sheehys – created what he called 'a formative ambivalence'. This in turn was 'replicated in the generational educational culture to which the growing boy was exposed'.[1] His mother was a devout Catholic, his father mostly agnostic. The formation of the author's split mind originates, by his own admission,

> in the conditioning of the two cultures within which I more or less uneasily grew up. The two cultures were the nationalist one, variants of which all my family adhered, and the post-1920 southern–Protestant culture within which I received most of my schooling.[2]

While this is largely true, to see O'Brien as some kind of pre-1916 Edwardian Liberal refugee in a madly indoctrinating Catholic nationalist milieu, however, misses what made O'Brien seem radical and attractive to 1960s Ireland. It misses what made him different.

To see Cruise O'Brien's development in terms of a tussle between mother and father is to accept his own retrospective view of how he developed and not how it actually happened. While there is no doubt that his father left an idiosyncratic legacy, the main bulwark against what might be viewed as a standard nationalist Catholic upbringing was the influence of the Sheehy Skeffingtons, Hanna and Owen. It is interesting that in his personal narrative at the crucial juncture of his father's death, O'Brien sees the torch literally being passed from his father to Owen. On that fateful day O'Brien recalls he was rescued from the clutches of morbidity by the arrival of the Sheehy Skeffingtons. In his autobiographical pieces he also mentions the story where

Owen brought a light to him in school, after lights out had been de-
creed.[3] These snippets bring across the closeness of the two figures:
Sheehy Skeffington was eight years O'Brien's senior, and at a time
when both were fatherless, the elder cousin seems to have acted in
the   role   of
father figure to the younger cousin. This image of Owen bringing
the light to him as a young boy has also been used by O'Brien as
a symbol for the Enlightenment – Owen bringing more liberal, less
nationalist, more socialist, European strains of thought to O'Brien as
a young boy.

There are numerous references to Skeffington being perhaps the
formative influence in O'Brien's life. His dedication of *Writers and
Politics* to Owen, who he described as 'more than a brother to me', sums
it up. Contemporary accounts all refer to Owen as being a member of
the family. To O'Brien's mother, Owen, who she referred to as 'my
sainted nephew', was in the view of her sister 'like her son'.[4] Hanna
felt that it was good for the two only child cousins to 'both to have a
brother'.[5] Even if the teenage O'Brien felt Owen was domineering ('his
lecture room manner') he goes on to admit that, 'I felt in boyhood that
Owen was right about everything; the only objective standard'.[6] While
he asserted that he had outgrown this, there is a case that Skeffington
exerted a strong influence over O'Brien even after his death.

> As senator for Trinity College he had long been the most consistent and
> outspoken stripper-down of the many hypocrisies of the Catholic State.
> Also, despite his mother's republican associations, he had been an open
> enemy to what he called the 'crazy militarism' of the I.R.A. Owen's in-
> fluence on my own thinking had always been strong: it seems if anything
> to have increased after his death.[7]

Skeffington's influence was possibly as significant for O'Brien's
political outlook as that of his mother and father. What it also suggests
is that O'Brien is a product of a particular perspective. The similarities
between Sheehy Skeffington and himself are too recurrent to be
dismissed. When one reviews their correspondence, it would seem that
the only thing which they were in dispute over was the question of the
amalgamation of Trinity and UCD.[8] Their position on education,
perhaps Sheehy Skeffington's prime contribution, socialism, church-
state relations, or even more basically, the sharing of an absolutely

secular understanding of society, seems to suggest a strong political compatibility. This stretches back to their youth: similar education, in both school and university.

The pathway of Skeffington through the multi-denominational Sandford Park and later Trinity was the decisive factor in O'Brien being sent there. O'Brien states that he was always going to follow his older cousin. All of Owen's many grinds to Conor were undertaken with Trinity entrance and scholarship examinations in mind. It is tempting to see Skeffington as merely reinforcing the legacy of Francis Cruise O'Brien – the agnostic. But Skeffington seems to have added another facet to O'Brien's political development, a particularly republican twist. The result of this leads to an interesting tension, perhaps not so much when O'Brien was younger, but when the republican idealism met the train-crash of the Troubles, something had to give. In order to understand this more complicated and rewarding scenario, we need to discover more about Owen Sheehy Skeffington.

Francis Sheehy Skeffington, Owen's father, was murdered in 1916 by a British officer, Bowen-Colthurst. Sheehy Skeffington had been a high profile pacifist and feminist, and a regular newspaper contributor. Owen's mother, Hanna Sheehy Skeffington, was one of the most vocal critics of State policy from within republicanism. In 1927 she resigned from Fianna Fáil when de Valera took the oath, and throughout her days consistently espoused the republican cause, with a strongly anti-British bias.

Their son Owen was imbued with many of their ideals, but was particularly strong on the education and secular fronts. This is where he encountered stiffest resistance, and the ground upon which his most memorable battles, normally in *The Irish Times* letters page, were fought. It is in this vein that Seán O'Faoláin saluted Sheehy Skeffington at his funeral service with the words: 'Good-bye Owen, you won.'[9] The implication behind these words was that a secular society with 'a liberal ethic' had at last sprung from its previously confessional incarnation. It would probably come as no surprise to many that O'Brien and Sheehy Skeffington were cousins. Indeed to look at it from this angle, the picture of two outspoken cousins, one in the Seanad and the other in the Dáil, in the late 1960s when this culture change was coming about, seems to have a seamless convincing quality. O'Brien himself subscribes to this interpretation.

The education of Owen Sheehy Skeffington also seems to have introduced him to a wider variety of opinion than was normal at the time. However, against the notion that this alone informed Skeffington's political outlook, it should be remembered that while he did know many who were neither Catholic, nor nationalist (he was for example quite friendly with Beckett), he was in constant contact with many republicans. From his earliest days he played with his neighbourhood friend Ronán Ceannt, son of executed 1916 leader Éamonn Ceannt, and they remained lifelong friends. He knew many who were high-profile republicans: Tommy Hughes, Peadar O'Donnell and Frank Ryan, to mention a few. Moreover, in his early politics, while Fianna Fáil moved more into the mainstream, leaving behind their republican roots, Sheehy Skeffington joined the Republican Congress (1935–37), and criticized the drift of Government policy.

This aspect of Sheehy Skeffington has not been properly sketched. His wife Andrée, in her illuminating portrayal, is to an extent, reticent on this.[10] While she relates his acts of humanity in his appeals for clemency for IRA activists, she is keen to not leave her husband open to the charge of being an IRA sympathizer, and correctly stresses his stronger streak of pacifism:

> Partition did not form the mainspring of Owen's political motivation. He did not agree with the IRA's assertion that the Republic would be real only if it included all 32 counties. He quietly welcomed the break of the final political thread between Éire and Britain, especially as it happened without upheaval or bloodshed, and hoped it might take a little heat from the IRA campaign.[11]

While O'Brien quite rightly labelled Hanna Sheehy Skeffington an Irish revolutionary, it must also be pointed out that her son did not follow her in the more practical aspects of her politics. The pacifism which he inherited from his father prevented it. Nonetheless, it is demonstrable that he felt sympathy for those who were in the IRA and persecuted for it. On several occasions he argued against the severity of punishments meted out by the government. He held up de Valera's treatment of Seán MacHaughey – whom he refused to commute the death sentence for – as an example of his ruthlessness, his 'hate for arts by which he himself had risen'.[12] From both his writings and deeds it can be maintained that Sheehy Skeffington saw himself as standing in the Irish revolutionary tradition. In his outlook on education and socialism he was a conscious disciple of Pearse and Connolly. An example of this is the death-bed conversation Skeffington had with Hanna. She saluted Owen's excoriation of de Valera with the approbation: 'best thing you ever did, that Trinity speech'. She was recalling a debate which included de Valera and the son of Jan Masaryk, the son of Czechoslovakia's Prime Minister who later himself became Foreign Minister and died in suspicious circumstances in 1948. In his speech, Sheehy Skeffington pointed to Czechoslovakia's fidelity to its revolutionary ideals. He rebuked de Valera for having abandoned the ideals which he had once espoused. A phrase used in the debate was recalled in a later interview: 'Ireland's dead and Ireland herself were betrayed, not by those who died, but by those who survived.'[13] He charged de Valera with failing to have lived up to his professed ideal of 'radically altering the whole system'. To Skeffington it seemed 'we have continued the British capitalist system with a change of rulers, a change of shareholders, a change of dividends'.[14] This line of thought is recorded more fully in Sheehy Skeffington's article for de Valera's 80th birthday in 1962. On education, de Valera is again charged with failure:

> our primary school system has been allowed to remain, apart from the teaching of Irish – pretty well what it was when Pearse so vigorously condemned it as a murder machine. Economically and socially, de Valera is a full eighty years behind Patrick Pearse and a hundred behind James Connolly. John Redmond would have found nothing too 'advanced' in his plans and achievements in the folds of industry, commerce or agriculture.[15]

Sheehy Skeffington highlights the contrast between this failure, and de Valera's ideal in 1932 to 'organise our economic life deliberately and purposely to provide as its first object for the fundamental needs of all our citizens'.[16] Sheehy Skeffington asks:

> Have we thus radically altered our whole system of production etc.? Clearly not. Must we then stand condemned as having failed, 'cruelly and disastrously', to put our hard won political freedom to the only use for which it was ever intended by those who fought and died to win it, the service of the ordinary people of Ireland.[17]

Finally, he asks de Valera to:

once more examine his heart. He may find in it now the humble hope
that Irish men and women of another generation will see his early
economic and social dream realised, and Ireland brought some steps
beyond the stage of mere political independence to which Eamon de
Valera did so much to lead his people, and at which he has since been
content to bid them stand and mark time.[18]

When we come to view the connection between Sheehy Skeffington
and O'Brien, the possibility that O'Brien was also infused with the same
republican ideal presents itself. If we examine the outlines of the
critique presented by Sheehy Skeffington, with its recollection of the
murder machine, of radically altering the whole system of production,
and its sense that a disappointed and disillusioned generation were
'betrayed not by those who died, but by those who survived', we are
immediately led to O'Brien's 'The Embers of Easter 1916–1966'.
Published as a critical commemorative piece in 1966, it clearly takes
its lead from Owen Sheehy Skeffington's earlier article of 1962.

While stating this, it should be noted that O'Brien's piece is in many
ways different to his cousin's. It is less specific, concentrating not on
any one individual, but on the legacy of 1916. Another difference is
that it is more personal. It relates the views of a member of the
generation which grew up in the aftermath of 1916. It speaks less of
social and economic situations, and more of the enduring political
effects. It characterizes these effects as ones of deception, disappoint-
ment and malaise. In its analysis of the question of partition and language, it probes the impact of failing to achieve the objectives of a free
island and a Gaelic nation. Around these two issues, and to a lesser
extent the social objectives of Connolly, O'Brien sees the phenomenon
encapsulated in Yeats's lines:

> Fail, and that history turns into rubbish,
> All that great past to a trouble of fools.[19]

It is particularly illuminating in its conjectures of the psychological results of this failure.

> The greatest tragedy about the creation of a state on the basis of ideals im-
> possible to attain was the release sought through national fantasy. When
> the answer to Pearse's 'not free merely but Gaelic as well' turned out to
> be '75 per cent free and 0.6 per cent Gaelic' it proved impossible for

Pearse's followers to either accept these figures or to alter the realities they represent. A desperate game of let's pretend followed: Ireland is Gaelic – is not Gaelic the first official language? Ireland is free – does not the Constitution declare that the national territory consists of the whole island and its territorial seas.[20]

One could, in 1966, see the germs of his analysis in the 1970s and beyond. Reflecting on these pretences, O'Brien perceived the more subtle effects of these delusions:

> These propositions struck an answering chord in the bosom of the Irish lunatic ... Gaelic! *Bas do'n Bhearla* is chalked on a wall: death to the English language! Free! 'Six divisions, sixty minutes, six counties' read a poster. And a few who were not lunatics but brave and logical young men went to their death for Pearse's Republic, in whose attainability they had been allowed and even encouraged to believe. They saw clearly that the national territory was not being re-integrated by semantic exercises; they tried force, sanctioned as they believed by the example of Pearse and Connolly, and they died for the fantasy of a United Ireland at the hands of one or other of the governments which rule the Ireland of reality. The Government in Dublin continued to propagate the fantasy while punishing those who acted on it.[21]

These highly perceptive observations mirror Sheehy Skeffington's remarks concerning IRA volunteers: that they were brave misguided idealists, punished by a hypocritical state.

However, a fuller reflection of Sheehy Skeffington comes in the more personal part of 'The Embers of Easter 1916–1966' where O'Brien remarks that the 'action of 1916 was not a programme: it was a challenge, to conscience and to courage'.[22] One of the areas where O'Brien explicitly saw this 'challenge' taken up was the stance of the Department of External Affairs from 1957 to 1960, on the vote concerning the representation of China in the United Nations. Seasoned O'Brien observers will know that this was a policy devised by O'Brien in response to Frank Aiken's desire to maintain an independent voice in the UN. In his 'Embers of Easter' article O'Brien points out that upon his resignation from the Department this independent line was abandoned. The Irish representation could now be regarded as a safe 'Western' vote. Whatever about O'Brien's actual role in this situation, even if one were to argue that he had no seminal role at all in this stance, the interesting thing is that he takes pride in this stance as a conscientious and courageous response to the challenge of 1916. The implication is inescapable. Not only is this article 'intellect directed benevolently, critically and correctively to the condition of the nation … in the tradition and spirit of the Irish Revolution',[23] to employ the phrase of Desmond Fennell, it is an article which O'Brien used to outline his own feelings toward 1916. He expatiates on the relevance of that spirit to the Ireland of 1966, and proudly proclaims his own actions to be a response to the challenge of 1916. In short he declares himself to be an intellectual descendant of 1916. What seems unthinkable to a reader forty years after 'The Embers of Easter' was written, is staring them in the face: O'Brien was a republican.

The death of Owen Sheehy Skeffington in 1970 broke the last thread with O'Brien's upbringing. The rashness and urgency of many of his criticisms would still have presented itself and found its outlet even if Skeffington were alive. On the other hand I feel it is a good deal less certain that the focus of the later years – where the 'challenge of 1916' became a talisman for terrorism; where 'a hypocritical and punishing government' not only colluded but inspired; and where 'the brave and logical young men' of 1966 became the epicentre of evil of 1977 and beyond – would have arisen. It seems that O'Brien could not in good faith write such things when the example and writings of Owen Sheehy Skeffington would argue the contrary. It seems unlikely that Sheehy Skeffington would have altered the debate on Northern Ireland had he lived another ten years (one can think of quite a few articulate pacifist republicans). He may, however, have had the effect of making O'Brien more sensible to his previous incarnation, and the extent to which this too was a Sheehy inheritance. Above all there would have been Sheehy Skeffington's 'enlightened' example which could denounce the 'crazy militarism'[24] of the IRA, while maintaining the benevolence and direction of his intellect.

O'Brien's 'The Embers of Easter 1916–1966' essay contains another personal aspect. This revolves around O'Brien's anti-partitionist activities in the Department of External Affairs in the early 1950s. As he says himself of these writings which 'he blushes to recall',[25] they served the purpose of deadening the pain of the torturous divide between the ideal and reality. Nonetheless by sketching his subsequent attempts to realize the ideals of 1916 through his stance at the UN, he is outlining what to his mind appears a good or faithful attempt to face the challenge. In presenting his less good attempt to do so with anti-partition propaganda, he is nonetheless testifying to its genuineness at the time. Apart from raising the text which he wrote for the anti-partition campaign above the level of idle musings of those who 'would have been better off playing tennis',[26] it presents the possibility that O'Brien is a victim of the national psychosis which his *Embers* article is in part an attempt to relate: that he was once a faithful son to Cathleen ní Houlihan as well as to Francis Cruise O'Brien. What should also be borne in mind is that these are not conditions which any individual casually shakes off. They are in the marrow in many cases, and their removal is a painful process. It could in part explain the vehemence and shrillness of later writings. Certainly the mind which can instance St Patrick as a 'national apostle',[27] and some forty years later write a book excoriating Ireland's holy nationalism, must contain some interesting tensions. The feeling expressed by many that O'Brien's writings have an almost unreal quality of detachment could in a paradoxical way be related to this.

The milieu from which O'Brien sprang appears a little more complex now. No longer can Protestant institutions, agnosticism, a European outlook and Enlightenment culture be cited to the exclusion of the more normal and accepted (in an Irish context) value of secularist tenets with a socialist programme and strong anti-clerical tendencies that was the fitting outlook of an early-twentieth-century republican. To complicate matters further, however, O'Brien, it seems, wasn't just any early-twentieth-century republican. We have seen how to an extent he carries within himself arguments for two ideas of nationalism. Something which could tip the balance in this intellectual equipoise needs to be explored. For the first time we have come to the point in O'Brien's development where he steps out from the skin of his family – forebears, father, mother and 'brother' – and into the wider world. And when he steps forward he finds himself almost accidentally in resolute opposition to all and sundry: party, country and religion. Something which demonstrates this quite vividly is his battles as a young man with one of Ireland's foremost writers: Seán O'Faoláin.

NOTES

1. Richard Kearney, 'Ulysses Returns to Ithaca', review of *Memoir. Times Literary Supplement*, 15 January 1999, p.6.

2. Quoted in Richard Kearney, 'Ulysses Returns to Ithaca', review of *Memoir: Life and Themes* (Profile), in *Times Literary Supplement*,15 January 1999, p.6.
3. See O'Brien, 'Foreword' in Andrée Sheehy Skeffington's biography of Owen, *Skeff: The Life of Owen Sheehy-Skeffington, 1909–1970* (Dublin, 1991).
4. Hanna Sheehy Skeffington (HSS) to Andrée Sheehy Skeffington (ASS), 28 February 1938. Sheehy Skeffington Papers (SSP), National Library of Ireland (NLI) MS 41,176 /22.
5. HSS to Owen Sheehy Skeffington (OSS), 29 July 1929. SSP NLI MS 40,484 /4.
6. O'Brien, College Notebook, O'Brien papers, UCD, P82/328/48. Owen gave Conor a lot of books to read 'in swaps and as birthday presents'. As O'Brien pushed into his late teens he began to assert his independence from Owen, although this was a delicate and difficult departure: 'Your sermon left me feeling much as I used to feel after a rugby practice in Sandford when I used to play at forward crushed, tired and humiliated. I can't talk about the 'interest' you take in me and so on for I feel all embarrassed and standing-on-one-foot.'
7. Conor Cruise O'Brien, *States of Ireland* (London, 1972), pp.220–1. Written two years after Skeffington's death – 7 June 1970.
8. O'Brien, 'A Laager of Liberalism?' and Sheehy Skeffington, 'Fluctuat nec Mergitur', *The Irish Times*, 11 October and 18 October 1968.
9. Quoted in O'Brien, 'Foreword', to Sheehy Skeffington, *Skeff*, p.3.
10. Sheehy Skeffington, *Skeff*, p.137.
11. Ibid.
12. Owen Sheehy Skeffington, 'Eamonn de Valera', *The Irish Times*, 13 October 1962.
13. Quoted in Sheehy Skeffington, *Skeff*, p.137.
14. Sheehy Skeffington, 'Eamonn de Valera'.
15. Ibid.
16. Ibid.
17. Ibid.
18. Ibid.
19. Conor Cruise O'Brien, 'The Embers Of Easter 1916–1966', *The Irish Times*, 7 April 1966.
20. Ibid.
21. Ibid.
22. Ibid.
23. Desmond Fennell, *Heresy: The Battle of Ideas in Modern Ireland* (Belfast, 1993), p.254.
24. Owen Sheehy Skeffington, quoted in O'Brien's 'Foreword' to Sheehy Skeffington, *Skeff*, p.3.
25. O'Brien, 'The Embers of Easter 1916'.
26. When the possibility of publication fell through, O'Brien commented on the amount of outside office hours spent assembling this work. If the result was to leave it to rot, then he felt he 'would have been better off playing tennis'. See O'Brien to J. Brennan, 21 May 1951. DEA, 305/14/112.
27. O'Brien, 'The Story of Ireland'. See DEA, 305/14/112.

5

Seán O'Faoláin

Seán O'Faoláin in the mid 1940s and early 1950s was at the head of the tiny clique of Dublin liberals involved in the journal which he was the founding editor of: *The Bell*. It was in this role that O'Brien both looked up to O'Faoláin and appealed to him for advice and direction. The advice he received would send him on a career trajectory of critic and historian. But it also put O'Brien at odds with O'Faoláin – an unusual divergence given what we might imagine to be a harmony of views. This tells us much about key differences with O'Faoláin and how O'Brien related to the world and Ireland's place in it. However, as ever with O'Brien, his differences with O'Faoláin can really only be explained within the context of a particularly personal rejection.

In his diary from his college days, dealing with a host of issues such as his mother's death, his father's memory, his personal dreams, the outbreak of the Second World War and French literature, there is a curious entry: 'Killed by Cork realists September 1940.' The reference is to a letter written by O'Faoláin to O'Brien telling him to give up the poetry. O'Faoláin removed any illusion that O'Brien might make his mark in that field by telling him that what he had sent O'Faoláin were 'congeries of one man's ideas and another man's style, both misunderstood and misused, which constitutes your sole originality'. Some fifty years later O'Brien professed gratitude for having been told to 'stop trying to be a writer I could not be'. At the time, however, it was a blow to his vitals to which he did not take kindly.[1] It is possible that this injury to O'Brien's fierce pride led him to take an overly negative view of O'Faoláin's prose when the opportunity presented itself.

In the years following the 'murder' of his poetry, O'Brien was double jobbing in the Department of External Affairs and undertaking his doctorate on Parnell. He was also assembling a series of essays on Catholic writers such as Péguy, Mauriac, Waugh, Greene and of course his compatriot O'Faoláin. The first two of these were published in *The Bell*, which O'Faoláin was still editing at the time. *The Bell* articles were O'Brien's first serious foray into criticism. When he reflected on O'Faoláin's role in his life he refers to the area in which he knew O'Faoláin best:

> The first number of *The Bell* came out in October 1940. The final words of the first editorial ran: 'Whoever you are then, reader, Gentile or Jew, Protestant or Catholic, priest or layman, Big House or small house, *The Bell* is yours'. As we read those words today that first pairing, 'Gentile or Jew', doesn't especially stand out. But when they were first published, they did stand out. In October 1940, all of Continental Western Europe was at the feet of Adolf Hitler. The then Secretary of the Department of External Affairs had advised the government, that summer, that Germany had won the war, and that Ireland must begin to adjust to that. Sean 'who thought world', was well aware of that. In those circumstances, and in the light of that knowledge, the words 'Gentile or Jew' take on special significance.[2]

He draws similar inferences from the fight O'Faoláin waged with what he calls the 'sinister influences' within the Gaelic League, who at the time felt that from 'certain Continental movements we have much to learn'. In the course of saluting O'Faoláin's bravery, O'Brien stated that O'Faoláin applied this to the excesses of Irish nationalism. In his recognition of imperialism in a new guise – 'the International Left's annexational tendencies' for Eastern Europe – O'Brien doffs his cap to O'Faoláin's prescience. Appropriating O'Faoláin's own definition of the ideal Irish writer, 'who thinks World and describes Irish', O'Brien felt that 'Seán thought world and his novels and stories, together with those of his friend Frank O'Connor, are an emerging part of the world's heritage in the English language'.[3]

O'Brien in 1991 could give the older writer, Ireland's first man of letters, his due regard. However, almost half a century earlier the relationship was somewhat marred by what can best be described as healthy scepticism to received opinion. On the one hand O'Brien was directing his withering gaze at the received opinion of what was regarded as the Irish intellectual vanguard of the day: the embattled clique of the writers for *The Bell* and its editor. In 'A Rider to the Verdict' of Vivian Mercier's criticisms of *The Bell*,[4] O'Brien refers to

Mercier as 'comrade', perhaps signalling a dislike for what O'Brien saw as their propensity for becoming too entrenched. More seriously he suspected that the journal was clichéd to the point that its contributions were all predictable. This is reflected in the tone and content of a parody of what were the all too familiar protestations of O'Faoláin in editorial mode.

What was more barbed than these semi-jocular jibes was the zeal with which O'Brien attacked O'Faoláin's more serious writings; not just in non-fiction, but in his novels and short stories as well. The various encounters had an oedipal quality to them, much like the relationship with O'Faoláin's own mentor: Daniel Corkery. We can get a flavour of the battle when we see that O'Brien felt that he had to dissociate himself from what he saw as the 'idolatries' of O'Faoláin's mind.[5] The particularly vehement language arose in a series of letters that followed from a review by O'Brien of O'Faoláin's *The Irish*. A condensed example of the more vitriolic aspects of the exchange indicates that whatever about the content, a certain amount of exasperation and indignation was felt on both sides:

> O'Brien: 'Mr. O'Faoláin is a difficult pair of writers for a critic to deal with.'[6]

> O'Faoláin: 'With so prehensile a seizer upon words as Mr. O'Donnell I must protect myself.'[7]

> O'Brien: 'The not unexpected result has been that the other Mr. O'-Faoláin, the ferret-eyed Cork realist (Phelanus depressus) has snapped at my pen-hand.'[8]

> O'Faoláin: 'I really must protest at having such balderdash attributed to me.'[9]

It has been suggested that this involved O'Brien in an almost unacceptable level of disrespect towards Ireland's leading intellectual of the day. One suspects that there was an element of self-aggrandisement involved: what his biographer Don Akenson refers to as 'painting graffiti on a national monument'.[10] There is some truth to this – it is totally in keeping with O'Brien's temperament to try this kind of high level debunking. But there is no doubt that the two writers were disputing a genuine point. The substantive issue seems to have been the question of intellectual horizons, and closely linked to this, the proper place of nationalism. We can see this most clearly if we turn to one of O'Brien's first works of serious literary scholarship: *Maria Cross*.

This collection contains very little Irish content with the exception of the essay, 'The parnellism of Seán O'Faoláin', which examines O'Faoláin's longer fictional works. In it we can see a whole range of O'Brien's own preoccupations. Church and country, the cloying hands of a failed revolution, and the excessively nationalist thinking of Ireland's literary class are all brought to bear firmly down upon the crown of O'Faoláin. Linking in with the motif of dispossession, O'Brien begins by declaring his intention to analyze that near past, 'which never quite belongs to the rest of history',[11] and its interaction with O'Faoláin's fiction. 'The degree in which we possess that sense of continuity and the form it takes – national, religious, racial or social – depend on our own imagination and on the personality, opinions and talkativeness of our elder relatives.'[12] This 'peculiar traditionalism', and its effect upon O'Faoláin's work, is the object of O'Brien's essay. In choosing *Bird Alone* and *A Nest of Simple Folk*, O'Faoláin's first two novels, O'Brien asserts that they share the common theme of atavism. In both novels the significant figures are an old man and a boy; in each the old man is a being of power, an accumulation of rage and lust, an ex-Fenian and an ex-fornicator; and in each the boy under the old man's influence becomes an outlaw in the world of his parents. For O'Brien:

> The Irish rebels of the nineteenth century, so regularly condemned by the hierarchy, were the inevitable heroes for the spirited son of a pious and 'loyal' family. Prometheus and Faust were remote and tenuous symbols, but the Fenian dead to punish whom, in that treasured episcopal phrase, 'hell was not hot enough nor eternity long enough', lived in people's minds. In their names, revolt which was otherwise doomed to futile isolation, found a way into the open, a fissure in the wall of acceptance. And even mightier than theirs was the name of Parnell, whose struggle not only against Church and State but directly against the power of sexual prohibition made him the essential hero of rebellious youth.[13]

O'Faoláin's *Bird Alone* captures the skirmishing about Parnell, the priests and notions of purity. In the case of the novel's hero, Corney, such scenes helped, 'along with his grandfather's example, to establish a firm connection between the separate ideas of national, spiritual and sexual emancipation. As one name will be needed for the triple association we shall call it "parnellism" (as distinct from political Parnellism).'[14] O'Brien proceeds to show how, in a minor episode of *Bird Alone*, Corney has to admit to a liaison with his girlfriend Elsie in order to exonerate himself from a political charge. As a result Elsie's father forbids her to speak to Corney and he broods upon this, until 'my contempt spread to so many people that I felt that what had happened to me was an image of the far worse that had happened to ... the Fenians, to the Land Leaguers, to Parnell'.[15] Of this O'Brien comments:

> Here 'parnellism' is passive, an extension of self pity. It can be dynamic, as in *A Nest of Simple Folk* which is planned to show the apotheosis of 'parnellism' in a moment of historical decision. The 1916 rebellion frees Denis from his family and at the same time justifies the life of old Leo Donnel. The young rebel and the old, and their private rebellions, are merged in the national insurrection (in which their creator took part, at a later stage). Thus they break out of their loneliness and recover through patriotism the unity with the people which they are unable to keep in religion. For them, and for almost all Mr. O'Faoláin's central characters, this unity, perhaps because it is so difficult to achieve, is profoundly important, a condition of spiritual life, almost a religion in itself.[16]

Further examples of 'parnellism' can be found in *Come Back To Erin*, where the central character pursues a rapprochement with his Irishness and his Catholicism, only to despair and drown himself. Finally, 'parnellism' itself mutates with the progress of time, inflicting a slow death as the poverty, submission, abstinence, and resignation from which it arose reassert themselves (*A Purse of Coppers*). The dynamic which comes increasingly into focus is the head of Catholicism eating the tail of nationalism; the unity sought for turns out to be a cancerous husk.

This recessive unity, seen as 'almost a religion in itself', proves to be the stumbling block of this essay, as O'Brien's pursuit of the Catholic imagination, the motif of *Maria Cross*, finds him increasingly at odds with O'Faoláin. The common ground between O'Faoláin's recessive unity and O'Brien's 'Catholic imagination' is negligible. The result is a resoundingly negative judgement of the writer's work by his critic;

ultimately O'Faoláin is taxed with parochialism. This seems unjust, and
it tells us a good deal about O'Brien if we discover how O'Brien reaches
this conclusion. In his correct portrayal of O'Faoláin's search for a
unity, paralleling his character's search for an 'image of life that would
fire and fuse us all',[17] O'Brien conjectures, perhaps correctly again, that
O'Faoláin fails to find this image because he has continued to trawl
history for the answer: 'digging deeper into the "racial mind" to find
again the rebellious unity that Leo Donnel sought'.[18] All his full-scale
biographies, *King of the Beggars* (1938) and *The Great O'Neill* (1942),
develop and illuminate his half-mystical ideas of the nation.

> In *King of the Beggars*, his life of Daniel O'Connell, he speaks of 'that
> most powerful of all emotional pistons known to man, a blazing love of
> place and a fond memory for the lost generations of his tribe, the
> ineradicable *pietas* of all submerged peoples'. Again and again he
> mentions 'the mind of the race ... the racial genius ... the native instinct
> for life'.[19]

For O'Brien, the inherent difficulty with mapping this line of thought,
what O'Faoláin labels 'delphic nationalism', onto the Ireland of the
twentieth-century is that 'it cannot go far without being deflected by a
fundamental contradiction – the impossibility of making a race-religion
about a "race" that already has a quite different religion of its own as
moulder of its "racial character".'[20]

O'Brien then goes beyond this 'mark of heavy mental stress', and
investigates the implications for O'Faoláin that are built upon these
shaky foundations. O'Brien does this by comparing O'Faoláin with
Francois Mauriac (another of the subjects in *Maria Cross* and a firm
favourite of O'Brien) in terms of the following common dispositions:
piety towards ancestors; love of place; spirit of revolt and hate; born
Catholic and sources of scandal; and finally their use of the church as
their central challenge. Ultimately, O'Brien adjudges O'Faoláin's fiction
to be inferior: the previously mentioned parochial. In Mauriac's case,
O'Brien argues, the challenge of his fiction is accepted.

> If his characters revolt it is against God through the family; if they are
> oppressed or debauched it is by their own sins or the general sinfulness
> of man; even if they have a secret anti-Christian religion it is usually a
> universal one, like pan-theism or sunworship. They do not usually revolt
> against the Gironde; they are never frustrated by France ... The piety of

place is properly subordinated; man stands in direct relation to the universal affirming or denying God.[21]

O'Brien then contrasts this with O'Faoláin who 'neither affirms nor denies anything of universal importance. He manufactures a substitute religion for local consumption.'[22]

Whatever ones feelings about O'Faoláin's novels, O'Brien is being deliberately unfair to his subject. There is a process by which someone else's 'ism' is denigrated through the practice of the 'irregular noun'. Thus someone else's nationalism becomes tribalism. An exact duplicate is being put forth here. In this case what for one is universal becomes in the eyes of another local. O'Faoláin's genuine nationalism becomes for O'Brien a 'Heath Robinson historical apparatus', or a 'glorified parish-pump'. This becomes even more pronounced when we see what O'Faoláin's conception is contrasted with in order to belittle it. For O'Brien, Yeats's 'messianism' and Dostoyevsky's 'apocalypse' are universal, they become 'a vehicle for a general idea'. Yet in the course of the essay O'Brien himself instanced two such 'general ideas' arising out of O'Faoláin's life: 'Freedom was a word of one indivisible meaning ... the Irish-speaking districts of West Cork were a pagan Arcadia'.[23] To somehow view utopianism or arcadianism as being inferior to Dostoyevsky's apocalyptic perspective or Yeats's 'messianism' makes little sense.

This lacuna has its basis in two mistaken presumptions. The first is the obvious incongruity between the objectives of Mauriac and O'Faoláin. In the case of Mauriac, 'place', 'fellow men' and 'France' find, for O'Brien, their proper subordination. O'Faoláin's characters, however, don't necessarily affirm or deny God. They may do, but it is not their purpose; it is not O'Faoláin's motif. What his characters seek is unity with their fellow men. The relation between O'Faoláin's 'fellow men' and God is best described by the hierarchy between God and another of O'Brien's subjects, Péguy: '*et quand Dieu le voudrait ce n'est pas son affaire*'. We must also acknowledge that it is largely because O'Faoláin portrayed his unity as recessive that he is labelled parochial, as he did not affirm anything of universal importance. But the worth of O'Faoláin's fiction is that he was faithful to this unity, which ultimately proved to be recessive, at great cost to him in terms of personal trauma.

The second presumption of O'Brien's is that the universal in question is undermined on the basis that it is historically contingent.

Thus O'Brien sees O'Faoláin's ideas as correct 'within a limited historical field, a period ending in the 1930s – during which a powerful revolutionary tradition ran not only against the Crown, but against the Church also'.[24] But what kind of basis is this from which to evaluate fiction? Because 'delphic nationalism' failed, because it ceased to act upon the imaginations of a considerable body of men, and because it never had real political effect, it is dismissed by O'Brien. The notion that the worth of an idea, its nobility and seductiveness, should be written off simply because it never saw the statute books or fell away politically, is a very suspect stance for a critic. The point is highlighted by the fact that throughout O'Brien enmeshes O'Faoláin's history and fiction, his editorials and his stories. The editorials may indeed be derided for living in a haze of unreality, if O'Brien so feels. The same charge makes no sense when applied to O'Faoláin's novels or short stories. Indeed this 'haze of unreality', the growing distance between a people's dreams and actions, would later become an obsession for O'Brien in articles such as 'The Embers of Easter 1916–1966', and it is fair to say that twenty years later in 1966, O'Brien would subsequently arrive at many of O'Faoláin's earlier conclusions.

This then would seem to complicate the relationship with O'Faoláin. In the historiography of that era, O'Faoláin is generally deemed to have exercised a highly valuable and prescient role through his editorship of *The Bell*. The persistent sniping by O'Brien would indicate that there were those who felt that, iconoclastic as O'Faoláin was, he did not challenge the central tenet of the time: that the nation was the *summum bonum*.

After this essay was published, O'Faoláin wrote O'Brien a letter, thanking him for the criticism. In replying he honed in on one of the central concerns that O'Brien was trying to get across. As O'Faoláin put it:

> There are as you rightly observe, only two urges in Ireland – nationalism and religion. The second is a monster. One can't dodge nationalism. It has to be written about. Analysed out of existence. The mistake, I think, is not to write of it seriously. To be so bored with it that one is amused, clinical remote. I'm sure I'll write and think about it to the end of my days.[25]

The irony is that O'Faoláin might well have been describing O'Brien's own œuvre. Over the years he would be shaken out of the unserious literary disdain for nationalism that was his original position, to the point where it would become the sole obsession of his writings. What is all the more intriguing is that O'Faoláin's two monsters were exactly the same demons that O'Brien both ran from and fought throughout his life.

However, to leave it like this would be to slip into the all-too easy trap of assuming O'Brien would arrive in 1972 with *States of Ireland*. In seeing O'Faoláin as an example, two significant qualifications must be inserted. Firstly, O'Faoláin's mantle was crafted in a furnace, and O'Brien would need to 'find his own' to have anything of similar worth to say. Secondly, the nation of Ireland was too small a thing to poke the conscience of. He would take his own advice to O'Faoláin, 'and fly to the ends of the world'.[26] But before we accompany O'Brien on this journey it is worth pointing out that it has taken him a great deal of emotional energy just to travel outside of his own circle of family and friends, and beyond the mores of his Catholic nationalist home. While many would argue that he was conditioned through his father and college to adopt this cosmopolitan outlook from the very beginning, this overlooks the more prosaic reality that it was long a Sheehy tradition to leave Ireland and spend exchanges and educational trips abroad in France. This was something that O'Brien was engaged in frequently since his early teens (but only after several summers spent in the Gaeltacht in Ring, Co. Waterford). In taking these trips he was following in the footsteps of his mother, aunts and grandfather. The Sheehy's French connection explains the choice of French and Irish for his degree in college, and also explains the naturally European outlook of the young man. In order to understand how O'Brien sought to combine his fascination with politics and literature along a particularly Francophile trajectory we must examine one more intellectual legacy, that of Albert Camus.

NOTES

1. See correspondence with O'Faoláin. O'Brien papers, UCD, P82/520.
2. Conor Cruise O'Brien, 'Memorial Address', in *Seán O'Faoláin 1900–1991: The Cork Review* (1991), p.95.
3. Ibid.
4. Conor Cruise O'Brien, 'A Rider to the Verdict', *The Bell*, May 1945, pp.164–7.
5. Conor Cruise O'Brien, 'The parnellism of Seán O'Faoláin', in Donat O'Donnell, *Maria Cross: Imaginative Patterns in a Group of Modem Catholic Writers* (London, 1953), p.102.

6. D. O' Donnell, *Envoy* 1 (February 1950), p.89. At the time O'Brien was writing under his pseudonym Donat O'Donnell.
7. S. O'Faoláin, *Envoy* 1 (January 1950), p.90.
8. O'Donnell, *Envoy* 1, p.89.
9. O'Faoláin, *Envoy* 1, p.87.
10. D.H. Akenson, *Conor: A Biography of Conor Cruise O'Brien* (Montreal, 1994), pp.118–23.
11. Conor Cruise O'Brien, *Maria Cross* (London, 1963 rev. edn), p.87.
12. Ibid.
13. Ibid., p.94.
14. Ibid., p.95.
15. Ibid.
16. Ibid., p.104.
17. Ibid., p.97.
18. Ibid., p.98.
19. Ibid.
20. Ibid.
21. Ibid., p.113.
22. Ibid.
23. Ibid., pp.101–2.
24. Ibid., p.102.
25. Letter from O'Faoláin thanking him for *Maria Cross* essay. O'Brien papers, UCD, P82/520.
26. O'Brien, *Maria Cross*, p.107. The final words of his essay on O'Faoláin.

6

Camus

For the final, and perhaps most influential 'mentor', we must turn to Albert Camus. O'Brien, as we will see, owes a great deal to Camus. Furthermore, Camus can tell us a lot about the development of O'Brien. From the various views which O'Brien held of Camus, we can see how O'Brien's mind evolved. In some cases events led him to agree with Camus: what O'Brien found uninteresting, or wrong in the late 1950s, he later came to identify with. There is a frank admission by O'Brien of Camus' importance to him:

> The real significance, and the source of the appeal, of the work of this period [the 1940s] is not one of revolt but one of affirmation. To a generation which saw no reason for hope it offered hope without reason. It offered a category: the absurd – in which logical, psychological, philosophical, and even social and political difficulties could be encapsulated and it allowed the joy of being alive, in the presence of death, to emerge. It was neither a revolutionary message, nor a specially moral one; but it was a singularly sweet and exhilarating message to a whole generation who were also pleased to think of itself as revolutionary and moral. I belonged to that generation and if I scrutinise that message now with the wary eyes of middle age, I am no less grateful for having received it in my youth.[1]

This passage is important for a variety of reasons. I think that from the frankness and honesty of it, we can say that Camus had a profound effect upon O'Brien both intellectually and emotionally.

The first thing to note is that O'Brien's primary concern was for a considerable time bound up with somehow trying to be both 'revolutionary and moral'. And the key to this can be found in his writings on Camus. The best place to assess O'Brien's estimation of Camus is O'Brien's 1970 monograph *Camus*. This book, which has been described as O'Brien's best, is an overview of Camus's œuvre and

life. It is written very much with the colonial perspective in mind and
continually interrogates the output of Camus against the background of
his birthplace, Algeria. The book itself has three stages, corresponding
to the years surrounding each of Camus' best known works – *L'Étranger*,
La Peste and *La Chute*. Each of these chapters needs to be examined in
order to demonstrate the relationship between Camus and O'Brien. If
we remember that Camus and O'Brien were roughly coevals, it is tan-
talizing to flirt with the notion of Camus as an evolving mentor to
O'Brien.

To begin with, O'Brien's opinion of *L'Étranger* is not that high. From
a 1970 perspective *L'Étranger* is seen as flawed. The main reason for
this negative judgement is the colonial perspective that O'Brien
employed to evaluate the effect of Algeria on Camus. To put it simply,
O'Brien felt that Camus' representation of Algeria was untruthful. The
second chapter on Camus, 'The Plague', deals with the period
surrounding the Second World War and the Resistance. For O'Brien, *La
Peste* is an allegorical sermon. It deals with a town stricken by the
plague of Nazism during the occupation of France. O'Brien sees a flaw
in the novel's inability to recognize all the forms which a plague can
take. In this criticism he is again referring to the prime concern in his
monograph: the relation of Camus to Algeria. For O'Brien, the irony
is that although the action takes place in Oran in Algeria, the Arab
population, indeed any colonial appreciation, are nowhere present.
O'Brien points out that Camus never included these Arabs in his fiction.
Although the Arab quarters are mentioned, they are never visited and
play no role in the story. O'Brien surmises that this oversight
encapsulates Camus's attitude to the colonial predicament. This
detachment from the actual conditions of Algeria reflects Camus's
outlook, and informs an aloof style. According to O'Brien, the power
of *La Peste* lies in its impersonal tone, and the solemnity this offers to
Camus's warning, which O'Brien was to use in *States of Ireland*.

> The bacillus of the plague never dies or disappears, it can remain for tens
> of years dormant in furniture and linen .... and perhaps the day would
> come when, for the misfortune and instruction of men, the plague would
> wake up its rats again and send them off to die in a happy city. Eight
> years after the publication of *The Plague* the rats came up to die in the
> cities of Algeria, with the eruption of the boils and pus that had been
> working inwardly in the society, and this eruption came precisely from

the quarter where the doctor, and by implication Camus, never looked. The source of the plague is what we pretend is not there and the preacher himself is already, without knowing it, infected by the plague.[2]

In the immediate years after the Second World War, Camus was 'the most brilliant and influential figure on the non-communist left in France, and his fame had spread through Europe and the United States'.[3] Through his works he had come to represent a figure of Godless holiness, and to be seen by some as the archetype of the 'just man'. O'Brien's interest lies in taking a contrary vein to the typical view of Camus and to focus more on the singular path which Camus then began to take. Camus was highly sceptical of the various forms of anti-communism, a view O'Brien was to share with Camus for many years. As the war grew more distant, Camus began to focus his attention increasingly on the threat of violence to the state and society. His reaction to this began to take an expressly anti-communist form. As O'Brien says, he 'grows to forget'[4] his distrust of political anti-communism. Against the backdrop of the beginnings of the Cold War, revelations of Stalinist practices and a blurring of the truth on behalf of both communist and anti-communist camps, Camus came to the viewpoint that 'lies and violence have their home with communism because it is legitimised by a philosophy of history'.[5] This was to be expanded upon in his essay *L'Homme Revolté*, or *The Rebel*.

The publication of *L'Homme Révolté* in 1951, with its formulation that 'violence and lies have their home in Communism',[6] led to the famous split between Sartre and Camus. However, this split was to magnify with their diverging responses to crises in Indo-China, Suez, Hungary and ultimately the Algerian war. In these situations, the implications of Camus's estrangement from the Left can be seen. Sartre's position was that Frenchmen who hated terror and oppression – the 'lies and violence' that were obsessing Camus – should turn their attention first to their own war: Indo-China, and after the French capitulation at Dien Bien Phu, Algeria. It is this question of priority, psychological as well as political, that came to press most heavily on Camus. Innocuous as it may sound, it is only when viewed in the light of the actual situations that this choice of priority came to be paralysing.

Camus's position in the fifties was one of extreme intellectual and emotional difficulty and tension. He had written about freedom, justice, violence, and revolt in abstract terms and asserted principles which he presented as both of fundamental importance and universal application. He never altogether abandoned this language and he continued to write about politics in the tones of a severe moralist. Yet his actual positions were political and partisan. The violence of the Hungarian rebels and of the Anglo-French expedition in Egypt raised no problems. It was 'violence on the right side': precisely the logic he rejected on the grounds of a rigorous morality, in relation to revolutionary violence. Freedom was an absolute for the Hungarians and their violence in asserting their will 'to stand upright' was 'pure'. The violence of the Algerian Arabs, who thought that they were making the same claim, was 'inexcusable' and the nature and degree of the freedom to be accorded to them was a matter to be decided by France, in the light of its own strategic needs – a plea which was irrelevant when made by Russia.[7]

For O'Brien, Camus tacitly supported the repression in Algeria 'since he consistently opposed negotiation with the actual leaders of the rebellion, the FLN'. Camus maintained that negotiation with the FLN (Front de Libération Nationale) would lead to 'the independence of Algeria controlled by the most implacable military leaders of the insurrection; that is to say, the eviction of 1,200,000 Europeans of Algeria, and the humiliation of millions of Frenchmen, with the risks involved in that humiliation'.[8] What was needed was the suppression of the FLN, and after this process of 'pacification', a period of 'Free association' would follow. Camus foresaw that this required French military victory over the insurgents. For O'Brien, Camus

> remained in fact a Frenchman of Algeria and what seemed to be the increasingly right-wing positions of his later years were latent in his earlier silences. The only public statement of Camus on the subject of the Algerian war which has the ring of complete candour is one that he made in Sweden in December 1957 just after he had received the Nobel Prize: 'I have always condemned terror. I must also condemn a terrorism which operates blindly, in the streets of Algeria for example, and which one day may strike my mother or my family. I believe in justice but I will defend my mother before justice.'[9]

It is only in the light of this that we can understand what, for O'Brien, is Camus' greatest work: *La Chute*. What concerns us, in the terms of the novel, is a conversion from 'something of a superman' to a 'penitent judge'. It begins when the main character, a lawyer – Jean-Baptiste Clamence – begins to hear laughter from nowhere. His self-assuredness and confident outlook begins to crumble, and he imagines laughter coming from all sides, even from those who held him in high esteem. As the fabric of his life is shaken, he hears a splash and a cry for help as he crosses the Seine. He does nothing about it. These two occurrences and their persistent gnawing upon his mind, lead him to exile from his previous life, and the notions and images of himself which he held dear.

With this character Camus seems to grow apart from the left-wing intellectuals and the aspirations they once shared. The universals which infused his language are set aside for what O'Brien describes as a 'more conservative, more organic'[10] view of life. In delivering this Clamence, Camus produces an artistic response to his own political quandary. He manages not only to close the circle with his estranged relationship with Algeria, but to also present it in a manner that is personally compelling for O'Brien's own political quandary. Camus 'faces his dilemma between mother and justice with unmatched imaginative integrity'.[11] Camus's defection was 'a defeat for an entire generation', and a political move that led many to 'feel horror at the moral capital of *The Plague* supporting Algerian repression'.[12] Yet as O'Brien points out, 'it was in the very personal circumstances of Camus's life that this choice had to be made. And although Sartre's choice in defending the Algerian cause, involved the risk of his life, Camus's choice was the harder for it involved his entire life's moral, emotional, and intellectual capital.'[13] In *La Chute*, Camus faced his quandary as an artist and out of it produced an ironic mirror that dissolves our smugness, reminding us that our own universals could equally become undone.

What, it might be asked, has this to do with O'Brien? From what we have encountered already in his writings certain similarities can be pointed out. In the 'Introduction' to *Writers and Politics* we can see a persistent trait of O'Brien's which derives from his reading of the Sartre and Camus controversies: the question of priorities. This notion – that intellectuals must look to their own area of responsibility before condemning others – can be seen quite clearly in the rationale behind many of the essays of the late 1950s and 1960s. For O'Brien, the task of western intellectuals during the time of the Cold War was to tackle the situation from within.

> The liberation of the communist world, and of the poor world, from
> their crude forms of mendacity, will have to proceed from within and
> that the liberation of the Western World from its subtler and perhaps
> deadlier forms of mendacity will also have to proceed from within ....
> From the other side we can hear a few writers, Poles, Russians, Hungar-
> ians and others, busily chipping away. What might help would be that,
> from our own side also, should be heard the sound of chipping.[14]

This 'priority' is a strong influence on O'Brien, but Camus's example
goes deeper. There is a very interesting parallel between Algeria and
Northern Ireland, and so too between Camus and O'Brien. The choice
of mother before justice is intoxicatingly simple. Many might be
tempted to see O'Brien's own conversion, or decision to criticize the
history and society of the Republic, as a similar choice. If we consider
the Cruise O'Brien legacy, from the 1890s to the present, it could be
argued that under the heading 'father' instead of 'mother', a case can
be maintained that he chose his inheritance instead of the universals
which he had espoused in the 1960s.

For the moment it must be stated that the parallel is not valid.[15]
Northern Ireland is not Algeria. The analogy could possibly hold in the
Anglo-Irish war period, when it was a case of two historic entities, and
a process of decolonization. In 1970's Ireland, with three governments,
two of these at varying stages in the process of decolonization, and with
different claims being put forward, it is a little harder to see an analogy
with the Algerian colony's fight for independence. Even if we allow the
parallel, O'Brien's relation with Northern Ireland is not similar to
Camus's with Algeria. For O'Brien to claim the mantle of Camus –
interestingly a thing he never did – he would have to be a London-
based Northern Protestant.

If O'Brien's writings up to 1970 were to be examined, taking into
account his role as anti-partition propagandist and anti-colonialist, his
choice of mother would lead to one of active support for the
nationalists in Northern Ireland. His choice of 'father', with its more
selective assessment of his past would admittedly not necessarily lead
to this support. As previously stated there is a certain intellectual
equipoise involved in this. O'Brien to an extent carries conflicting
arguments within himself, which are almost antithetical. It would seem
that outside factors were pivotal in determining his choice between
mother and justice. Viewed in this light, the crucible of a choice

suggests the importance of personal histories to O'Brien. It also clearly illustrates why it has been necessary for O'Brien to stress certain aspects of his legacy to the detriment of others. Why, for example, the legacy of 'father' is accentuated from the 1970s on.

To return to the situation itself, we can see that O'Brien's initial reaction was to actively support the nationalists in Northern Ireland. Furthermore, if Camus were a Republican Nationalist, he would, according to his writings, not have to make a choice between mother and justice. They would be one. To see why O'Brien took the road he did, we need to go beyond this mother-justice choice. We need to go back to Camus's earlier writings. We need to look at what Camus said in *L'Homme Révolté*. By doing so we can, if nothing else, understand what is meant by justice.

As stated, the publication of the essay *L'Homme Revolté* in 1951 was the cause of the break between Sartre and Camus. O'Brien's initial opinion of *L'Homme Révolté* when he first reviewed it was not that high.[16] Years later in his 1970 monograph on Camus, he accords it far more weight. But even then there is a certain distrust of it as it is explicitly anti-communist. Nonetheless, it can be shown that *L'Homme Révolté* is the bed-rock upon which O'Brien's subsequent critiques of the IRA and of Irish history are founded. It is significant that while he was working on Camus, the violence in the North was beginning to escalate. It was also at this time that he co-wrote *A Concise History of Ireland*, while also keeping notes which would appear in *States of Ireland*. Rather than examine *L'Homme Révolté* in its entirety – a very difficult task on account of the variety of thinkers within the considerable time-span of the book – I will concern myself only with what O'Brien is on record as having deduced from it.

Writing about *L'Homme Révolté* in 1970 O'Brien refers to the view that came to obsess Camus in the Cold War period: 'the idea that violence and lies have in some special sense their home among the communists because they are legitimised by a philosophy of history'.[17] O'Brien goes on to say that the central argument of the very long first part of *L'Homme Révolté* resembles that of Yeats's short poem, 'The Great Day':

> Hurrah for Revolution and more Cannon-shot!
> A beggar upon horseback lashes a beggar on foot.
> Hurrah for revolution and cannon come again!
> The beggars have changed places, but the lash goes on.[18]

'Camus unlike Yeats, approves the revolt of the beggar on foot. What Camus rejects is the continuation of the lash, and more especially the justification of the lash in terms of the philosophy of history, the super-man, or the dictatorship of the proletariat.'[19] Now in Ireland there has not been much scope for the superman, or the dictatorship of the pro-letariat. There has, however, been a philosophy, or interpretation, of history which has given rise to many an action. It is this philosophy, and O'Brien's interpretation of it, which constitute the motif of all his later writings.

An example of this can be seen if we examine O'Brien's analysis of Camus's play *Les Justes*, which explores the conditions under which violence becomes justifiable. Both *Les Justes* and *L'Homme Révolté* are seen as moral critiques of violence. 'Politically, they are a critique of revolutionary violence and – most especially – of violence legitimised by the ethos of past revolution. The question falls heavily on the question of the morality of violence used to secure social and political change.'[20] It is when we read *L'Homme Révolté* as questioning the notion of 'violence legitimised by the ethos of past revolution'[21] that the whole inspiration and content of O'Brien's rationale for criticizing republican violence and Irish history, can be seen to derive from the concerns of Camus in *L'Homme Révolté*. The text of *L'Homme Révolté* itself is replete with examples of the language which O'Brien would introduce to an Irish audience. In borrowing the language, he swapped republicanism for communism and translated the violence and lies legitimized by a philosophy of history into a specifically Irish context. O'Brien would alter just one insistence of Camus's argument. This was the stipulation that 'the only thing that can justify violence is that he who inflicts it should lay down his life'.[22] In the Irish case, with O'Brien's critique of the Pearsean blood-sacrifice and its unfortunate role as exemplar to latter-day republicans, the idea that this would ex-onerate a terrorist collapses. It would appear that O'Brien saw an Irish parallel with the themes in *L'Homme Révolté*, and distilled and mapped them onto Ireland. The ethos of past revolution, the phi-losophy of history, the specific language and accusations about vio-lence and lies deriving from past precedent, however well they fit, however apposite they may now sound to Ireland in the wake of O'Brien's critique from the 1970s, all came from Camus and especially *L'Homme Révolté*.

At present there is some awareness of the influence of Camus in O'Brien's development, although this still revolves around one reading, which is the mother–justice choice.[23] As stated, the parallels between Ireland and Algeria are unsatisfactory. It belongs to an earlier period of Irish history, and would look better above the head of Shaw or Yeats, if it is to be anyway analogous to Camus's relation to Algeria. Moreover, to force a choice between mother and justice is to entirely miss the O'Brien critique. What does O'Brien do in 1971 and after? However sceptically some may view it, he, adapting Burke, loves his 'own platoon': his family, friends, neighbours, his compatriots, the Republic. It is only when the repercussions of violence in the North are felt in the South that O'Brien chooses. His critique is for the Republic in terms of audience, and it is initiated by events in the Republic, such as the Arms Trial. It is intellect directed 'critically and benevolently', according to his lights, toward the nation.[24] In short he, like Camus, chooses 'mother'.

We might also ask, what is justice in an Irish context? Does O'Brien supposedly dispense with it? Certainly most of the universals which infuse his writings of the 1960s, and especially the collection *Writers and Politics*, are jettisoned. The view which he comes to accept is the 'more organic, more conservative' one of Camus, which can also be seen in O'Brien's fondness for Burke. It must be pointed out that when Camus wrote about justice in *L'Homme Révolté* in 1951, he was not addressing colonialism or Algeria, he was addressing communism. The text of *L'Homme Révolté*, which is an enquiry into what legitimised the Nazis and Stalin – philosophical murder – is riddled with the word justice. The important thing to note here is that this is exactly what O'Brien concerns himself with from 1970 on. Justice and 'the philosophy of history' are, according to Camus, and as interpreted by O'Brien, incompatible. By locating 'the philosophy of history' in the tradition of Tone, the Fenians, Pearse and the IRA, by squaring up to 'the ethos of violence legitimised by past revolution', and by using the language of *L'Homme Révolté* in all subsequent writings on Ireland, O'Brien is explicitly and consciously choosing justice. Viewed from this angle, one could, without irony, say O'Brien chose mother *and* justice.

While O'Brien might consciously or otherwise have adopted Camus's critique and to an extent tried to borrow his mantle of the 'just man' (before being exasperated with the opprobrium it brought

him and threw it away with some well-timed detonations in 1970's Ireland), they are very different writers. Despite O'Brien's attempt to base
his critique on Camus, there are significant differences in their manner
of conceiving the world. While Camus is described as 'hardly a philosopher at all',[25] he shows that he is not only conversant with all the
philosophers of his time and before, but that he is acutely interested in
the intellectual capital behind the events. He may view things historically, but it is only to provide a scheme for his probing of the thoughts
that concern him. O'Brien, on the other hand, is profoundly historical.
While interested in the notions in people's heads, the results of this
probing are used to inform his historical conception. Possibly the most
basic difference between the two is simply that of originality. Camus is
an artist, O'Brien is a critic. Camus conjures up provocative solutions,
while portraying people and problems which pervade and endure.
While he may reach his metaphysical position of hope through intelligence, the inspiration which guides it, and the aspirations contained
within, rely on a rare perception informed by pure intuition. O'Brien,
who is no less intelligent, gets nowhere similar. There is exhortation
but it rings hollow. The positions of eminent worth are derived from
others. The tone is of prohibitive ethics, the scope is limited, its substance negative.

This is not a criticism. Readers can determine for themselves the
value of O'Brien's œuvre. They may make their own decision regarding its provenance, and according to their own tastes judge its originality. They should not, however, have doubts as to its effectiveness. If the
limited scope does not make for art or permanence, it found its audience. The ethical stance was necessary when the civic notions of the
public were being appealed to over the more attractive allure of sentiment and history. The negativity arises out of the context, and perhaps
also from the selectivity of the writer. That selectivity, a bleak
Manichean impatience, what we might call O'Brien's 'vision', is addressed in the following chapters.

NOTES

1. Conor Cruise O'Brien, *Camus* (London, 1970), p.32.
2. Ibid., p.51.
3. Ibid., p.52.
4. Ibid., p.54.
5. Ibid., p.53.

6. Ibid.
7. Ibid., p.75.
8. Ibid., p.74.
9. Ibid., p.75.
10. Ibid., p.83.
11. Ibid., p.85.
12. Ibid.
13. Ibid.
14. Conor Cruise O'Brien, *Writers and Politics* (London, 1965), p.xii.
15. He himself rejected the parallel twice. See Letter to *Irish Press*, 18 May 1970 and also the essay, 'Violence in Ireland: Another Algeria?' *New York Review of Books*, 17, 4 (23 September 1971). Also see draft of 'The People have risen', O'Brien papers, UCD, P82/259(4).
16. O'Brien, 'Monsieur Camus Changes his Climate', *Writers and Politics*, pp.65–71.
17. O'Brien, *Camus*, p.53.
18. Ibid., p.51.
19. Ibid., p.55.
20. Ibid., p.59. Almost the exact words O'Brien uses in his 'Introduction' to *Herod, Reflections on Political Violence* (London, 1978).
21. Ibid., p.54.
22. Ibid., p.60.
23. See Declan Kiberd's discussion of Camus and Cruise O'Brien in *Inventing Ireland* (London, 1995), pp.558–60; and Terence Browne, *Ireland: A Social and Cultural history 1922–2002* (London, 2004), pp.272–5.
24. Desmond Fennell's term in *Heresy: the Battle of Ideas in Modern Ireland* (Belfast, 1993).
25. O'Brien, *Camus*, p.60.

PART II
The Mind of Conor Cruise O'Brien

7

Overview

'Dr O'Brien, I would like to thank you for what you did ...
whatever it was.'[1]

Our response to O'Brien surely demands more than this. If we
inspect the various roles throughout O'Brien's life an impressive
list presents itself. External Affairs official, diplomat, journalist, literary
critic, historian, professor, university head, anti-war activist, social
critic, civil-rights activist, dramatist, TD, government minister, senator,
newspaper editor, university fellow, biographer and pro-Union negotia-
tor. Expanding upon this we discover that his education was quite distinctive: Sandford Park, French exchanges, Trinity, a doctorate on
Parnell and, to an extent, a thinker on Catholicism. To examine his earlier political views, we see a brief involvement with the Labour party,
an expressed affinity for socialism, and a parallel trajectory to his cousin
Owen Sheehy Skeffington, who started O'Brien off on a similar path,
yet unlike O'Brien held strong socialist views all his life.

As a government official, he headed up the Irish News Agency while
also involving himself in the conception, formulation and distribution
of articles and pamphlets which argued forcefully against partition. In
this dissemination of counter-information he could without difficulty be
labelled a propagandist. This sketch, however, would miss his capa-
ciousness within External Affairs. He also headed up the newly formed
UN section and, upon his return from New York in 1960, was for a
while put in charge of the Northern Ireland section. He was then
seconded to the office of the Secretary General in New York, and was
sent to Katanga as its representative, where he fulfilled the role of
peace-broker, or trouble-shooter (the double-meaning possible in this
term aptly sums up his role there). It is interesting also that he was
proud of the fact that he was the first individual to ever order UN
troops to employ force as part of an offensive action.

As university head under Kwame Nkrumah, he did his best to protect academic integrity. From Ghana O'Brien moved to the Albert Schweitzer Professorship in New York. Here he wrote on colonialism and the effect of power on the intellectual. Through active involvement, not just with intellectuals such as Chomsky and Arendt, but also with sit-ins where he was kicked by police and arrested, he was forced into practical reflections on revolution, war and civil-rights. However, this part of his life, the apogee of his socialist and liberal thinking, is also the point at which he retreats from his loose-cannon and internationalist incarnation upon his return to Ireland. While this may have been a personal decision, possibly influenced by his wife Máire MacEntee, it was also a choice where disillusionment with New York, the United States and Vietnam must be balanced against his keen interest in Irish politics.

With his election as Labour TD in 1969, his focus returned to issues such as the North and Irish foreign policy, but also socio-political questions such as the role of the church in Ireland. At various points throughout the 1970s he encountered the wrath of the hierarchy, most especially in a series of clashes with Bishop Jeremiah Newman. But he also brought intellectual critiques on the abuse of power to the more homely setting of land deals in Dublin. He fought the ascendancy of the Minister for Finance, Charles Haughey, who was to be O'Brien's erstwhile foe until Haughey's retirement. While giving some attention to the Biafran crisis in Nigeria, his main focus outside of the Dáil was Northern Ireland, following the outbreak of troubles there in 1968. As he said later, albeit underplaying the extent of his involvement, he 'gave some small support' to the Civil Rights Movement.[2]

However, from the position of a stalwart defender of civil liberties O'Brien would within a few years draft legislation which would lead to their restriction. In 1977 he lost his Dáil seat and was elected senator for one of the Trinity seats. In his two years he made practically no contribution, and, after becoming Editor-in-Chief of *The Observer*, resigned his seat. He held this position briefly, before becoming a freelance journalist, writing a book on Zionism, and receiving fellowships to American universities. The result of one of these was his book on nationalism, *God Land*. In more recent years he produced a well-received study on Edmund Burke, and stood for election as a United Kingdom Unionist Party candidate. He continued to write practically up until his death in December 2008 at the age of 91.

This familiar biographical sketch of O'Brien is less convincing if we view his life through the lens of 'position' rather than 'role'. Firstly, there is O'Brien the 'post-colonial critic'. In frequently writing anti-colonial pieces, he seemed to imbue the entire 'post-colonial' critique. He made his audience in Ireland and abroad aware of this approach, while offering some original contributions in this field. At one point in the aftermath of his role in the Congo one reviewer in the *Times Literary Supplement* greeted his new book, *Writers and Politics,* with the words, '"We have no ships to bring the Negroes Yeats". But the United Nations brought Dr O'Brien to Katanga instead.'[3] From this ridiculously exalted position there was nowhere to go but down. Perhaps inevitably he would, in subsequent decades, arouse the ire of those who could be labelled under the 'post-colonial' bracket. His positions on Northern Ireland show a similar progression. At one point he was sufficiently critical of Northern Ireland's status quo in the late 1960s to write that 'support for the equality of rights and the abolition of Stormont's institutionalised *caste system* is another matter. Its destruction would be a human achievement of more than merely local significance.'[4] From this he moves to the position where he would lacerate the Civil Rights Movement, and be highly critical of nationalists, North and South.

He crafted an interpretation from this which implicated not just violence, but gestures of rejection or refusal of the Northern state as utterly immoral. Moreover, he voiced concerns which questioned the legitimacy of the aspirations of Northern nationalists. Connected to this, he challenged the long-held belief in the rightness of the unification of the island of Ireland. He would ultimately reject this, firstly as unwinnable, and subsequently as a pernicious enterprise. The cumulative effect of this was that he came to question all the tenets of Irish nationalism. He broke the final taboo with his accession to the United Kingdom Unionist Party: O'Brien became a unionist. We might ask the question: did he ever hold principles which were the converse of Unionism; was O'Brien ever a republican? If we view his writings in the 1960s, especially his seminal essay to commemorate 1916, 'The Embers of Easter 1916–1966', we can say he definitely saw himself working in this vein, and that for a considerable portion of his life he held the challenge thrown down by 1916 to be a noble one.

In much the same way as his anti-colonial critique by and large evaporates, so too did his 'power and the intellectual' arguments fall to dust. In the late 1960s he successfully sued *Encounter* magazine in defence of his inference that it was affiliated with the CIA. Within years O'Brien's position evolved and embraced positions which would argue the opposite of a previous stance. An example of this is neatly brought across in the official biography of O'Brien by Donald Akenson, where O'Brien retracted his highly trenchant criticisms of Arthur Schlesinger Jr's role as a Kennedy aide and contributor to *Encounter*.

> Now at the time of the debate with Arthur Schlesinger I'm afraid that I felt quite self-righteous about my own participation in these matters. But pride cometh before a fall and at that time I had not myself been engaged in active democratic electoral politics in my own country.[5]

By the 1980s he was happily writing for not just *Encounter*, but a host of other hard right publications.

The core of this seemed to be an association with Israel which developed in the 1980s. As many of his obituaries indicated, this relationship was tested severely on many an occasion by the brutality of Israel's treatment of Palestinians and its actions in the Lebanon, especially in the aftermath of the Sabra and Shatilla massacres. What is less often observed is that O'Brien even went further than this, and in the late 1980s was articulating highly neo-conservative positions – again largely as a result of his political affiliation with Israel. In *Passion and Cunning*, a collection of essays from the 1980s, he clearly advocates that it might be necessary to invade Iraq, Iran, Syria, Libya and South Yemen as a necessary means of defending Israel![6]

If his roles were varied throughout his life, and if his positions evolved until they contradicted what he espoused earlier in life, there remains a possibility that there was an internal consistency within O'Brien. I am not referring to the view expressed in his *Memoir* where he claimed a lifelong consistency in his opposition to imperialism. I am reflecting more on the basic categories of O'Brien's mind which lead to the many sparks and circles of his event-filled career. The temptation when writing about a life is to present a seamless whole. The process however often leads to a papering over of the outstanding feature of most of our lives: we simply don't know what will come next. While every historian works with the knowledge of retrospect s/he must endeavour to place him/herself in the mind of the person whom s/he writes about as if this knowledge did not exist. By separating the choices of O'Brien's life from their circumstances, by juxtaposing the unionist with the nationalist regardless of time and place, the peculiar context behind each thought and deed is lost. This study has not attempted to piece together anything more than the initial influences and the key arguments in his life. But one example of a fundamental category in his mind would be his obsession with consequences. *States of Ireland* can be read as an essay on the consequences of Irish nationalism. His essay on Yeats's politics, 'Passion and Cunning', revolves around the consequences of Yeats's poetry. It is one of the features of Burke and Camus which he constantly chose to highlight. A similar thread can be seen in O'Brien, especially in the writings which arise from his concern with legitimacy.

What these categories of his seem to be able to point to is that if the political positions have changed nearly as much as his career, there does seem to be an internal coherence not in what he says or does, but in how he perceives things. The consistency that O'Brien claims, while highly subjective, does seem to exist. The second part of the book then tries to explore not just the political arguments, but the categories and criteria that his mind brings to any given situation. They may be skewed, slanted and biased according to another's position, but they are quite simply his way of looking at the world.

NOTES

1. Kwame Nkrumah's reported parting shot to O'Brien upon his departure from Ghana. Quoted in D.H. Akenson, *Conor: A Biography of Conor Cruise O'Brien* (Montreal, 1994), pp.270–1.
2. Conor Cruise O'Brien, *States of Ireland* (London, 1972), p.7.
3. 'Only Commit', *Times Literary Supplement*, 23 December 1965, p.1195.
4. Conor Cruise O'Brien, 'Holy War', *New York Review of Books*, 6 November 1969, pp.15. My emphasis.
5. Quoted in Akenson, *Conor: A Biography*, pp.461–4, and pp.533–4.
6. He did not actually come up with this list himself. It was created by Benjamin Netanyahu, but in the course of the essay O'Brien endorses the view that these invasions might be necessary. Conor Cruise O'Brien, 'Thinking about Terrorism: II', in *Passion and Cunning* (London, 1990), pp.309.

8

The Siege

There is a canonical view of *States of Ireland* that it is O'Brien's most influential work. One critic has it that in writing it O'Brien 'embarked on a complete rethinking of his nationality, rejecting in this brilliant polemic ... the sacred principle of the thwarted Republic: unity of North and South'.[1] It is generally acknowledged that this highly successful book was a key text in re-educating the Republic into a better understanding of their Northern neighbours. Others went a step further and accused O'Brien of crossing the fence. John Hume's 1972 review in *The Irish Times* did just that when he said that, 'Conor Cruise O'Brien's case is a more effective and subtle defence of Unionism than any that has come from any Unionist quarter'.[2] At the time O'Brien was a minister in an Irish government. Whatever his sympathies may have been with the unionist view, to be labelled one was 'a political death-sentence'.[3] The relationship between O'Brien and Hume was destroyed. O'Brien never forgave him, and both parties went out of their way on several occasions to outmanoeuvre the other. Within a week of the review O'Brien returned with interest when he criticized the SDLP proposals for a new Ireland and stated that, 'their insistence on unity without the agreement of the Protestant community was – although unwittingly and unintentionally – a formula for civil war'.[4] The irony is that many years later O'Brien was happy to pay tribute to Hume's ability to spot the nascent unionism that appeared in *States of Ireland*: 'Looking back on it, over a gap of about a quarter of a century, I can see this was quite a perceptive diagnosis.'[5]

Regardless of the rights and wrongs of this spat between O'Brien and Hume, there is little doubt that *States of Ireland* is a conscious attempt to introduce O'Brien's Southern brethren to the mindset of the Northerner so that they may understand it that bit better. Many have ventured that it is a badly written hodgepodge of differing styles and narrative threads. They see it as part biography, part reportage, and part philosophical musings, mixed with a large part of history of the *tour d'horizon* kind. Some have claimed that its confused and jarring execution are perfectly matched with the political situation of the day; 'the mess is the message' as one commentator put it. These points are all true, but they should not deflect from the substance of what Hume touches upon. In terms of its design it very subtly and quite effectively brings us into the mindset of the Northern Protestant. And behind this effort lies a simple message that revolves around one key idea: 'the siege'.

The notion of a siege is something that is not new to any discourse on unionism or Northern Protestants. O'Brien himself used it on occasion, as in 1969 when he took stock of 'The Irish Question'. Back then he stated that 'even with some help from Mr. Lynch' there was no escaping the fact that 'the "siege" has been off for years and that it is hard to pretend that it is still on'.[6] Three years later, however, by the time he was writing *States of Ireland* his perspective had changed considerably. At regular and particularly important junctures O'Brien put forward the notion of a siege as the reason and excuse for the historical patterns that sadly had resurfaced once more. Furthermore, when reading *States of Ireland* it becomes clear that the entire relationship between Catholics and Protestants is characterized in terms of a siege.

However, if you examine the index for a less impressionistic pattern, you would be no wiser: 'the siege' receives no entry. After trawling through the text itself, there are twenty-nine separate references to the notion of a siege.[7] The idea of the siege as a signature theme in O'Brien's work is further strengthened by the presence of O'Brien's 1988 book *The Siege: The Saga of Israel and Zionism*.[8] The title alone suggests a strong connection between nationalism and this metaphor. When one considers that a good deal of O'Brien's foreign critiques derive from his experience of Irish nationalism, an opportunity to observe the circumstances that created this persistent mental pattern of his could tell us a lot about O'Brien.[9] There are several senses in which the siege metaphor operates in *States*. The two instances where it is employed in the literal sense, references to the siege of Derry and the breaker of that siege, Percy Kirk, are the least important. The next sense, the usage of 'the siege' in the demographic or physical sense, starkly illustrates the entire argument of *States of Ireland*. The references appear in the 'Foreword' and in the 'Epilogue', making them a kind of argumentative frame. O'Brien claims that 'the siege', corresponds to the denominational proportions in the island, and not to the proportion of Protestants to Catholics within Northern Ireland. There is also an interesting discrepancy between the two frames. Speaking of the two to one ratio of Protestants to Catholics in Northern Ireland, O'Brien argues: 'Protestant fear and suspicion of Catholics in Northern Ireland do not correspond to these proportions, but to the proportions between Catholic and Protestant in the entire island of Ireland, by which Protestants are outnumbered by Catholics by more than three to one.'[10] Then at the end of the book in the 'Epilogue' he speaks with greater simplicity: 'Above all the Ulster Protestant's response is proportioned to his concept of a siege conducted by a majority in the island.'[11] It is fair to say that some distance has been travelled by one so careful in measuring his words when we contrast 'outnumbered', with, 'a siege conducted'. This, in a way, is the point of the book.

The next sense in which O'Brien employs this metaphor is a religious one. Although not crucial to his thesis, the religious instances are important for illustrative purposes. The first reference is to what O'Brien sees as the historical commonplace that reformed religious communities suffer from a pervasive feeling of insecurity or are to some extent surrounded. 'The old fears of besieged Reformed communities have been kept continuously alive in Ulster – by the reality of the siege – and made even more lively by certain modern developments, such as democracy and birth control.'[12] The second religious reference explains how the context of a siege determines the manner in which voice is given to religious differences. 'In the much more nearly homogenous Republic, all the political parties are overwhelmingly Catholic in membership, support and representation. The church has good reason to be satisfied with this situation, no desire to see Catholicism used obtrusively as a political weapon.' The corresponding situation in the North, the existence of 'a straight forward siege situation',[13] is the explanation offered for why religion is so obtrusively employed in the North.

The final and most important area in which the metaphor of 'the siege' operates is the historical. This requires quite a lengthy exegesis. To begin with we must turn to the time of Parnell. The place which

Parnell occupies in O'Brien's historical interpretation cannot be over-stated. It is interesting that the first mention of 'the siege' occurs when O'Brien discusses Parnell, and at the point where Northern Ireland is introduced into the narrative. Here O'Brien asserts that the legacy of Parnell had been to awaken the very real possibility of Home Rule and the danger to Ulster from this movement.

> The liberal leader, whoever he might be, would someday blow the dust off Gladstone's speeches. Ulster had to be prepared against that day. Siege operations had been suspended, but it was clear that they would be resumed. Protestant Ulster was well prepared for such a contingency. The siege-mentality had been its heritage from the seventeenth century, when the conquerors had followed with imperfect success a counsel of Machiavelli's.[14]

The seventeenth-century settlements failed Machiavelli's basic test, as set out in *The Prince,* since the injuries inflicted by various princes proved not to be of such a kind that there is no fear of revenge. 'That fear was there from the beginning. At different times it has faded away, only to return; it is there now.'[15] O'Brien asserts that the early colonists were aware of the dispossessed natives biding their time. 'The farmer in his tidy holding in the valley had to keep an eye out for the Catholic outlaws in the hills, and for signs of treachery among his Gaelic Catholic servants if he had them.'[16] Stopping to draw parallels with settlers in New England and Dutch Calvinists in South Africa, he illustrates how the whole character of the seventeenth century was one of unmitigated settler–native hostility. The result of the roll-call of battles and tribulations were the penal laws, of which he observes that the 'victory was so complete that the old siege-mentality relaxed, and almost seemed to disappear'.[17] This is a good example of 'the siege' as a twin aspect device. Not only is it a potted history, but it is also a narrative that is tailored to effect an understanding of the Ulster Protestants' mentality. The next reference endorses this particular reading. Speaking of Wolfe Tone, O'Brien states how he is not concerned with Tone's role at the centre of the 'cult of modern Catholic Republicanism' (hardly a neutral way of describing Irish nationalism), but rather with 'the place of his movement in the history of the Ulster Protestant siege-mentality: first as apparently breaking down that mentality; then as re-establishing it'.[18]

At this point, the outline of three arguments which O'Brien will repeatedly use when analysing the following centuries is apparent. Firstly, the situation of the seventeenth century was in essence the same as the twentieth. Secondly, the character of this immutable sentiment or reaction was one of fear. Thirdly, this relationship involved a dynamic by which all gain for one party had an axiomatically negative impact upon the other party. The next reference to 'the siege' asserts that the rising of 1798, 'did more than any other single set of events to divide Irishmen, and to re-establish among Protestants the old siege-mentality of the seventeenth century'.[19] By the time O'Brien arrives at the Famine, 'Protestant Ulster now seemed to have little to fear, its besiegers (were) dispersed by hunger'. However, by

> a strange reversal it was as a result of the Famine that the Catholic Irish themselves began – initially in a most modest way – to share in another great success: that of America. It was from America that the materials came for the renewal of revolt: renewal from Protestant Ulster's point of view, of the siege.[20]

We have now returned full circle to our point of departure: Parnell. O'Brien closes his argument with another reference to Machiavelli, whose counsels had been imperfectly carried out as the 'injured' had not been sufficiently depleted in terms of numbers or wealth. Nor had they been absorbed or placated. The wound was deep but not fatal, and there were grounds to fear revenge. 'For Protestant Ulster, the 1880s constituted the renewal of the siege, in a more dangerous form than at any other time since the seventeenth century.'[21] This was because Parnell had brought about what seemed unthinkable to Ulster Protestants: the conversion of a British Prime Minister to the idea of self-government for Ireland. 'Self-government after Catholic Emancipation and universal suffrage: implying domination of Protestants by Catholics.'[22] It was in this era that the Orange Order's commemoration of the Boyne became the great mass demonstration that it is today. Again we return to the fall of Parnell. O'Brien interprets it as meaning that 'the besiegers had been driven back. But they were still around.'[23]

The Boer War is the next instance in which the siege metaphor is employed. The Afrikaner character was 'in fact very like itself, dourly Protestant, thoroughly besieged, sure of its God-given superiority, slow, suspicious, determined and tough'.[24] Then O'Brien explains how the Tory policy of 'killing Home Rule with kindness' had actually strengthened the forces working for self-government:

> The Tory democratisation of the local government in Ireland in 1898 meant that there were now Catholic majorities on all the local bodies outside of the core of Protestant Ulster, and these bodies were ready to pass disloyal resolutions on any topical subject whether it was technically within their competence or not. In Ulster itself many Protestants, outside the densest area of the Bann, experienced a sort of foretaste of 'Catholic rule' through this democratisation of local government. It was from an Ulster Protestant point of view, another turn of the screw: a constriction of the siege.[25]

This goes some way to indicating the extremes O'Brien was beginning to occupy in order to maintain his position. As an argument for Ulster Protestants, and against democracy, it surely is not that well intentioned. Nor is it without implications. In later years, this scenario of once again asserting the rights of one group, at the expense of another, will reappear.

He next moves to those events concerning the independence of Ireland. 'The Easter 1916 Rising was a blow struck against England, and struck in circumstances that precluded all hope of military victory.'[26] He concedes that with the focus almost entirely on England, Ulster probably seemed far from urgent to nationalists. While this may be so, '1916 and its aftermath affected Ulster too. It was another tightening of the siege.'[27] However, the election of 1918 deserves even more prominence. Nationalist Ireland voted out the old Irish Parliamentary Party, and voted in its place for Sinn Féin.[28]

> From the point of view of Protestant Ulster, the significance of the shift in nationalist (Catholic) opinion was that the Catholic leaders who had reluctantly accepted partition, and the idea of remaining within the Empire, had fallen, and been replaced by men who totally rejected partition and the Empire, and who were committed to the use of force for securing full independence for an island unit. This was – from an Ulster point of view – an open proclamation of a siege which had long been more covertly conducted.[29]

The remaining paragraphs of O'Brien's chapter outline how the

formalities of partition came to pass and the disintegration of the
United Kingdom and Ireland was completed. Brief mention is given to
the pogroms against Catholics in the North; the guerrilla warfare
against the British; the enactment of the Government of Ireland Act of
1920; the Treaty dissension, and the Civil War. 'By 1922, the essential
framework of Lloyd George's Government of Ireland Act had been
accepted, at least de facto, in both parts of the partitioned country.'[30]

As the narrative of *States of Ireland* progresses, it becomes less event-
centred and leans more toward a treatment of the mentalities of the
parties involved; these mentalities are again governed by the siege
metaphor. Once the historical stage has been set, the pace slows down
and becomes more focused on themes which reinforce the idea of a
siege. The real critique is of post-Independence Catholic Ireland, and
its role in 'the siege'. Within this new thematic inquiry, the siege
metaphor is employed twice. When Cumann na nGaedheal, the pro-
Treaty faction of Sinn Féin, was replaced by Fianna Fáil in 1932, it
'marked a more or less open renewal of the siege'.[31] This is reflected in
the withdrawal of official recognition from the Northern Ireland state.
Furthermore, the effect of the 1937 Constitution was to repudiate the
Boundary Agreement and formally lay claim to Northern Ireland.
Articles 2 and 3, and Article 44.1.2 (special position of the Holy
Apostolic and Roman Church), led O'Brien to write that it 'would be
hard to think of a combination of propositions more likely to sustain
and stiffen the siege-mentality of Protestant Ulster'.[32] Therefore, this
political shift in the 1930s constitutes in the words of O'Brien a
'standing vindication of the Unionist Party's call for unremitting
vigilance'.[33] An example of why this was necessary is seen in the 'chapel
gate collection' of 1949 where 'the siege' arises again.[34] The only real
look at Northern Ireland itself comes when O'Brien refers to the 'vested
interest of the Unionist Party and the Orange Order in maintaining the
tautness of the siege mentality'.[35]

When O'Brien switches from historical enquiry to contemporary
events he employs the siege metaphor as a bridge between two quite
separate narratives. Reflecting on the late 1960s, he observes: 'It was
much less easy to predict what would come out of the civil rights
struggle. One thing, however, was certain, for anyone who had an idea
of the character of the besieged state ... was that much blood would be
shed.'[36] Having employed 'the siege' extensively up to now, it is perhaps

puzzling why O'Brien should use 'the siege' only once in describing the situation of the late 1960s, which takes up two thirds of *States of Ireland*. It seems that O'Brien drew back from the implication of 'the siege' when mapped onto the contemporary.

Regardless of what he said in 1969 – that the siege was off – we can definitely say that on any reading of *States of Ireland* he saw the Ulster Protestants as besieged. But from various articles, his statements in the Dáil, and from the tentative way in which he uses 'the siege' in the contemporary part of *States of Ireland*, he does not seem to have been convinced that the Republic was actually besieging Northern Irish Protestants. This would eventually change. It could be added that this is the real value of Hume's review in that he saw the natural implication of O'Brien's drift, even if it was not actually explicit at the time. The seeds of his ultimate certainty can be seen here for the first time. In the final analysis we can see now that *States of Ireland* is a kind of interpretive portal that allowed some Southern Irish people to make a new mental approach to Northern Ireland. Through its 300-plus pages it makes its readers confront the thinking of Northern Protestants.

There is no question but that O'Brien wants the reader to infer that 'the siege' is a history of 'the relations between Catholics and Protestants, and between the two political entities created by those relations'.[37] From the evidence assembled by O'Brien, can we say that the construct of 'the siege' is an accurate presentation of their experience? An initial investigation pursued at the almost pedantic level of actual statements corresponding to an emotional or cognitive standpoint yields limited results. We have the solitary example of Mrs McTier. As the sister of William Drennan, a leading figure in the United Irishmen, she had 'been like him, an ardent believer in United Irishmen ideas, (and) was frightened by "a singing procession of Catholics". "I begin to fear, these people", she wrote, "and think, like the Jews, they will regain their native land".'[38] Interestingly, this is the closest O'Brien comes to producing testimony to substantiate 'the siege'. In synopsizing the 1880s, the purportedly apocalyptic decade, he offers as conclusion: 'Drennan's sister's nightmare'.[39] Is it reasonable to enquire how representative Mrs McTier actually is, and if one utterance does four hundred years of a province make?

In its persistent interaction with the text, the unquestionably overriding usefulness of 'the siege' lies in its subjectivity. As with all things of this nature only the subjects can determine their vision. In this case, with O'Brien as interpreter, he alone can arbitrate as to what constitutes a siege. There is a sense in which *States of Ireland* is quite positive. In writing within his agreed framework, O'Brien puts forward an argument and creates a novel vocabulary. This vocabulary forces the reader to maintain pace with the book's argument. It manifests itself almost unconsciously, to the extent that a reader might take issue with the premise of *States of Ireland* and yet follow and ultimately agree with its conclusion. Even if one disagrees with the manner in which it arises, the creation of a vocabulary must be acknowledged as significant. We could characterize it as the language of single effect, that of the effect of any given event upon Ulster Protestant perceptions. The analysis of O'Brien's 'siege' leaves little doubt as to the axiomatic relationship characterized in this history: that of Catholics impinging upon Protestants. Ultimately it can be said that O'Brien set out to write a book explaining the Northern Ireland situation which would at each stage of the narrative force us to internalize, as well as understand, the Ulster Protestant worldview.

The audience receives a chronology of events which amounts to an apologia for Ulster Protestant actions. *States of Ireland* concentrates almost exclusively upon their tradition, their long-established existence and their obsession with the Catholic Irish. Because they are a minority, because they are not agents and are merely reacting to others, their role in bringing about the present-day situation is minimized. In terms of agency he focuses almost exclusively on the responsibility involved in Catholic Irish words and actions. His concentration upon the Ulster Protestant mentality in both the past and the present represents an unbalanced history and an unbalanced critique of the then contemporary conflagration. Perhaps the most viable explanation for this was that he felt a moral onus to deal with what he viewed as a re-enactment of the past. This obligation to alter the undercurrent of dislike which had surfaced once more can be seen to be one of the primary motives in subsequent writings. There was a very serious task at hand for people in the Republic of the 1970s. As he put it in an address to the Irish Association of Civil Liberties some four years later:

> We ought to undertake whatever part of that work we can, in whatever part of this island we live in, without preconditions, and without waiting

for someone else in another part of the island, and in another community, to begin. Peace begins at home.[40]

NOTES

1. Maurice Walsh, 'A Talent to Offend'. *New Statesman*, 1 January 1999.
2. John Hume, 'Review of *States of Ireland*', *The Irish Times*, 9 October 1972.
3. O'Brien's term when referring to the effect of Hume's review in *The Irish Times*. Conor Cruise O'Brien, *Memoir: My Life and Themes* (Dublin, 1998), p.339.
4. Quoted in Richard Deutsch and Vivien MacGowan, *Northern Ireland 1968–1973: A Chronology of Events* (Belfast, 1973), Saturday 14 October 1972.
5. O'Brien, *Memoir*, p.339.
6. Conor Cruise O'Brien, 'The Irish Question', *The Irish Times*, 21 January 1969.
7. This makes it the second most referred to subject, by a clear margin, in addition to being the most diffuse. Jack Lynch has the most entries, but they are concentrated in the final third of the book.
8. Conor Cruise O'Brien, *The Siege: The Saga of Israel and Zionism* (London, 1986).
9. For a good discussion of this, and some of the strange alleys this leads into, see D.H. Akenson, *Conor: A Biography of Conor Cruise O'Brien* (Montreal, 1994), p.534.
10. Conor Cruise O'Brien, *States of Ireland* (London, 1972), p.11.
11. Ibid., p.308.
12. Ibid., p.168.
13. Ibid., p.194.
14. Ibid., p.34. 'So any injury a Prince does a man should be of such a kind that there is no fear of revenge'.
15. Ibid., p.36.
16. Ibid.
17. Ibid., p.37.
18. Ibid., p.39.
19. Ibid., p.41.
20. Ibid., p.43.
21. Ibid., p.46.
22. Ibid.
23. Ibid., p.47.
24. Ibid., p.66.
25. Ibid., p.77.
26. Ibid., p.99.
27. Ibid.
28. Ibid., p.100–29.
29. Ibid., pp.100–1.
30. Ibid., p.102.
31. Ibid., p.137.
32. Ibid., p.121.
33. Ibid., p.137.
34. A collection carried out at the time in order to aid the anti-partition campaign. O'Brien suggests that the fact that the Church endorsed the collection summed up everything that was wrong about the South.
35. O'Brien, *States of Ireland*, p.137.
36. Ibid., p.156.
37. Ibid., p.9.
38. O'Brien, *States of Ireland*, p.42.
39. Ibid., p.46.
40. Statement on 'Church and State' by Dr Conor Cruise O'Brien TD, Minister for Posts and Telegraphs, delivered to IACL, 28 Feb 1977. P 82/327 (10).

9

Religion: Church and State in Ireland

When O'Brien returned to Ireland from New York in 1969 he successfully ran for election to the Dáil as a Labour candidate. If one compares the newly elected TD of 1969 with the outgoing minister who failed to get re-elected in 1977, the difference is quite startling. Popularity aside, in the later case we have the 'scourge' of the IRA and the arch-critic of nationalism. In the earlier instance it is difficult to ascribe any sketch of immediate relevance to Ireland, based on this returned professor from New York, anti-war demonstrator and civil-rights activist. If there was one area in which some friction could be expected, it was far more likely to come in the province of religion than of nationalism. O'Brien was, after all, the first *divorcé* and avowed agnostic to enter the Dáil, no minor milestones in their own right. Perhaps of greater significance, he had in 1965 labelled the Irish church, 'the heart of darkness of the ecumenical movement'.[1] O'Brien then, can be viewed as one of the figures whose vocal presence gives an impression of a thaw in Irish society in the late 1960s. There is a plausible argument that if O'Brien had been allocated the portfolio of Minister of Education in 1973, I believe our impressions of him, and possibly his critique, would now to be totally different. The probability is that his resignation would have been forced in some re-enactment of the Mother and Child crisis over the church and schools, rather than a general distaste for his contributions on violence and broadcasting and sympathizing with the IRA. However, events in the North were to divert attention away from this more gradual secular evolution. O'Brien's concentration on more immediate concerns north of the border altered both O'Brien and the public's perception of him. Bearing this in mind, the church and state debate can be seen as something of a lost theme.

It is nonetheless notoriously difficult to try to establish a fixed point in O'Brien's view on the church. It is fair to say that he was an agnostic and was interested in working towards a secular state. Instinctively he had an inherent suspicion of religion and would have preferred to see less of it in Irish society. Intellectually speaking he was without a doubt anticlerical. That said, he was not hostile to the church as a collection of individuals. His personal papers in UCD are testament to the reasoned, polite, considered fashion in which he dealt with queries and points by various members of the clergy. Moreover, he personally developed from a young vehemently anticlerical student to a more balanced critique of the 1960s where he could acknowledge that Ireland had moved on from its post-Independence incarnation of being priest-ridden and opposed to ecumenism. A good illustration of this is how in 1966 he agreed to allow an essay of his from 1956, 'The Church of the People', to be reprinted. While he was content to re-publish it unchanged, he wanted the following footnote to be added to reflect the developments over the ten years.

> Important changes have occurred, not so much in formal rules and institutions as in attitudes and atmosphere. Criticism of the social and educational role of the clergy is made publicly to an extent that would not have been acceptable ten years ago. The subject of birth control, which was then almost completely taboo, can now be freely discussed even in a popular paper with an almost entirely Catholic readership. The censorship of publication – a clerically inspired move for which the clergy never took formal responsibility – has been relaxed to the point at which serious works are now seldom affected.[2]

He went on to say that a lot of these changes were coming from within, due to social forces and rising living standards. At the same time a great deal of the change was coming from without: the ecumenical movement. The prime example of this filtering through for O'Brien was the piece of advice from Cardinal Conway to young priests to 'avoid paternalist attitudes'.[3]

However, some fifteen years later, a critique more in tune with what he had been saying in the 1950s resurfaced. Writing in the early 1980s, there was, he felt, an extremely disturbing nexus between the Irish and their religion, and he compares it to the Taleban of Afghanistan. The image he conjures up leaves us in little doubt about the effect of the Troubles on O'Brien's view of Irish society.

What we have on our hands, I have been arguing, in reality is a Holy
War and the reason for the sinister durability of the provisional IRA is
that many people, in some part of their psyche, view those men as the
equivalent of what the Moslems call Mujahidin, those who fight the
Jihad – the Holy War. That's there in the basement, and we can hear it
if we listen carefully.[4]

Clearly something savage happened to force an acute mind to offer an
opinion so utterly out of tune with the increasing secularization and
decreasing relevance of the church to Irish society from the 1980s on.

The following pages, then, attempt to ascertain the extent to which
religion features in O'Brien's treatment of both Northern Ireland and
Irish nationalism in *States of Ireland*. More precisely, I hope to offer
substance to the elusive link between religion and O'Brien's core
politics – an appreciation that will allow us to establish his basic position
on the church in Ireland above and beyond what Erskine Holmes called
the 'politics of the last atrocity'.[5]

In doing so, I am limiting myself to two crucial areas of *States of
Ireland*: the chapter entitled 'The Catholic State', and the 'Epilogue'. As
previously mentioned, O'Brien shifts focus from historical narrative to
an ideas approach, and these two pieces are highly indicative of this. In
the chapter 'The Catholic State' he concentrates mainly on the years between 1922 and 1937 and begins with a tongue-in-cheek discussion of
the ironies posed by the nomenclature of the Free State, the Republic,
and its constitutions and territories down the years. While good at
outlining the disparity between wish and fact, his approach is primarily
a vehicle for introducing the question of the designation of what is
generally thought of as the South, whatever its appellation, as a
Catholic state. This focus on designation, a Catholic state for a Catholic
people, is the spine of the entire chapter. In the relation between
religion and politics, O'Brien maintains that 'the Catholic state'
accurately sums it up. It also provides the necessary ambience for the
assertion that: 'Democracy in Ireland must always be taken with a
tincture of theocracy.'[6] This then is the point he wishes to tease out: was
post-Independence Ireland secular or theocratic?

As with so many of his other writings, the chapter 'The Catholic
State' begins with a sustained autobiographical piece. It all leads up to
an image of his mother forced to seek priestly dispensation through the
chink of a door, which quite understandably leads him to reflect upon

'the oppressive pieties of the Catholic Church'.[7] He then embarks upon an analysis of the role of religion in Irish society. His method is perhaps best illustrated by observing what he chooses to abjure. A simple case-by-case-history approach is inadequate. The most notable example of this approach, the work of Paul Blanshard, 'may be accurate enough in detail, but leaves a false general impression, excessive in darkness'.[8] On the other hand some critiques of the Blanshard position, also literally accurate, also end by giving another wrong impression: 'too bright, too sweet, too light and airy'.[9] A different approach, exemplified by John Whyte's *Church and State in Modern Ireland*[10] would, in contrast to Blanshard, dispute such terminology as the 'Catholic State'. Whyte's work is referred to in glowing terms, and it would be fair to say that there is very little contradiction between the two. While there are differences of opinion upon certain points which I will come to later, the main point to bear in mind is that the 'Catholic State' chapter of *States of Ireland* is designed largely to circumvent the problems inherent in the case-history approach.

O'Brien wonders if the Ulster Protestant point of view is correct: does Home Rule mean Rome Rule? For O'Brien, this slogan 'represents the substance of the reason why Ulster Protestant workers and farmers reject, despise and fear "the Free State" which claims jurisdiction over them'.[11] While he asserts that Home Rule did not mean Rome Rule, he argues that no-one ever contended this in the literal sense. Rather 'what the slogan implied was the general condition of being priest-ridden, the over-riding authority of Catholic bishops and priests, the Catholic State'.[12] He explores why the Free State never proclaimed itself a Catholic State, and chooses to do so upon the evidence of Parnell, Southern Protestants, the Free State Constitution and legislation. For instance, he claims that in 1922 'the Irish Free State could not have declared itself a Catholic State because the conditions through which it became a State at all precluded it from having any other kind of Constitution'.[13] This secular spirit did not last very long, according to O'Brien:

> The Catholic hierarchy had supported the Treaty, and had excommunicated those who opposed it in arms. The Government, therefore, appeared to be 'better Catholics' than their opponents and they encouraged this image of themselves. They introduced and carried a motion preventing divorce, in 1926. It is not clear whether they were

asked to do this by the hierarchy, either officially or informally, or whether they sensed it was expected of them or acted in accordance with their own consciences (trained, by Catholic instructors, to abhor divorce), or whether they judged it politically expedient, as strengthening their de facto alliance with the clergy and reinforcing the respectability of their image. Probably a combination of several of these elements was at work.[14]

Here we have a departure from Whyte. Whyte specifically states that there is no evidence to support the view that the legislation prohibiting divorce was introduced at the hierarchy's instigation. In contrast we can see O'Brien's speculation not so much as an attempt to ignore this, but to assert that his concern is that there must have been some interaction of minds. It is this implicit understanding, some form of social telepathy, which is the nub of Ireland's complicated history of church and state.

O'Brien's inspection of the position of Protestants of the Free State in the face of divorce legislation is perplexing. He describes how the Protestants equivocated when it came to 'the power of the priests'. Distaste for superstitious priests was mitigated by their own fondness for the role of priests when it came to thwarting extreme nationalists. Furthermore, in subsequent years, 'Protestants were middle class, and most middle-class people supported the Free State government against the republicans, and were glad to have the Catholic clergy as their powerful allies.'[15] All this is quite incisive, if a little esoteric, in explaining how O'Brien arrives at the definition of 'the Catholic State'. Speaking of the evolution of Protestant attitudes to the legislation of 1925, O'Brien says:

> in the Ireland of the 1920s, divorce was a very nasty issue, socially speaking, to have to take a stand on. In the Parnell divorce crisis over thirty years earlier, Catholic Parnellites had been only too apt to say that, whereas adultery and divorce were forbidden to Catholics, Protestants were 'different' (i.e. could not be expected to know or behave any better). Protestants naturally resented this and it became accepted doctrine among anti-Parnellites, whether Catholic or Protestant, that 'decent Protestants' were just as opposed to divorce as Catholics were.[16]

It has to be said that this sketch is at best unhistorical, and could fairly be described as a blatant piece of dissimulation. Ireland was not up in arms at the prospect of the O'Sheas divorcing, but Parnell and adultery. In *Parnell and his Party* O'Brien on several occasions points to: 'Catholic Ireland, which was interested in the truth or falsity of the adultery charge.'[17] It also stretches credibility that the considerable time-lag of nearly a year, between divorce being filed and the returned verdict, was insufficient time for the phantom opposition 'to divorce' to grasp the substantive fact that the O'Sheas would ultimately be divorced. But of course this is not what was at issue, nor is it what any person would infer from the situation, least of all a respected historian of Parnell.

A similar transformation can be observed in his critique concerning the Cumann na nGaedheal Government. 'Subsequent Free State sectarian legislation – against contraception, and setting up a Censorship of Publications, to exclude "immoral and obscene" literature – presented Protestants with the same kind of problem as the divorce legislation.'[18] However, O'Brien had seen the 'problem' of how to deal with this literature in a very different light five years previously:

> The reality of censorship – in schools and colleges and municipal libraries and in the life of the countryside and in small towns generally – had existed long before Independence. The state censorship, when established in 1928, was notoriously incompetent and eccentric.[19]

This corresponds with a general shift discernible in *States of Ireland*, in contrast to previous works, of ignoring the continuities between pre- and post-Independent Ireland. Sadly the historian in O'Brien gave way to the needs of the polemicist.

The problem of legislating for Catholic thought (summed up in de Valera's statement 'we are a Catholic nation') and what O'Brien calls de Valera's 'sectarian legislation',[20] is resolved in an unusual and original manner. The problem of the religious and the political is to be found if we consider 'the peculiar nature of Irish nationalism, as it is actually felt, not as it is rhetorically expressed. The nation is felt to be the Gaelic nation, Catholic by religion.'[21] This has to be viewed in light of how it appears to Ulster Protestants – his 'siege' perspective – and how the siege colours his historical perspective. Bearing in mind 'the siege' then, his particular reading of a 'Catholic State' is very persuasive. 'Northern Protestants tend to think of democracy in 'the Free State' as a farce. The real rulers are the Catholic hierarchy: since they can tell the voters what to think, they can tell the government what to do.'[22] The great exhibit in support of this view is the 'Mother and Child crisis' of 1951. This for O'Brien does not prove that 'the church are the real rulers of country'.[23] Quite the opposite: 'the party which expelled Browne was shattered at the next election, Browne himself increased his personal vote and was, when O'Brien wrote, still a force in politics. Fianna Fáil which maintained an austere silence throughout the crisis, were the prime beneficiaries, and ultimately enacted much of the substance of Dr Browne's scheme.'

Ultimately, the truth between the Northern Protestant view of Irish society and the reality demonstrated by the Mother and Child crisis is captured in the question of contraception. This is viewed as a borderline case, 'since the churchmen concerned are known to be genuinely convinced that contraception is a moral, not a political issue. At the same time, the State laws are products of a political assembly, and church pressure on this assembly to maintain them makes the enforcing itself political.'[24] The resolution of this particular question, not contraception itself, but the political enactment of moral conviction, amounts to nothing short of a political test of faith. O'Brien's inclinations in this matter are quite clear. What is of great originality is the interpretative framework which he crafts from the interaction of his 'beliefs' and Ireland since Independence. He attempts to define the problem in the following terms: 'the influence of the Church on the State should be measured – if in fact it were measurable – not by the frequency or intensity of confrontations, but by the assiduity with which politicians avoid such confrontations'.[25]

Further to this he cites the answer of the then Minister for Justice, Micheál O' Móráin, who in response to questions about adoption law, informed the Dáil: 'There's a stone wall there'.[26] O'Brien's appraisal of this 'stone wall' bears consideration. His first difficulty is not just with the cryptic nature of the remark, but with the fact that it was immediately understood and passed without demur. It is unacceptable to his mind that the state abdicates its responsibility by allowing the church to insist upon where it feels the stone wall runs. The state has never disputed the right of the church to draw this line. The whole problem for O'Brien is that it is the bishops who decide whether religious or moral issues are involved, and they have a very wide view of when a political matter is also a moral or religious one. Upon these terms then the state is 'a Catholic State'.

The 'Epilogue' to *States of Ireland* poses equally intriguing questions. It attempts to outline his concerns regarding the increasingly ominous developments in Northern Ireland. It opens with the very straightforward question about the Troubles: 'Is it a religious quarrel? I believe the answer is "yes", but with significant qualifications.'[27] Those significant qualifications exist in two spheres. Firstly, according to O'Brien, there are the less important issues or interpretations which affect the character of the 'quarrel', without taking away from the essentially religious nature of the 'quarrel'. The second sphere is given over to the precise manner in which it is a religious quarrel. In answering this he delineates his worldview as well as defining his concept of religion's role in Irish society.

It would be better, according to O'Brien, to acknowledge the existence of a conflict between groups defined by religion.

> This does not mean it is a theological war. It would not even be exact to say that it is a conflict between IRISH Catholics and ULSTER Protestants. More immediately, of course, it is a conflict between Ulster Catholics and Ulster Protestants and, as we have seen, southern Irish Catholics are not involved in it in the same way.[28]

And it is here in the 'Epilogue', where the wealth of the book is distilled, that the theory of religion is combined with his concept of a siege. By viewing the quarrel as an essentially religious one, O'Brien endorses the interpretation of a menacing Irish Catholic monolith, whose theological antipathy besieges its neighbour. 'Above all, the Ulster Protestant's response is proportioned to his concept of a siege conducted by a majority in the island.'[29]

This bald assertion is tempered by several distinctions which his 'Catholic State' critique is filtered through.

> Firstly, the actual religions – the systems of belief and of feelings about those beliefs – are distinct in reality from those practised elsewhere. Secondly, these actual religions are an amalgam of the strictly ecclesiastical body of doctrines and practices, and of other doctrines and practices derived from the history of Irish Catholics and Ulster Protestants. A cult of the ancestors enters into both, and is acted out in the annual commemorative rites at Bodenstown, Finaghy and elsewhere. Thirdly, in theory the religious and political heritages are separate, though they are however in practice not so easily compartmentalised.[30]

O'Brien's critique comes into its own in the following paragraphs. He begins by taking to task the observations of Mary Holland, who is inclined to give religion a prominent role also: 'the tightly knit loyalties built around chapels and schools, the fact that the whole identity of the community, its tribal senses, centre on being Catholic'.[31] O'Brien whole-heartedly agrees with this focus. It is 'the reason why the division between the two communities can never be defined in purely political terms, and why it is ridiculous to dismiss religion as "irrelevant"'.[32] However, O'Brien disagrees strongly with Holland when she infers from the events that a clash between the Official IRA and the church is imminent – and that this will by necessity be a good thing. According to O'Brien, the clash between those bodies, which he groups together as the Fenians and the church, is not about to happen. It has been happening for at least a hundred years. The differences and interactions are neatly encapsulated in the following:

> The Fenians and the Church never really meet head on. This is because they are involved in different sections of the 'Irish Catholic religion', as broadly defined above. The Church are concerned with the Catholic end of Irish Catholicism: the Fenians, belonging to the Irish end, are felt to fall outside the Church's sphere of jurisdiction, in respect of their Irish patriotic activities. So when a Bishop condemns the IRA, and an IRA man replies 'Mind your own business', Irish Catholics generally listen to this traditional exchange with monumental placidity.[33]

Holland gets another rebuke for what he sees as her simplistic analysis of how the Official IRA will replace the clerical influence; a replacement which will involve some kind of liberation with its vaguely internationalist and progressive rhetoric. O'Brien clearly insists that in removing one plague he is not inclined to invite another, whose use of the power they have, and the fact that it 'grows out of the barrel of a gun', is surely more weighty than vague aspirations adumbrated in politic phrases.

In support of his charge of an 'Irish Catholic religion' with two sections, Fenian and clerical, he moves to consider the amount of historical collusion between the two. What he had in mind was not the individual priests (who he sees more as representative of the community), nor the ecclesiastical representatives from Cardinal Conway down (who have been unequivocal in their condemnations), but more the 'role of the Churches in encouraging, exalting and extending the kind of tribal-sectarian self-righteousness which forms a culture in which violence so easily multiplies'.[34] Examples of this can be seen in the pope-baiting divines on the Protestant side, but for O'Brien it is more subtly encased in the hierarchy's 'need' to have separate schooling. This insistence is but a part of the whole system whereby, over time, 'the Irish Catholic clergy systematically fostered, not a militant, overt anti-Protestantism, but a well-enforced avoidance of social contact with Protestants, a sort of creeping freeze-out'.[35]

Finally, he turns his attention to the essentially religious quality of Irish society; a view shared by him and also Cardinal Manning who stated that 'Irish society, both Catholic and Protestant, is not a secular society; it is a deeply religious one'.[36] O'Brien points out that in asserting what 'the basic values' of Irish society are, Manning reflects an interpretation which is inimical to conciliation, on the basis that these values reflect an adherence to 'the Catholic point of view'. In the instance of divorce, it is the Cardinal who interprets its continued prohibition as 'a religious aspect', even though it is objectionable to many Protestant and some Catholic spokesmen.

> Protestants (or Catholics) who find that the possibility of legal divorce in certain circumstances is quite compatible with their concept of the 'moral law' do not count as being 'deeply religious'. In the last resort it is the Cardinal who decides not merely what the proper outlook is for Catholics, but also which Protestants are religious and which are not.[37]

He acknowledges that this has an Ulster Protestant corollary and it is these twin intolerances which feed on one another.

These assertions by O'Brien can be seen either as very broad generalizations or as a pithy summary of the role of religion in Irish politics. That it was more the latter is hinted at again by Mary Holland who, some three years after *States of Ireland* was published, reflected on O'Brien's contribution to the debate on religion and Irish society and credited him with having initiated the call to secularization. 'The present debate was sparked off by Conor Cruise O'Brien (who else?) ... who made an eloquent plea for rational public discussion on such issues as contraception and divorce.' There was still an aspect of 'sectarianism which was less violent than that which afflicted the North, but intended to be conducted not in a roar but in a sort of pervasive whisper, interspersed with pregnant silences and occasionally worded admonitions'. The value of O'Brien's probing was to force the church out of its comfortable silence. As Holland put it, 'there was nothing whispered about the Church's response to this ... the advocating of a secular state in Ireland was something the Church would fight to the end'. In the words of one leading bishop, Jeremiah Newman, the church simply had to 'give leadership to the people to stand up against a secular state and those who represent it'. The problem was that while most Irish people had now moved on from agreeing unquestioningly with Newman's procrustean approach, they couldn't quite chime in with the good Dr O'Brien either.

> In many ways Dr O'Brien sounds more like an English humanist, accusing them of being superstitious, narrow, in thrall to their priests, than one of themselves. Many Irish Catholics agree that the Church's dominance of Irish life, particularly in the sphere of personal relationships, should be challenged, but given the choice of lining up with Conor Cruise O'Brien or their own parish priest, a lot of them feel more comfortable with their parish priest.[38]

If they were not quite yet willing to give up 'the Catholic state' and join O'Brien in his secular idyll, he could acknowledge with some satisfaction at his own role that they had come some way in a short time.

> It would be foolish to ignore the extent to which life in the Republic reflects the Catholicism of its population. There is however a clear division between church and state, and changes within both society and the church have reduced and are reducing the extent to which the Republic is a conformist society. Certainly a visitor often feels a more relaxed atmosphere in Dublin than in the dual but separate conformisms of Northern Ireland society.[39]

In the final analysis he had diagnosed the problem that had bedevilled an independent Ireland. And even by the admission of one of his sternest critics, he had managed to nudge it that bit closer to a less paternalist, authoritarian relationship between the church and its people.

It is ironic, then, that the person who gave him the most credit for his role in diluting the confessional nature of Irish society should find herself dismissed under O'Brien's watch as Editor-in-Chief of *The Observer*. It probably speaks to his own weighting of nationalism as being the more dangerous of the twin foes of mother church and mother Ireland. Holland, in O'Brien's unfair view, showed too much of the latter and was fired. It is perhaps testament to how traumatic the loss of his Dáil seat was upon his psyche. It also indicates that the reasonableness of his earlier positions had by the early 1980s become a thing of the past. He had by then given over to foaming at the mouth not just about Haughey and a nationalist junta, but had descended to his characterization of the Irish population as a silent forbidding Talebanesque monolith. In many ways the Irish had regressed to a position more akin to the Penal Law era than the post-Catholic state one he was credited with having helped to bring about. Something which could possibly explain this is O'Brien's view of Irish history which changed significantly in the 1970s. I referred earlier to 'a bleak Manichean impatience' in order to describe O'Brien's latter day 'vision'. It can be seen in the way he began to engage in his 'craft' – how he thought and wrote about history. Increasingly his writings betrayed a fondness for polar opposites and a brusque (some would say careless) treatment of facts and figures, actors and ideas. How he came to the technique and approach behind all the works of his final thirty years is the subject of the following chapter.

NOTES

1. Conor Cruise O'Brien, *Writers and Politics* (London, 1965), p.xvi.
2. O'Brien Papers, UCD, P/82/162.
3. Ibid.
4. Conor Cruise O'Brien, 'Religion and Politics'. The New University of Ulster 10th Annual Convocation Lecture, 1983, p.10.
5. Holmes was the Chairman of the Northern Ireland Labour Party. When O'Brien demanded a withdrawal of British troops in the wake of Bloody Sunday Holmes berated him for giving in to 'the politics of the last atrocity'. As quoted in Conor Cruise O'Brien, *States of Ireland* (London, 1972), p.283.
6. O'Brien, *States of Ireland*, p.123.
7. Ibid., p.110.
8. Ibid. He is referring to Paul Blanshard, *The Irish and Catholic Power: An American Interpretation* (London, 1954).
9. O'Brien, *States of Ireland*, p.110.
10. J.H. Whyte, *Church and Society in Modern Ireland, 1923–1970* (Dublin, 1971).
11. O'Brien, *States of Ireland*, p.110.
12. Ibid., p.111.
13. Ibid., p.112.
14. Ibid.

15. Ibid., p.114.
16. Ibid., p.115.
17. Conor Cruise O'Brien, *Parnell and his Party, 1880–90* (Oxford, 1957), p.280.
18. O'Brien, *States of Ireland*, p.116.
19. Conor Cruise O'Brien, 'Two-Faced Cathleen', *New York Review of Books*, 29 June 1967, pp.19–21.
20. O'Brien, *States of Ireland*, p.124.
21. Ibid.
22. Ibid.
23. Ibid. In this example he chooses to adhere quite closely to Whyte's interpretation of the debate.
24. Ibid., p.125.
25. Ibid.
26. Ibid.
27. Ibid., p.305.
28. Ibid., p.308.
29. Ibid.
30. Ibid.
31. Mary Holland, 'The Church and the IRA', *The New Statesman*, 2 June 1972.
32. O'Brien, *States of Ireland*, p.310.
33. Ibid., p.311.
34. Ibid., p.312.
35. Ibid.
36. Ibid.
37. Ibid., p.313.
38. Mary Holland, 'Conor Cruise O'Brien and the Church', *The New Statesman*, 30 April 1976.
39. Conor Cruise O'Brien, Address to Historical Society, Portora Royal School, Enniskillen, 8 December 1975. O'Brien Papers, UCD, P82/314.

10

Histories

Yes I'm an historian, partly by training, but more and more by in-clination. I find that almost everything I read now is history in some form or other. The historian interprets, but there are great brute facts which he can't interpret away.[1]

The only requirement of the scientific spirit to which I have tried to conform is that of respect for the facts.[2]

To make sense of O'Brien a critical approach is necessary. All critiques of the O'Brien position bring with them a certain amount of baggage, which they then apply to familiar areas which make up the O'Brien edifice: his upbringing, the Congo, the North etc. This is inescapable, even when one recognizes it to begin with. The only solace I can offer is that my angle of approach is predicated on the assumption common to O'Brien and all his critics: historical know-ledge. To the reader who would question this exaltation of history I would assert that one can only understand O'Brien on the ground he himself has chosen to operate on. Furthermore, it is my understanding that both the mind of O'Brien and Irish society are deeply historical. And in order to understand this nexus, 'history writ large', we must first work through some of the nitty-gritty of his historical texts and how he has composed them.

In order to write a cogent study of O'Brien, we must deal not just with the writings, but with the historical frames that he imposes upon these writings. If we examine the O'Brien of the 1950s and the O'Brien of the 1990s we come up with certain parallels. If, however, we examine the political stances behind this simple sketch we can see utter opposition. On the one hand we have a person who wrote anti-partition treatises. On the other hand, the O'Brien of the 1990s writes about the pernicious interaction of religion and nationalism in Ireland. Furthermore, in these later essays and articles he outlines his pro-Union views as well as his anti-nationalist ones, to say nothing of his views on Irish partition, which are utterly opposed to his 1950s incarnation.

To examine this further, we need to look at what has been described as 'the lost book of O'Brien': the term used by his official biographer Donald Akenson to describe the book which O'Brien wrote for the Anti-Partition campaign in the late 1940s/early 1950s. It seems that an influential US Congressman, Ed Flynn, was disposed to lend his name to whatever treatise the Department of External Affairs deemed fit for the campaign. By the time it was written – 1950 – Flynn had lost interest in adding his name to the Irish cause. O'Brien was initially incensed and tried quite vigorously to get it published independently. 'The Story of Ireland', as O'Brien called it, makes for perplexing, if entertaining, reading when one contrasts it with O'Brien's subsequent positions.[3]

In its three chapters, there is a sustained attempt to lay the blame for partition at the door of England.

> The history of the partition of Ireland is, in brief, the story of the many and varied efforts of the British Government to 'settle the Irish question': or in plainer language, to keep Ireland under British rule with the minimum of trouble. So long had Ireland proved herself unwilling to become part and parcel of England; so long had she struggled against the might of an empire to regain the freedom and independence which had been hers in her most glorious days and so roused had world opinion, especially in America, become that, at last, a grudging admission was forced on England's Government that some effort must be made to find a solution to the problem. And so began the series of negotiations, of party manoeuvrings for political expediency by which the problem was finally brought to a head. It seems not only unworthy but stupid of a nation of England's calibre that she could for internal political reasons, create in another country an artificial secession which was destined to become one of the greatest blots on her own record. And, in effect, that is what did occur.[4]

Writing in 1944 about the Home Rule Crisis he felt that:

> When it became apparent that the Ulster Protestants would not willingly enter a Home Rule Ireland, Irish nationalists insisted that it was the constitutional duty of the British Government to oblige the Protestants to accept Home Rule. The word coerce was not used (see above,

'dissimulation') but that was most certainly the idea ('persuade' is the euphemism in use in 1994). The British declined, for adequate reasons: British public opinion would never have approved the use of force to induce people who wanted to remain in the United Kingdom, to leave its jurisdiction. Once the British rejected the use of force, partition was inevitable ... This is what would have happened if the British disengaged, and if the British were to disengage now [in 1994], that is also what would happen.[5]

If these excerpts are not a total contrast, they very nearly are. And if they are not, it is because of a difference in focus.

To take another example, if we view what the two O'Brien's have to say about the national mood regarding sentiment towards the Irish Parliamentary Party and those involved in the 1916 Rising, the clear opposition becomes apparent. Writing in 1994, again in *Ancestral Voices*, he muses:

But that Irish nationalists should support the British war effort in 1914 has to seem extraordinary, in the retrospect of modern Irish nationalism, powerfully conditioned as that retrospect is, both by the events of 1916 and the subsequent cult of Pearsean nationalism. But the political nationalism of most Irish people, in 1914, was not remotely Pearsean.[6]

Compare the above with his estimation in 1950:

It must not be imagined that these constitutional and parliamentary efforts to gain Ireland's freedom were the only signs of the desire of the Irish people to achieve that end. The inauguration in November 1913 of the Irish volunteers marked the culmination of many trends towards a more vigorous nationalism. By this time the younger generation of Irishmen, inspired by the vision of a regenerated Gaelic Ireland, found the ideal of limited 'Home Rule' to be a fading one. Armed force had been made an issue – the dominant issue – in Ireland's struggle and a determination arose to grasp for the rights either totally denied or grudgingly admitted by England. The rapid growth of the Volunteer force was sufficient indication of the dissatisfaction with which Ireland's young men and women regarded the bandying about of the question of Irish freedom by Britain's political parties.[7]

To these examples of two opposing O'Briens many more interesting contrasts can be added.

The acknowledged propaganda of the early 1950s finds its exact opposite in the 'historical' work, *Ancestral Voices*. What then prevents us from calling this propaganda also? Did not O'Brien join the United Kingdom Unionist Party the year after its publication? Could his writings not be said to provide this party with the perfect reasoning for their pro-Union policy? Is not *Ancestral Voices's* treatment of evidence, its exclusive focus, and its highly dubious use of induction an example of the very methods which O'Brien employed when he wrote the nationalist propagandist tract 'The Story of Ireland'? While there is validity to this contrast and the questions they raise, to merely juxtapose the variant texts of O'Brien is to take the pedant's path. It does not lead to a greater understanding of O'Brien, and we must therefore look a little deeper. What we need to do is to evaluate certain themes. In this thematic analysis we need to critically evaluate one of the most important criteria for historical writing: the use of evidence.

The relevance of evidence can be seen if we examine a frequent preoccupation of O'Brien's critics: 'the O'Brien conversion'. This 'debate' basically entails ascertaining why, and when, O'Brien chose to begin his critique of Irish society. The basic inference is that in doing so, he dumped his nationality, his liberal convictions and all common sense and decency. The critics differ as to the location of his apostasy. For some it stems from his time in Katanga. For others it was his brutal mugging at an Apprentice Boys march in 1970; or his entering into government, or his Broadcasting Amendment Act. There is some truth in all of these. But to assume a conversion, you must not only know what the conversion is to, but also what O'Brien converted from? This is where history becomes so important, for it presents us with a benchmark which allows us to show in his own words what 'great brute facts' O'Brien tried, if at all, to 'interpret away'.

O'Brien's ability to 'interpret away' is clearly apparent if we look at his recurring fascination with Yeats. Throughout his many books he has used snippets of Yeats to explain and to reduce a complex history to a few pithy lines. A classic example is the number of different interpretations by O'Brien of a famous observation Yeats made upon his play *Cathleen ni Houlihan*. What is interesting is that O'Brien's treatment of Yeats's observation changes according to the deterioration of the situation in the North. In 1967 O'Brien reviewed a study of the literature and politics of early twentieth-century Ireland and wrote about the complex way that human imagination interacts with human action.[8] This for O'Brien is encapsulated in Yeats's famous question:

> Did that play of mine send out
> Certain men the English shot?

To which O'Brien replies: 'There can be no sure answer to the question that troubled Yeats on his deathbed'. He adds, '*Cathleen ni Houlihan* did powerfully affect "certain men" who took part in the Rising of 1916. One of them has recorded that for him and his friends the play was "almost a sacrament". Yet it could not have had this effect, if it had not touched a stock response.'[9]

In 1975, reflecting again on the interaction of the political and the literary, he instances Yeats's play once more. On this occasion he quotes Constance Markievicz for whom the play 'was a sort of gospel to me'. Following on from her, O'Brien reasons:

> Another revolutionary who saw it, P.S. O'Hegarty, called it 'a sort of sacrament', and a spectator who disapproved came away asking if such plays should be produced, unless one was prepared to go out to shoot and be shot. To the question of the dying poet, 'Did that play of mine send out certain men the English shot?', it seems that the probable answer is 'Yes, it did'.[10]

Gone is the mitigation that was present in 1967. What he once viewed as an improbable scenario – men shot each other because of what Yeats wrote – is asserted contrary to what he once felt and on the basis of nothing other than authority.

Some fifteen years later, in 1989, O'Brien once more poses Yeats's 'question':

> More than 20 years after that, the dying Yeats asked himself the question:
> Did that play of mine send out
> Certain men the English shot?
>
> I believe, not only that it clearly did, but that it is still sending them out.[11]

In total there are three different interpretations upon the one great Yeatsian question. In 1967 Yeats's play could not have incited men to rebel. By 1975 it did. However by 1989 it not only sent men to take up arms in 1916 and to be shot for it, but over seventy years later it *continues* to send men to their death.

In the short space of time between 1967 and 1975, O'Brien underwent a reversal in opinion, and this change substantially altered the manner in which he both viewed events and interpreted evidence. Why the change? Was the brute fact of the Troubles sufficiently brutish to go back across decades and send men out in 1916 to be shot by 'the English'? And if we accept that 'the Troubles' of the 1970s cannot be accepted as 'a brute fact' in the events of 1916, is it not fair to assert that at some stage O'Brien threw off the accepted criteria for evaluating the 'stuff' of history.

The wider implications of O'Brien re-interpreting not just Yeats's play but the chronology, personalities and events that make up Irish history are quite serious. The basic point would be that the rules of history allow change: a 'conversion' like O'Brien's is 'allowed' in history, but only if it meets certain criteria. The 'apostate' would need some new historical evidence upon which to base his 'new testament'. In addition, the works previous to the 'apostasy' would be invalidated as a result (in the eyes of both the writer and audience). To put it another way, history does not admit the possibility of two antagonistic interpretations. Two interpretations are indeed possible – history is a crazily exaggerated version of this normally – but they cannot logically occupy the same mind. Thus if the O'Brien of 1969 writes of several causes of violence, he cannot in 1972 ascribe the same violence to a single factor without some new evidence.

If we look at O'Brien's interpretation in 1969, social structures, Protestant supremacy, the Civil Rights Movement, the United Kingdom's lack of will and interest, and Dublin's lazy irredentism are adduced as the causes of violence in Northern Ireland. Within a few short years all these reasons drop from sight with the exception of the Civil Rights Movement and the Republic. The Civil Rights Movement became, for O'Brien, the agitational arm of the IRA. The Republic of Ireland's history and present-day interference legitimized the 'Provisional's war'.[12] In order for such an interpretation to be plausible, the evidence would in this case have to diminish the role of one factor and increase the role of another. Furthermore, to operate without this evidence and support this new thesis is to be unhistorical, or to propagate an historical untruth. To many these categories might seem harsh and unwilling to admit of the role of interpretation of evidence. A valid argument can be made that not everybody would accept just one way of writing history or of making historical judgements. O'Brien is one such individual and it is worth observing the special character of his earlier historical accounts to try to get to grips with this.

In his 1948 essay, 'The parnellism of Seán O'Faoláin', O'Brien puts forward his view of Ireland in that decade. It 'is the least romantic and the least revolutionary of countries. It is one in which the Church and State exist in harmony, as inexpugnable bastions of the family.'[13] That picture has not changed much by the time of his return from New York, some twenty years later. 'What really happened was that the exalting sense of Ireland's exceptional destiny which had existed before 1922 simply faded into the sheer ordinariness of a paternal, pettifogging, fairly decent little Republic.'[14] This is reinforced in another essay 'The Embers of Easter 1916–1966', which reaches essentially the same conclusion as his essay of 1948. Of these two analyses, we could say that the particulars of his portrait of the post-revolutionary period remained constant; the historical analysis as far as he is concerned holds good. His assessment of crucial areas, the 'great brute facts', had not aged. He was clinging to his interpretation and in this he is not uncommon. We could say he was merely being properly historical. It does not seem unjust then, that we should attempt to come to grips with O'Brien's original view of Ireland before we comment upon his later reputedly distorted writings. Basically it is the aim of this chapter to be able to construct a valid interpretation of what O'Brien is saying.

A good place to start is the essay 'Timothy Michael Healy', which underlines this point. The essay is an unsympathetic appraisal, some would say it's a bit of a hatchet job (perhaps not difficult with Healy), in that it exults in the psychological portrayal of an embittered and volatile mind. The penultimate paragraph which describes the family man, 'who pleases without effort',[15] conveys more of a sense of schizophrenia than balance. What is most striking about this essay is the debatable thesis that not only did Healy bring down Parnell, but he single-handedly created the 1916 Rising: 'It was he more than anyone who brought the Irish Parliamentary Party into discredit, and so cleared the way for Sinn Féin.'[16] He managed this because to 'hear Healy speak, to read what he wrote, must have had the effect on many of disgusting them with cleverness and oratory, of turning them towards self-discipline and the idea of violence that was cleaner for not being wholly verbal'.[17] But the Healy essay also embodies a political affiliation and a harking back to a particular time, which betrays an attachment that explains a great deal about O'Brien. O'Brien's clear-cut political affiliation comes in the final paragraph when O'Brien contrasts the two ways of viewing Healy:

> If one adopts the historical retrospect of Sinn Féin, one can regard Healy as a sort of salutary plague, speeding the rot of parliamentarianism: clearing the ground for a new and better Ireland. If on the other hand one feels, as I do, that the destruction of the movement which Parnell had created maimed Ireland in some important ways, then one is likely to echo the phrase with which Tom Kettle, years ago, saluted Healy: 'A brilliant disaster'.[18]

When O'Brien wrote this in 1955 he was a counsellor in External Affairs, and generally, though not in this case, felt it necessary to write under a pseudonym. By the standards of the day it would have been viewed as quite an unguarded expression to label the events of Irish independence as somehow disastrous or to extol the virtues of Home Rule before Ireland was 'maimed' by Sinn Féin. It is interesting to explore further the 'disaster' conjured up by the 'brilliant' Healy. We might also ask what are the implications for O'Brien's work should he continue to pursue his family-based political prejudices further into other more considered pieces. It is interesting to explore whether these 'dispossession' traits are also evident in his doctorate and other writings on Parnell.

If we look at *Parnell and his Party*, *The Shaping of Modern Ireland* and a review of F.S.L. Lyons's *The Fall of Parnell* it can be argued that these form an interpretative whole, spanning the years 1952 to 1961. In the 'Foreword' to *The Shaping of Modern Ireland*, O'Brien deals with the period 1891 to 1916, which for him seemed to be 'an interval between a verdict and a sentence. The return of nationalist MPs in every constituency bar the North East of the island (and TCD) implied one simple message. Thenceforward the 'basic political facts of Irish life – long doubted or denied – were incontrovertibly clear'.[19] The people of the era can be seen to have 'lived out their lives under a shadow of some kind of political reckoning'. This is explained in terms of the conflicting necessities, 'which were to turn Ireland into two armed camps'. The 1916 Rising is a convergence of these necessities, and given the factors one could discern the 'inherent probability of such an outcome'.[20]

As editor, O'Brien contributed two essays to the collection. The essay, '1891–1916', goes a great distance in grappling with the complexities of the period. He characterizes the interlude between Parnell's death and 1916 as 'a sort of crease in time, a featureless valley between the commanding chain of the Rising and the solitary enigmatic peak of Parnell'.[21] He compares the frozen social scenes of Joyce's *Ulysses*, which looked through Ireland and saw nothing beyond, to the middle-class, whose main focus of interest on Easter Monday 1916 was of course Fairyhouse racecourse rather than the GPO. Despite this, O'Brien argues that many important things were going on: 'a revolution in land ownership, the beginning of a national quest for a lost language and culture, and the preparation of the two successful rebellions which were among other things to tear Ireland in two'.[22] The peculiar quality of the zeitgeist is illustrated:

> As soon as we turn in this direction, we see of course that there was an unusual amount of mental activity, an unusual degree of intensity and self-dedication, not in the people as a whole, but in quite sizeable groups of people. This excitement and dedicated loyalty had perhaps something to do with the romantic loyalty which the figure of Parnell, and especially his fall, had evoked in many.[23]

He instances Yeats, Griffith and the revolutionary movement. 'This generation bore the mark of rebellion and rejection or that of the cult of the hero and of heroism', and 'while this should not be exaggerated we should be aware of its presence and its ability to take unexpected forms'. He cites the GAA which replaced what had been a 'servile spirit' with the spirit of 'manliness and freedom'; the Gaelic League which succeeded more than any other movement in crossing 'invisible religious and social barriers'; the industrial unrest which gave 'the middle-class a different, and we are likely to think, better relation, between capital and labour'; the propaganda of Irish Ireland which first made nationalist Ireland think of itself under this term, and which had for its target the Irish upper-classes, who in turn, partly initiating, partly reciprocating, replied with 'a tone of sovereign contempt'.[24] In the spirit and utterances of these movements O'Brien traces a certain obtuse identification with the wrong enemies. There is a corresponding lack of thought about the hostages to fortune they were surrendering for a future reckoning. At this stage he makes the valuable point that while it is well to talk of intention and conscious effort, we must remember that one of the most remarkable features was that 'Modern Ireland did not take the shape that any of its shapers wanted'.[25]

Throughout he has managed to strike an intoxicating balance between the discordant aspirations, motives and methods. This is the 'way in which history exists as opposed to the way in which we try to tidy it up afterwards'. Vitally, he asserts that the distinctions under different appellations were 'usually found together, in different forms of association, in the same people'. It is just this blend of conviction and restraint, affirmation and doubt, which indicate that in addition to a fine grasp of the various equations, he had the ability to convey them:

> One could believe simultaneously that Ireland had particular virtues springing from its rural way of life and also that it ought to be industrialised. Or one could in Ulster pride oneself on one's loyalty to Britain and to the King and also on one's readiness to revolt against His Majesty's Government. The confusion of the time was rich and explosive. And it was the man of action rather than the man of moderation who flourished in it. The caution of an Archbishop Walsh, the constructiveness of a Horace Plunkett, the moderation and inclusive view of a John Redmond, came to seem irrelevant or even tarnished values. Through the mouths of Carson and of Pearse all Ireland heard ancestral voices prophesying war. Different ancestors and a different war.[26]

However, as beautifully crafted and stimulating as these essays are, they nonetheless contain a plot that betrays a firm objective. The piece entitled '1891–1916', could just as well have taken for itself the sub-title: 'Why Ireland did not achieve unity'. Beneath the contrasts and confusions, there is a simple thread which connects most of the movements. The GAA carried into cultural fields the political method by which the Land League achieved victory in the agrarian struggle: the principle of the boycott. He sees the Gaelic League as containing 'a generosity of spirit which is the one essential element in any real movement towards Irish unity'.[27] In the case of Irish Ireland and D.P. Moran: 'a price has to be paid for all polemics and Irish Ireland never accurately reckoned the cost of its attitudes. We cannot afford, said Parnell, to give up a single Irishman. Moran and his friends, including many Sinn Féiners and even an increasing number of Gaelic Leaguers, acted as if they could afford to lose a million.'[28] As O'Brien points out, these polemics were mainly cast against their perceptions of West Britons who fairly drove them to it. Even if this were the case, he reminds us that there were a million West Britons who did not conform to the stereotype, and who they alienated nonetheless.

The second trace of emplotment is that the essay explains the actors in terms of 'a political reckoning'. Thus there is a violence of language and predictability in the selection of the incidents which tends to reflect this. The die of the 'verdict' is cast in very particular terms:

> the effects of the sordid, scurrilous struggle on the spectators were also destructive of the hopes of moderate men. Among the young in Ireland the spectacle engendered contempt for constitutional politicians; among the English it fostered contempt for the Irish. The contempts converged in the ruin of the Irish party and the rise of Sinn Féin.

Conversely, the Rising is foreshadowed by the 'necessities and conflicts which were to turn Ireland into two armed camps'. Ultimately the voices which call Carson and Pearse are ones which prophesy war, albeit different ones. Significantly there was only one way that the unity issue could have been resolved. This is located in the genius of Gladstone and Parnell.[29] When that avenue no longer remained, the die of violence was cast.

The final point to make is that the whole essay can also be seen as an attempt to rationalize the jettisoning of the Irish Parliamentary Party. Struck by romanticism and the cult of the hero, the country plotted in Parnell's ruins the seeds of violence, which would eventually, with proleptic irony, ruin the party he moulded. This particular interpretation has, as we have seen, a personal resonance for him, as it is the point at which the Irish Parliamentary Party falls and with it the 'house of Sheehy' also. Trying to understand this could be taken as the motif of his historical work. And it is at this point that we can state that from his earliest writings there has been a real connection between Irish nationalist politics and the histories he has written. Nothing sums this up better than his view that 'people are apt to look back to the period before the Rising, not in any way nostalgically but with thoughts of salvage'.[30]

One of the problems that obscures an appreciation of O'Brien's many historical approaches is his writing 'style'. He writes fluidly, coherently and persuasively. The result is a composition married to intent. This writer can only marvel at the almost paradoxical balance between restraint and luxury, which is the result of O'Brien's focused arguments. Any typical O'Brien essay will select a few arguments, and at an almost laconic pace, pursue, with logical and interesting references, a conclusion which has been ordained from the beginning. However, one of the more noticeable aspects of O'Brien's style through the years is its flexibility. It could be argued that there is no one style. This itself is a style in its own right. If pressed to name it, one could call it a style according to ends. There seem to be two determinants of this style: audience and purpose. These are concerns with most writers, but they are paramount in the case of O'Brien. We have the mannered recounting of *To Katanga and Back*, the exhortations and ramblings of *Sacred Drama*, the textbook critical method of *Camus*, and his Introduction to Burke's *Reflections on the Revolution in France*; the historical narrative of *Parnell and his Party* and *A Concise History of Ireland*, and finally the probing of mentalities mixed with biography of *States of Ireland*.

In all these writings O'Brien is acutely concerned with ideas. He is quite original in the sense that from an early age he focused on more democratic and realistic forms of thought. As opposed to the thought of politicians, philosophers, economists and diplomats, O'Brien probed the imagining of events, the shared misconceptions, the mindsets of opposing groups, and the 'telepathy' of similar groups. His gloss on Yeats's verdict on 'the event' of the fall of Parnell is quintessential O'Brien:

> The event was one thing, the way the event was imagined was another thing, and more powerful. And there were men and women who lived through the event, and through the imagining of the event. Their lives marked by this double experience, marked mine. And both the event and its imagining, and the consequences of the way in which it was imagined, helped powerfully to shape what happened in Ireland in the early twentieth century, and what is happening now.[31]

In this alone you have a great leader, a great poet, a pure event, and its dynamic aftershock. More importantly you have the only O'Brien paragraph 'you will ever need'. Without saying anything specific, you have the entirety of twentieth-century Ireland. Furthermore it is all based on personal reminiscence: his understanding as a child is re-presented here. The forces used are of the fantastic hyperbole scale. The event was powerful, but the imagining was even more powerful, and these two combined to create consequences, which 'helped powerfully to shape'. This apart you have those almost throwaway words at the end: 'and what is happening now'. Just as Yeats's play sent out and continues to send out 'certain men', just as Pearse's words incited a sacrifice, and still do, now Parnell's fall continues to exert its triply powerful influence on Ireland.

This brings us to some of his other traits when writing history. He can be seen to use counterfactuals: Lenin's feeling that the 1916 Rising was premature, or indeed his own musings as to how Ireland might have turned out had there been no 1916 Rising. Perhaps more fundamentally these counterfactuals underline a pronounced tendency to speculate. There are three aspects to this which are worth noting. First is the feigned circumspection. It is the apparent ramblings of the luxury and restraint mentioned earlier, which hide a definite purpose. This tends to take him to the dubious territory of speculating as to what others might have thought or said or done. This circumspection has its merits. However, in a writer like O'Brien who reasons general rules from particular instances, a writer who always operates by the method of induction, this can have repercussions. That he is given to masking a definite purpose with circumspection becomes more dangerous still when we take into account his use of evidence. A writer who has a demonstrable tendency to use evidence selectively, who can push this even further with a selection of 'what ifs' and 'we can imagine', allied to a seemingly unshakeable belief in the rightness of induction – where an individual can be said to represent all individuals of his values, whether they can be proven to be shared or not – has to be handled with the greatest of care.

We can better understand how he arrived at this unusual historical approach by examining the influence on him of the French historian, Jules Michelet. In 'Michelet Today', an extended article written in the mid 1950s, O'Brien juxtaposes the arguments of 'history-as-science' against what he feels to be the higher worth of 'history-as-art'.[32] By critiquing the defects and inconsistencies of present historians who cling to an interpretation which is primarily scientific, he manages to offer a defence not only of Michelet, but of the political nature of his own historical work.

O'Brien introduces us to Michelet by referring to the arguments of Michelet's detractors who decry his penchant for polemics. Some of these detractors would deny him the title '"historian" altogether, call *The French Revolution* an epic pamphlet, a work of art inspired by historical events, anything but history, for accuracy is the essence of history, and accuracy is said to require scientific detachment, not passionate involvement'. O'Brien refutes this by asserting that while these harsh judgements ('Absolutist thinker', 'illusionist' and 'self-deceiver') can be sustained, Michelet remains 'not merely a very great historian but, within certain limits, an exceptionally honest one'.[33]

For O'Brien, the root of Michelet's greatness was that he felt passionately about history. What distinguishes him is that he said clearly and openly what he felt. O'Brien contrasts this with the case of 'some Buster Keatons of historiography who can attain genuine and total impassivity: they record the facts and nothing more. Yet what facts, and why record them? How select the facts if you care nothing about them, one way or another?' O'Brien then sketches the scenario, an increasingly familiar one nowadays, of a fallacious separation which is accepted by historians. This is where the 'opinions hot and strong, go into newspaper articles, radio, television; the serious historical writing is tightly buttoned, ostentatiously unemotional'. For O'Brien, to accept this belies any grasp of human psychology. To reasonably expect historians to manage this, is to believe in 'fabulous creatures'. In truth, what 'history-as-science' historians rebuke in Michelet is his unguarded expression of prejudice and emotion, which O'Brien thinks we should be grateful for, as it puts us on our guard. In a line that O'Brien would adopt as his own, Michelet tells us precisely where he would have stood, beside whom he would have sat, and where he would have fallen on all the great issues of the day.[34] Yet to call Michelet 'an honest historian would be only a play on words unless he is also found honest in relation to the facts, unless he consistently relates events which do not suit his thesis'.[35] At this point O'Brien makes a distinction between Michelet as historian of the Revolution, and Michelet as historian of the general events outside the Revolution. In the former, he is 'remarkably honest, because he is anxious to be just to all parties, is acutely concerned and even torn by their disputes'.[36] In the case of the latter, he clearly fails, because for Michelet 'international relations is hardly more historical than a Punch-and-Judy show'.

For O'Brien, Michelet's critics have however insisted on this aspect too much. Surely he should be considered on the basis of the bulk of his work. In writing as he did, Michelet ignored the point of view of the enemies of the Revolution, because he was too busy trying to understand the revolutionaries' concerns and psychology. When viewed on this basis, he manages to be just and skilful to all parties. In addition, by not identifying with any one leader, Michelet achieves what no subsequent French historian managed. In the crucial area of displaying the explosive mutability of the political positions – where survival was made difficult, if not impossible, as a result of the changing political circumstances – Michelet comes into his own. In all this O'Brien taxes the scientific historians with themselves being prone to the very same emotionalism. O'Brien points to one sentence where a critic found Michelet's attitude to Robespierre and his cohorts 'positively repulsive ... sentimentality about the bloody maniacs'. Another example relates to those historians who *blame* Michelet for '"helping to form the intellectual background of French communism"'. This, as O'Brien neatly points out, is one of those unscientific lapses into 'judgements from the standpoint of today'.[37]

Ultimately, O'Brien contrasts the two types of history. 'History-as-science' is seen as a 'sedative, leading to the resignations of agnosticism'. 'History-as-art on the contrary is a stimulant, enriching and embittering contemporary conflicts.'[38] The explanation of Michelet's passionate involvement is to be located in the simple cultural difference between the French view (seeing their historians as themselves involved in the historic process), and the Anglo-Saxon or Nordic critic who sniffs at such emotionalism. The conundrum for O'Brien is that:

> in practice the man who believes himself to be prepared to modify his opinions in accordance with the evidence cannot help interpreting the evidence in accordance with his opinions. If he is scrupulous the dilemma will paralyse him. Acton's knowledge was not inferior to Michelet's but his production was vastly inferior ... the classical contrast between an honest Englishman, tongue-tied by his inhibitions, and a voluble, unscrupulous Frenchman.[39]

The French, he points out, have a tradition of *l'histoire engagé*, where history is 'part of the long blood-feud, which runs from the Great Revolution and 1848 through the commune to the collaborations and liberations of the last struggle'.[40]

This particular dualism seems to be a persistent train of thought with O'Brien. In *To Katanga and Back* he put forward a slightly different combination. On the one hand you have the proud legatees of 1688, with their attachment to liberty and freedom and the society which they think has crafted these virtues. On the other hand, you have the Irish, whose relation to these notions of liberty and freedom is quite different. They realize that many of these achievements were attained at their expense, or were enjoyed while they themselves were subjugated. The polarities are pithily expressed by O'Brien in the following: 'Of history and its consequences it may be said: "Those who can, gloat; those who can't, brood."'[41] O'Brien at the time was referring to the relationship between an Irishman and an Englishman.

If we return to 'Michelet Today' (which was written three years before *To Katanga and Back*), what is subliminally at odds with the Anglo-Saxon view, could easily be interpreted as not just the French tradition of '*l'historire engagé*' but also an equivalent Irish historical tradition. The Irish view of history-as-art with its connection to the long Irish struggle with the English and its own tradition of '*l'histoire engagé*' from the seventeenth century to the present would receive unexpected validation. O'Brien would no doubt repudiate the essay today not only as a result of where it would put him in the Irish historical debate, but also because of the idea of historians validating and inciting what he would subsequently view as 'tribal self-righteousness and ethnocentric arrogance'.

This speculation aside, what remains is an enthralling view of one brilliant historian being re-interpreted by an aspiring one. O'Brien disdains prophecy, and yet sees Michelet's prophecies more as healthy curses. O'Brien demonstrates an '*et alors?*' attitude toward polemics: he is clearly signalling a belief that in certain circumstances the cost of vented spleen outweighs the non-defence of the values under attack. This aside, most of the fascination and the approbation is reserved for Michelet's honesty surrounding the Revolution itself. In conveying the dynamism of the flux and the fury of the French Revolution, we see O'Brien's enthusiastic endorsement of what he would try to achieve himself.

What, then, are the implications of judging O'Brien by his own criteria of what makes a great historian and great history? At its simplest, his writings indicate a disposition to identify with what has been neglected and what stimulates the historian's interest for whatever reason and to pursue this relentlessly. In this identification one might have to defend a misunderstood subject or, as O'Brien put it, to look back with 'thoughts of salvage'. These writings also gives a clear idea of what history is: Punch-and-Judy shows are out, as is chauvinism. Michelet is brilliant and honest in his analysis of the French Revolution because, although fully engaged, he did not take sides. He may have had his preferences, but they did not affect his judgement; in fact his judgement was honed by his enthusiastic participation. By concentrating on Michelet's preoccupation with the nuances of the French Revolutionary, O'Brien endorses Michelet's own historical template: to convey the varied interactions, the mutability of the characters and questions concerned, and the richness of the issues and opinions involved.

Can Michelet help us evaluate O'Brien's writings? Does he pass his own Michelet test? The answer depends on what we choose to see as O'Brien's French Revolution. O'Brien's writings should be evaluated in the light of a particular section of Irish historical writing over the past hundred years. If then we attempt to relate the criteria O'Brien applied to Michelet, can it not be said that we are being fair to O'Brien? To run the rule over his own evaluation of Michelet, we could say that in his portrayal of the Irish nationalist tradition, he certainly found something which stimulated his interest, and which he pursued relentlessly. In his identification with this tradition he for a time defended it well, and gave those of other traditions pause to think. While it can be said that O'Brien was brilliant and fully engaged, he always took sides and was not entirely honest. While it would never be fair to accuse O'Brien of chauvinism, can it be said that he never resorted to the level of Punch-and-Judy shows? His moral polarization of the parties in the contemporary debate certainly has hints of this. However excusable that was, the moral historicism surrounding his portraits of nationalists in the past often descended into pure pantomime.

It isn't until the 1970s that O'Brien stops asking certain questions and starts giving quixotic answers to others. O'Brien's approach, quite apart from his use of evidence, is a classic example of politically engaged prejudgement. In his writings on Parnell we can see the keen mind which brought the complexity and confusion of the epochs to our attention. However, even in these 'tightly buttoned' works, we can see a definite focus that demonstrates that he wrote while fully engaged.

Even with the simple example of Yeats's 'Did that play of mine send out / Certain men the English shot', he can be seen to prove himself less a historian and more a victim of history. If there is one thing which the reader should take from this survey, it is that O'Brien should be quoted less, and instanced as a result of the history of his time more. Finally, it would be hard to say that the participation honed his judgement. Sadly he ceased conveying the confusion of history as it happened and the nuance disappeared. The varied interactions, the mutability of the characters and questions, the richness of the issues and opinions, atrophied to a single explanation: religion; a lone culprit: the Catholic Irish; a sole judgement: wrong; and one future: doom.

NOTES

1. Interview with Conor Cruise O'Brien in Naim Atallah, *Of a Certain Age: Interviews* (London, 1991).
2. Conor Cruise O'Brien, 'Preface', in *Maria Cross: Imaginative Patterns in a Group of Modern Catholic Writers* (London, 1963), p.vii.
3. Both the correspondence and the text of O'Brien, 'The Story of Ireland' can be found in the National Archives of Ireland, Dublin, Department of External Affairs, 305/14/112.
4. O'Brien, 'The Story of Ireland', p.25.
5. Conor Cruise O'Brien, *Ancestral Voices* (Dublin, 1994), pp.92–3.
6. Ibid., pp.93–4.
7. O'Brien, 'The Story of Ireland', p.32.
8. W.I. Thompson, *The Imagination of an Insurrection: Dublin, Easter 1916: A Study of an Ideological Movement* (London, 1967).
9. Conor Cruise O'Brien, 'Two-Faced Cathleen', *The New York Review of Books*, 29 June 1967.
10. Conor Cruise O'Brien, 'Politics and the Poet', *The Irish Times*, 21 August 1975.
11. Conor Cruise O'Brien, 'An Exalted Nationalism', *The Times*, 28 January 1989. In D.H. Akenson, *Conor: A Biography of Conor Cruise O'Brien, Vol. II: Anthology* (Montreal, 1994), pp.285–8 (p.286).
12. See Conor Cruise O'Brien, 'Holy War', *The New York Review of Books*, 6 November 1969, and O'Brien, 'Introduction', in *Herod: Reflections on Political Violence* (London, 1978).
13. O'Brien, 'The parnellism of Seán O'Faoláin', in *Maria Cross*, p.102.
14. O'Brien, 'Two Faced Cathleen'.
15. Conor Cruise O'Brien, 'Timothy Michael Healy', in *The Shaping of Modern Ireland* (London, 1960), p.173.
16. Ibid., p.172.
17. Ibid.
18. Ibid., p.173.
19. O'Brien, 'Foreword', in *The Shaping of Modern Ireland*, p.1.
20. Ibid., p.2.
21. O'Brien, '1891–1916', in *The Shaping of Modern Ireland*, p.13.
22. Ibid.
23. Ibid., p.15.
24. Ibid., p.16.
25. Ibid., p.19.
26. Ibid., p.22.
27. Ibid., pp.21–2.
28. Ibid., p.17.

29. Ibid., p.18.
30. Conor Cruise O'Brien, 'The Fall of Parnell', in *Writers and Politics* (London, 1965), pp.116–18.
31. O'Brien, 'Foreword', in *The Shaping of Modern Ireland*, p.7.
32. Conor Cruise O'Brien, *States of Ireland* (London, 1972), p.23.
33. Conor Cruise O'Brien, 'Michelet Today', in *Writers and Politics* (London, 1965), p.46.
34. Ibid., p.42.
35. Ibid. 'A thing I always had in mind approaching it [history] was "What would you have done chum? – what side would I have been on?"'. Quoted in Fintan O'Toole, 'Profile of Conor Cruise O'Brien: the Making of a Liberal', *Magill*, April 1986.
36. O'Brien, 'Michelet Today', p.49.
37. Ibid.
38. Ibid., p.53.
38. Ibid., p.57.
39. Ibid., p.56.
40. Ibid.
41. O'Brien, *To Katanga and Back*, p.31. A.J.P. Taylor writing at approximately the same time took the following anonymous quatrain for his definition of Realpolitik: 'We cling to the simple plan/ That they shall take/ Who have the power/ And they shall keep, who can'. I like to think of O'Brien's rationalization above, which infuses all his writings, as Realmentalite. Although the pidgin neologism may not be acceptable, it does convey O'Brien's matter-of-fact acceptance of imaginings, notions, and misconceptions as an aspect of the 'stuff of history', which is of equal importance to any other consideration.

11

Legitimacy: Violence and Irish History

The little known collection of essays by O'Brien from the late 1970s entitled *Herod: Reflections on Political Violence* is something of a lost treatise of Irish political philosophy. In the current historiography *States of Ireland* is usually seen as O'Brien's signature work: his dramatic bolt out of the blue, with its irreverent debauching of Irish pieties that proved so popular and vital in helping to educate a whole new generation – the no to Articles 2 and 3 generation. This view is not necessarily wrong. Certainly in terms of influence, there is no comparison between *States* and *Herod*. It is, however, less of an actual, or what we might call an organic, view. Typically we see the mutation of O'Brien in the early 1970s less as a gradual development and more as a Sauline conversion. In many circles it is even characterized as a dramatic treason. To the extent that his change was heedless to what went before, then the Biblical allusion holds true. His transformation can be isolated to a particular year, 1970, and his thinking did jettison a large part of what he had previously professed. As broadly correct as this viewpoint is, its drawback is that it tends to obscure exactly what it was that O'Brien achieved in this decade. When looked at from the 'output' point of view (rather than isolating his prior 'input') we can discern a more reasoned basis to his political mutation. Ultimately we can see it as a form of philosophical analysis (albeit through his congenitally historicist lens). In the end it should be recognized, even by the many who disagree with O'Brien's analysis, as less of an attempt to excoriate Irish society and more of an effort to buttress the essentials of that society.

While he was still Albert Schweitzer Professor in New York University, O'Brien stood as a Labour candidate in the June 1969 General Election, contesting the Dublin North East constituency with

Charles Haughey. The eight years between his return to Ireland and losing both his Dáil seat and ministerial office were obviously tumultuous times. The best way to get an overview of his thought in these years is to turn to his collection of essays entitled *Herod: Reflections on Political Violence*.[1] O'Brien's writings in *Herod* are focused on the sole theme of legitimacy, an interest that can be traced back to the intellectual re-positioning that took place after he returned to Ireland from New York in 1969. In complementary and, occasionally, contradictory ways the articles in the *Herod* collection establish the centrality of legitimacy to his mind. While his concern for legitimacy hits its high point in the post *States of Ireland* phase of O'Brien, the period when O'Brien was a member of government, the essays in *Herod* give a good account of the changes in his thinking throughout this entire decade.

The 'Introduction' to *Herod*, penned by O'Brien in 1978, discusses the various events that made O'Brien a staple of public discourse in Ireland, and the far from subtle effects these events had upon his thinking. To put it plainly, the changes in *Herod* reflect the changes wrought upon O'Brien's mind by the politics of those days. This phenomenon can be seen most clearly in his play *Salome and the Wildman*,[2] which is an example of his flirtation with revolution.[3] It is also proof of a phenomenon that some of his colleagues in NYU drew attention to, which was that O'Brien was lured by some of the exuberant tendencies of his radical students. When O'Brien returned to Ireland it was with the dubious cachet of somebody who had protested against the US presence in Vietnam, had participated in student sit-ins and withstood horse charges by the New York police, as well as having been kicked by one of them. However, by the mid 1970s in another of his plays, *King Herod Explains*, his outlook is mired in the notion of a violent human condition that debases the mind and intentions of all – student, priest and politician.

The incongruity of some of the content, memorably described in another context by Joe Lee as 'O'Brien sober' commenting on 'O'Brien drunk'[4] allied to the inclusion of certain superfluous articles (mainly the book reviews), has led some critics, notably Tom Paulin and Don-ald Akenson,[5] to dismiss this collection. While there may be arguments for its critical dismissal, which have a good deal to do with the breakdown in the O'Brien hallmarks of coherence and fluidity, to ignore it would be to lose a vital key to the O'Brien mind.

To begin with, *Herod* is a collection of arguments that are loosely based on the concept of legitimacy but played out in different spheres. Some of these spheres are as far apart as, on the one hand, O'Brien's attempts at theatre to, on the other hand, his theoretical consideration of the origins of terrorism. Yet all his offerings in this collection, even the book reviews, are built around this notion of legitimacy. A look at the philosophical pedigree of legitimacy shows us that it appears to be one of those concepts whose centrality to human endeavour is not reflected in the volume of material written on it, which is only modest. This is doubly paradoxical in that legitimacy seems to occupy a pivotal place in any of the major national-political narratives. A further deficiency is highlighted by the fact that it appears, precisely in the areas most in need of enlightenment: the watersheds or the seminal events of the respective countries under scrutiny. In the situation of Ireland, legitimacy would seem to be the key term in the histories of, say, Lyons, Lee, Foster, Mansergh, MacDonagh and Boyce, when scrutinizing the 1916 Easter Rising and the surrounding years.[6] A similar situation would seem to pertain to the period generally known as 'the Troubles', which is the pivotal moment in the subsequent historiography of Northern Ireland. To demonstrate: 'Northern Ireland, on the other hand, failed to acquire legitimacy in the eyes of a sufficient number of its inhabitants to prevent itself being torn apart by what appears to be a variety of tribal religious war.'[7] It is for this reason that O'Brien's attempt in *Herod* to deal with the question of legitimacy in Ireland should be given serious consideration as it is, in effect, an attempt to grapple with the opposing political conceptions of Ireland in that decade.

O'Brien outlines his understanding of legitimacy by stating that 'if democracy includes placing "the monopoly of the legitimate use of force" under the control of elected representatives, as generally in Western Europe, then a clear distinction can be drawn between the legitimate democratic monopoly and all illegitimate competition'.[8] This excerpt, built around Weber's definition of the state, is taken from a 1976 O'Brien essay in *The New York Review of Books*. While it establishes in his mind the importance of legitimacy to the modern state, he seems quite happy to employ it to merely draw the distinction between illegal and legal. He is aware that for all the insight this affords into the basis of an orderly state, it is negligible in terms of aiding an understanding of the more fundamental nature of legitimacy. A true appreciation of legitimacy needs to grapple with the various conditions that precede the illegal/legal distinction, while acknowledging that any and all such distinctions flow from notions of legitimacy. This is borne out by O'Brien's essay quoted above, and indeed his whole treatment of legitimacy in the years prior to 1976. Certainly it should be established that Weber never dictated O'Brien's understanding, and it would not be too much to say that this first (and last) quotation of Weber appears almost as an afterthought.

One of the most intriguing aspects of *Herod* is that it attempts to get to grips with those fundamental criteria upon which legitimacy is based. In *Herod* O'Brien comes very close to answering some of the perennial questions surrounding legitimacy: are certain conceptual, social and political conditions necessary for it to be present? Does it precede the state, or does it proceed from the state? Need it be consistent with democratic principles? Where the state has been deemed to be illegitimate, what conditions are sufficient to prove this? Finally, when does violence become legitimate, or indeed is this proof of a state's illegitimacy?

Some answers to these questions are to be found in the classic political philosophers' writings, which 'are primarily concerned with building up a theory of the liberal state, its origins, establishment and constitution. Inevitably they wrestle with the problems of securing Governmental legitimacy and authority, political obligation and order.'[9] Against this background, problems have philosophically and historically occurred when these rights and responsibilities have collided with what from Aristotle to Locke has been described as tyranny. The most notable elaboration of this is provided by Hobbes in *Leviathan* where he gives primacy to the sovereign power. For him this should be unconditional and the first obligation: 'I think the toleration of a professed hatred of tyranny, is a toleration of hatred to the Commonwealth in general.'[10] Obviously questions of this nature fuel a perennial debate. I do not suggest that O'Brien deals with all these arguments or that he has any specific answers, but rather that his critique lies within this noble, if cryptic, discourse. This at least affords a manner in which to deal with the outlook of the later O'Brien and how he fashioned and, in turn, was himself shaped by the main political dynamic of Ireland in the 1970s: the quest for legitimacy. The validity of such an over-arching statement will become clear when we take a closer look at O'Brien's comments on the situation he returned to in Ireland.

Having arrived back from New York in 1969, O'Brien drew attention to what he described as the 'impenetrable cosiness' of the South's perspective of the North. 'What is peculiar in our situation is the need to think about the legitimation of violence in terms of the dominant assumptions of that society.'[11] He was also exasperated at the character of this 'legitimation': 'what was most oppressive was not the legitimation of violence itself, but the frivolity of this legitimation, the refusal to see it was legitimation, or that legitimation was important'.[12] Leaving aside for the moment the serious question of the Republic's role in this process, let us concentrate on the implications of O'Brien's use of the vocabulary of legitimacy to describe the Northern Ireland conflict.

Having left the riots and protests of 1960s America, the legitimation of violence reappeared much as it had throughout his involvement in the Vietnam debate. Looking back, he explained the evolution to his position of the late 1970s by asserting that:

> The Civil Rights Movement and Protestant vigilantes (including police vigilantes) had shaken the foundations of the Northern Ireland State. The ensuing events necessitated the introduction of British troops in order to protect Catholics from Protestant repressive violence which had taken a lethal form in Belfast. Subsequently, the IRA sought to break the Catholic fraternisation with the British troops and to present themselves as Catholic liberators.[13]

He reveals that he had sympathized with the Civil Rights Movement in its early stages, and given it some small support. Reflecting upon this movement, he felt that 'although non-violent, it was likely to provoke violence'.[14] In *States of Ireland*, and in other later writings, he reflected on the nature of the situation as 'frozen violence', and castigates himself for not having perceived the inevitable outcome when the rigid social structures of the North thawed. Nevertheless, the result of all this civil agitation and intense political turmoil was, in his opinion, 'the removal of the system of caste supremacy'. Despite this, 'the people went on killing children and others and legitimizing the killing of children and others'.[15]

This chronology and selection of events was chosen by O'Brien for its relevance to legitimacy, although it is fair to say that it is quite selective, and would be unsatisfactory for many. It should also be noted that O'Brien's own interpretation in the late 1960s was markedly different from the one he presented in the subsequent decade. Broadly speaking, the change came about because he was no longer looking for 'causes' and had interest only in why the violence persisted. The most notable difference is a generic one. This consists of the transformation in his writings from a critical yet positive stance, to that of a negative construct. Previously, O'Brien's object had been the dismissal and subsequent clarification of the various interpretations of Northern Ireland, most notably the Marxist interpretation and those critiques that dismissed religion. What we might call the negative construct arises from a change in focus, from Northern Ireland to the Republic. The 'constructive' element stems from O'Brien's view that the Republic played the main role in the creation of the Troubles. The negative aspect concerns itself with the removal of this political option, or as O'Brien phrased it, 'the dismantling of legitimation structures'. Although it certainly was not his goal when he entered politics at the beginning of the decade, this in a nutshell is what O'Brien ended up doing in 1970's Ireland.

There are two points to be made about O'Brien's chronology above that reveal the essence *of Herod*. O'Brien maintains that the rationale for violence became untenable with the 'removal of caste supremacy'.[16] An inquiry into how he arrived at this understanding – of viewing the removal of caste supremacy as the point of crystallization for what constitutes a legitimate or illegitimate action – is hugely beneficial to an understanding of O'Brien. That analysis belongs mostly to the theoretical sphere. The no less important second point of why the killing and legitimizing continued is largely a mélange between Irish history and its effect upon the contemporary events. Within this dynamic of past and present lies the essence of O'Brien, and his importance to Irish thought.

His primary concern, it seems, was to establish whether the violence was moral or not.

> The legitimation of violence (force) is not always wrong. It is contended that the legitimation of violence (force) as a lesser evil in any particular circumstance is a profoundly serious matter which has to be capable of being established and defended on rational grounds, in relation to those

circumstances, if it is to have any moral force.[17]

Expanding on this in his lecture 'Liberty and Terror'[18] he hints at the magnitude of the stakes involved. There was a very real possibility that the entire democratic heritage might be undermined; accordingly there was a huge responsibility on that generation to recognize the fragility of this tradition in the face of terrorist attacks upon it. The vital thread between legitimacy and democracy is found in a much-abused historical 'parallel'. Contrasting the Sinn Féin of 1921 with the Sinn Féin of the 1970s, O'Brien rubbishes the latter's claim to a valid parallel with the observation that 'the old Sinn Féin had, and retained, a genuine popular base. The importance of the distinction in terms of political morality is obvious.'[19]

But what of a situation that is not characterized by the democratic process, as many both in the North and elsewhere contended was the case? According to the 'early' O'Brien, the predicament of the Northern Irish Catholics was an example of this. 'The natives are deemed to accept their status. They have no means of changing it by ordinary democratic process.'[20] Nonetheless, the legitimacy of their recourse to violence can only be justified in certain circumstances. 'Only extreme circumstances can justify ... examples of such are the manifest failure and disintegration of formerly organised polities – as in Russia and China – and the existence of such conditions for whole communities ... such that no possible alternative seems likely to be worse'.[21] When these notions are applied to Northern Ireland, O'Brien asks:

> Did such conditions exist in Northern Ireland? It is argued that they did. The Catholics of Northern Ireland were and are in a permanent minority in what has always been run as a Protestant state. They were second-class citizens, discriminated against in jobs and housing, and often obliged to emigrate. Since the Protestant majority always voted *en bloc* for the Unionist Party, perpetrator of the discriminations in question, ordinary democratic process offered no hope for the Catholic minority. All this is true. What is not true is the idea that terrorism, the urban guerrilla, therefore represented the only way out – or any way out – for the Catholic minority.[22]

His earlier evaluation of the situation in 1970 instanced another factor that made violence unjustifiable. This was 'the deployment of British troops in August 1969 – an event which inevitably signalled the end of the old institutionalised caste system in Northern Ireland (Derry Corporation and all the rest)'.[23]

A question mark must remain over the view that the deployment of British troops was entirely sufficient, simply because he himself did not view it like this at the time. Three months after the British Army had arrived he penned an article for *The New York Review of Books* (where most of his considered pieces went). He wrote: 'Support for equality of rights and the abolition of Stormont's institutionalised caste system is another matter. Its destruction would be a human achievement of more than local significance.'[24]

However, reservations must be expressed as to whether Northern Irish Catholics perceived this as being sufficient for 'ruling out' the use of violence. If it did not appear to eradicate the caste system in his eyes back then, it surely would not have done so in the eyes of the inhabitants of Derry and Belfast. The discrepancy between his two differing views on this precise point of the institutionalized caste system is hard to resolve. Were one to argue for O'Brien, one could include elaborations upon various references to the past and future role of the British government, which he outlined in a later book *Neighbours: The Ewart-Biggs Memorial Lectures, 1978–1979*. But this is with the benefit of hindsight and clearly not how he saw it at the time. In any case those lectures say nothing about the basis of legitimate violence, which he had countenanced in 1969, and of which he had approved while in New York.[25] His later position took the shape outlined in *The New York Review of Books* of September 1976 where he argues: 'The cause of minority rights may be and probably has been served by episodes of token protest, blackmail, violence, but sustained political violence would be suicidal, almost by definition, for any minority population.'[26]

In O'Brien's mind the situation of the minority was insufficiently oppressive because 'a way out' was available through the intervention of the United Kingdom. The ability to petition the UK government was crucial in his view, in that it placed a moral onus upon the minority to abjure violence. 'Their legitimate complaint against the successive governments of the United Kingdom was that these governments had condoned, by ignoring, the oppressive practices in Northern Ireland.'[27] This tacit compliance was no longer possible as a result of the peaceful agitation set in train by the Civil Rights Movement. O'Brien adds: 'the continuation of this movement, therefore, represented by far the best hope of removing the disabilities of the Catholic community. On the basis of this new balance, a peaceful, if belated, resolution of the conflict could be arrived at.'[28] Continuing this utilitarian line he outlines how, ultimately, 'the coming of the urban guerrilla had the opposite effect: it alienated sympathies, and sharply increased the hostility between the two communities. The best hope of this community lies, in fact, in the disappearance from the scene of their "defenders".'[29]

It is interesting to note the discrepancy here between the above, taken mostly from 'A Global Letter', written in February 1972, and the 'Introduction' to *Herod* written six years later. The difference in O'Brien's later attitude to the Civil Rights Movement is striking. Writing in 1978 he is outright hostile. 'Why', he asks, 'with the disappearance of Derry, Stormont and the institutions of caste supremacy, did the killing and legitimising continue?' One of the explanations provided in 1978 is that,

> the left-wingers now emerged as the agitational arm of the IRA in converting what had been ostensibly a civil rights campaign (whose essential objectives had been achieved) into an overtly nationalist campaign ... This movement had in fact turned its 'non-sectarian', 'international', 'class-centered' rhetoric into material for the legitimation of tribal civil-war in Northern Ireland.[30]

Needless to mention, this is some way from the explanation he put forward in 1972 where he announced that the Civil Rights Movement 'represented by far the best hope of removing the disabilities of the Catholic community'.[31] In *States of Ireland* a good deal of effort is spent in outlining how certain elements, notably the 'ginger group' Peoples Democracy, frittered away valuable political capital andbreathing space with their actions at Burntollet. This could be adduced as the probable cause for the exasperation with the Civil Rights Movement were it not for the fact that this is not voiced in his other writings around this period, notably 'A Global Letter' from the same year. This hiatus tends to cast serious doubts on the reasoning that led to his unsympathetic analysis of the Civil Rights Movement. Again one is left to infer: the cause no doubt lies somewhere in their becoming 'the agitational arm of the Provisionals'. That this is not expanded upon anywhere seriously undermines the claim to sustained and thorough thought.

Another reason why he became disenchanted with this movement and Peoples Democracy has to do with his own drift from the radical outlook he brought back from New York with him. One of the theories he shared with these 'ginger groups' was the theory of institutionalized violence. Again it is another way of rephrasing the legitimacy question. As one of the legitimating structures operating in Northern Ireland it receives a healthy exposure in 'A Global Letter' and some attention in other essays, notably 'Liberty and Terror'. It is significant that it receives no mention in the 'Introduction' he penned in 1978. From this, it could be surmised that it is an interpretation that the O'Brien of the late 1970s viewed as having had its day. As an accretion of his time in New York and the new social critiques of the late-1960s, perhaps he felt that it was one of those intellectual tools which tend to obscure rather than reveal. Perhaps also it was part of the vocabulary of those groups whose actions he now found repugnant. Nonetheless, as it is the only real attempt to explain the society of Northern Ireland through the lens of legitimacy it is worthy of some attention.

O'Brien's definition of institutionalized violence is a useful start: 'Where there is social injustice, enforced by law, then violence is diffused through the institutions of the state, and it is hypocritical to object to illegal acts of violence, which are no more immoral than the daily ones at which we connive.'[32] It is probably no surprise that he was sceptical to the point of being caustic about such a *carte blanche* for violence. He acknowledges that institutionalized violence is endemic to all societies and that the great inequalities of all societies, such as wealth and power, are in the final resort defended by violence. The logic of institutionalized violence suggests that it is society which is to blame for the actions of someone who blows up a supermarket. The basis for this is that it is not the terrorist who is responsible but the forces of society that have driven him to it. It is the values that 'defend' the supermarket, and the laws that defend those values, which are guilty. In rebuttal, he accepts the existence of institutionalized violence as a reality. He nonetheless argues that this in itself is insufficient legitimation for violence. On that basis violence would be permissible in all societies, even in the societies that show no unhappiness with their institutionalized lot. He insists that there must be the aforementioned conditions of Sino-Soviet inequality and political breakdown. These oppressive conditions alone can free the oppressed from their moral bond to resolve their predicament peaceably.

There are some problems with O'Brien's application of his interpretation of legitimacy, especially as it is applied to Northern Ireland. As well as adopting a far less radical approach, and some might say less open-minded one, he attempts to translate the legitimacy deficit that has led to the Troubles into a readily understood message:

> Not everybody of course is up to the general theory of institutionalised violence. But most people can find significance in such a statement as, for example, 'violence is a by-product of partition'. The significance found by simpler ruder spirits is that when a Protestant is killed by a Catholic, he had it coming to him. This is the extended doctrine of institutionalised violence as seen at grass-roots level, for institutionalised violence has long been a Protestant monopoly. The other kind of violence is practised by both sides.[33]

Accepting this, we must ask why O'Brien would bother to mention institutionalized violence, if he intends to simply ignore it? By firstly acknowledging its existence: 'long been a Protestant monopoly', and then by developing the view that 'simpler ruder spirits' would reason thus, he is doing no more than stating that animosity precedes institutional violence rather than emanating from it. This amounts to ignoring the institutional problems. The presence of serious civil inequalities, allied to a long established belief in the illegitimacy of the Northern Ireland state, as the seminal factors in the reasoning behind the violence (O'Brien insists there must be one) cannot be overlooked. To deliberately invoke the vocabulary of legitimacy, one must come to terms with the reasons for the absence of legitimacy. The attainment of the objectives of the Civil Rights Movement, even within the terms of his argument, could not begin to change the fundamental perception of many at that time that the Northern Ireland state was without legitimacy. O'Brien is to be admired for his analysis of Northern Ireland on the basis of legitimacy. It must be said that having done so, he failed to accept the logic of his arguments, or rather he did, but not in the Northern Ireland sphere. The great pity of O'Brien is that by failing to engage with both sides, he failed to engage with Northern Ireland. Ironically, just at the point when he is most associated with the North in the eyes of most observers, he is actually in full retreat from it.

However, where he is fully engaged in these years is with the question of the legitimation of violence in the South. 'As far as our village is concerned, it is true, institutionalised violence is a far less potent concept for purposes of legitimation than are the prevailing myths of history and the cult of the dead.'[34] The strength of such a claim is reflected in the fact that his critique of the role of history is given far more space than institutionalized violence. O'Brien is far happier in this milieu, by way of training, and possibly through temperament. It is instructive that the only translation of institutionalized violence he provides – 'violence is a by-product of partition' – is itself a quote that, as he tirelessly points out, we have Jack Lynch to thank for. This underlines the notion put forward earlier that O'Brien's real motivation for invoking the legitimacy argument lies with the Republic's actions. It is in this arena that O'Brien pursues his argument of legitimacy to its utmost. Institutionalized violence was one of three excuses for violence that O'Brien ascribed to the IRA and its sympathizers in their attempts to legitimate violence. An example of the second type of argument is seen in questions along the lines of: 'When told they have no mandate for this recourse to violence, they ask: what mandate had the men in Easter 1916?' Allied to this they ask: 'was it not the threat of force in 1912–14 by Ulster volunteers which created Northern Ireland?'[35] O'Brien insists that these two questions, or variations upon them, are central to the legitimation of violence. Effectively he says that what must be grasped in order to comprehend the motivations of the various separate peoples, indeed the whole situation in Ireland, is how their thinking upon the civil strife is determined by their reading of the history of the previous sixty years.

By raising the relation of history to the legitimation of violence and the notion of an illegitimate state, O'Brien took the debate about the present into the past. In doing this he engaged in an unusual method. The discipline of history sees itself as a scientific endeavour, whose 'value', to quote Collingwood, 'is that it teaches us what man has done and thus what man is'.[36] With O'Brien's method we seem to have a conscious inversion along the lines of 'knowing what man is, we will teach ourselves what man has done'. This is no seismic travesty of all intellectual standards, and it is certainly not unprecedented. This teleological approach underwrites the disciplines of, for example, sociology and psychology. However, the presumption of motive in an attempt to frame the mind of a terrorist, or a sympathetic population, must perforce change the way one writes history. To be committed to this approach will affect your selection of evidence, limit or expand the parameters of your scope, and ultimately expose the transparencies and opacities of ideology. This is all the result of O'Brien's reasoning that in order to defeat the IRA in the present, one must debate them in the past.

An example of this in operation can be seen in his treatment of the phrase 'for this generation'. For O'Brien this is an example of a republican shibboleth where a simple phrase divulges a whole cast of mind. The implications of these words can only become apparent when viewed in the context of their original use and the background behind the phrase 'for this generation'. 'It is therefore necessary to say something here both of Irish history, as Irish Republicans conceive of it, and of actual Irish history, of which the Republican myth is part, but which contains other *vitally important elements which the myth ignores or distorts.*'[37] This leads him to setting up some counter myths of his own, the first of which is that Irish nationalism was split from its inception by the twin progenitors of rival factions, Tone and O'Connell. He posits that 'most Irish Catholics in the nineteenth century followed constitutional nationalists politically and gave almost no support to the military activities of the Fenians'.[38] Firstly it should be pointed out that this dichotomy is not entirely valid. A brief inspection of 'The New Departure', an area O'Brien is unquestionably an expert in, demonstrates that Irish nationalism was more the promiscuous mistress who admitted several suitors, rather than the virginal constitutional bride.

It should be noted of late nineteenth-century Irish nationalism, that there was a great deal of fluidity in a nationalist's position with regard to physical force. This is where his need to defeat them in the present forces the evidence in his debate with them in the past. O'Brien's concern with legitimacy hinges on morality, and when he speaks of the physical and constitutional factions, the moral eminence accorded to those who abjured violence is discernible. The problem with this is that it involves the imposition of a laudable sentiment upon a populace who would not have viewed it in such terms. Furthermore, according to the Catholic Church's teaching, and the accepted wisdom at the time, what made violence immoral was its hopelessness. Further pause for thought is given when it is realized that the role of physical force was evaluated solely on the criterion of efficacy and not morality. This can be seen in the statement of John Redmond in 1907: '"the methods of resistance" to be adopted remained merely "a question of expediency" and that an appeal to arms would be "absolutely justifiable" if it were likely to succeed'.[39] In addition, as O'Brien was fond of quoting William O'Brien's axiom that 'violence was the only way of securing a hearing for moderation' he would have done well to heed the admonitions to posterity of the same William O'Brien who maintained that:

> constitutionalism in a country whose grievance is that it possesses no constitution is an historical humbug. Parnell built up his movement not by railing at Fenianism in the spirit of a professor of Constitutional history, but by incorporating its tremendous forces in his ranks and acknowledging no criterium [*sic*] of the rectitude of his political action, be it 'constitutional' or 'unconstitutional' except whether it was in the circumstances the best thing to be done for Ireland.[40]

Having put forward an unsatisfactory glimpse of one century he moves on to the following one, where he informs us that: 'while nineteenth century attitudes subsist, new puzzles have been added to the old ones. One of the strangest is that the modem Irish state, the Republic of Ireland ... has been deemed to owe its origins to the actions of members of the IRB.'[41] This is where we encounter Padraig Pearse, who in the O'Brien template is the outstanding individual in Irish history (certainly in the malefactors' side of the pantheon). While there may be a case for Wolfe Tone, who it cannot be denied started the whole affair, Pearse is the linchpin upon which O'Brien's whole thesis of republican influence rests. 'But although the Easter Rising was in a tradition, it gave a new twist to that tradition. This was due to the strange personality, original genius and concentrated will of the most influential of the leaders of the rising, Patrick Pearse.' It is this 'twist' which O'Brien proceeds to investigate. 'What was special about Pearse was the intensity of his commitment to a sacrificial form of nationalism, his vision of the past as a long chain of sacrifices, and his imaginative understanding of the power over the future which further sacrifices could exert.'[42] In addition Pearse understood the powerful influence of funerals and is responsible for the fusion of the Divine and recurrent blood sacrifices. What he is not responsible for, according to O'Brien, is the character of the IRA. O'Brien instances the acts of faceless violence indiscriminately carried out by the IRA which Pearse would never have condoned. O'Brien reminds us that the 'Proclamation of 1916 specifically repudiated "inhumanity" and "rapine" as well as "cowardice"'.[43] He points out that there are profound differences, at a psychological level, between any IRA individual and Pearse. One might be surprised to see true respect in O'Brien for Pearse, but it is unquestionably present. He has no difficulty in illustrating the strange nobility manifest in the mystic poet, the chivalrous dreamer with a bent for self-immolation, who in terms of temperament, character and method, was superior to any contemporary IRA individual. This apart, O'Brien maintains that the Pearsean conceptual legacy motivates the IRA every bit as energetically as his personal example has been ignored. 'The *tactics* of the contemporary IRA can certainly not be justified by Pearse's *example*. But the *concept* of the IRA – the renewal of the bloody conflict until the connection with England is altogether broken for all Ireland – is fully in line with Pearse's *doctrine*.'[44]

For O'Brien, Pearse's interpretation of history is important in two ways. 'First of all, just as they (the IRA) are insulated against democratic repudiation by the whole elitist Fenian tradition, so are they insulated against failure by Pearse's interpretation of history.'[45] This has the implication of removing normal criteria of success, with the result that their efficacy is measured in terms of blood and carnage; or to put it in terms of their personal role: the production of more martyrs. The second way in which Pearse sustains violence, O'Brien argues, is that opponents to violence can have their arguments refuted as they derive from the same non-rational assumptions from which the IRA itself derives its mystique and continuity. All our assumptions are similar because 'Pearse's doctrine has long been accorded, and to a lesser extent still is accorded, quasi-sacred status in nationalist Ireland'.[46] The implication of this is that nationalist Ireland maintains a dangerous sentimentality. It is this sentimentality, leading to an ambivalence on the question of the political heritage of the Republic, which will be the basis of criticisms of his own generation.

Having dealt with how history legitimizes the IRA, O'Brien proceeds to demonstrate how ultimately the similar points of departure, the common ideological reference points, sustain violent elements under apparently dissimilar conditions. This is what he meant when he quoted Camus in *States of Ireland*. 'The bacillus of the plague can be dormant for years "in furniture and linen" and may one day "waken its rats and send them to die in a happy city".'[47] Referring to the subsistence of ambivalent attitudes in connection with the Fenians and the law in general, he points to other legacies which continue to endure. One such is 'that the modern Irish state, the Republic of Ireland, which condemns the IRA and is condemned by it, has been deemed to owe its origins to the actions of the Irish Republican Brotherhood'. He subsequently deals with the relation of the Rising to the present Irish state, which 'is of course much more complex and ambiguous than the conventional doctrine seeks to assert'.[48] An interesting manner in which to demonstrate this is to isolate the Rising. In line with this train of thought we are, in the essay 'American Aid to Freedom Fighters', introduced to what could be called the Irish Parliamentary Party historiographical tradition, or less clumsily, the 'Redmondite tradition'.[49] It revolves around a counterfactual, specifically: what would have been the outcome if there were no 1916 Rising? O'Brien clearly belongs to this tradition, although this statement in itself does not do justice to the complex inheritance comprising a legacy at once intellectual and visceral.

The counterfactual reads:

> The present Irish state was established not in 1916 or in absolute terms, but in 1921 on the basis of a compromise. The limited self-government (for twenty-six counties) obtained in 1921 was to develop into sovereign independence for the same area. I see absolutely no reason to suppose that the more limited self-government offered to the constitutional nationalists could not equally well have developed into sovereign independence for the same area, without the need for any violent uprising.[50]

There are many dangers involved in counterfactuals, one of the primary ones being an insufficient depth of approach. Essentially what is being argued pays no attention to the particular nature of either the Home Rule or Republican movements. It could therefore be interpreted as an article of faith arising out of O'Brien's background. It could be deemed a shallow, if relatively benign approach, were it not for the existence of several other contributions by O'Brien on this subject. The most notable of these is his article, 'The Embers of Easter 1916–1966'. Written in 1966, for the fiftieth anniversary of the Rising, it could be described as a critical commemorative piece. That article dealt with the sense of a missed opportunity and the perception of the Rising as a failure, as evinced by the truncated area of the state and the absence of a Gaelic-speaking nation. In a letter to *The Irish Times* five years later he again touched on similar subjects: the inevitability of partition, and how sovereignty could have been achieved without a violent uprising. 'Subsequent improvements on the treaty were won by negotiations and could, obviously, have been won in the same way on the basis of the 1914 Home Rule proposals.'[51] There are clearly problems of historical evidence with O'Brien's 'obviously', and the 'I see absolutely no reason', quoted above. Strictly speaking there is nothing obvious concerning the years 1914 to 1925 (the Boundary Commission). It could also be argued that there are plenty of reasons for viewing the Ireland that transpired as qualitatively different from the other possible outcomes.

An example of a non-republican mainstream viewpoint has been offered by Garret FitzGerald in an essay entitled 'The Significance of 1916'. It addressed those who would dwell on the evil effects of violent nationalism, while remaining oblivious to its more positive and less heralded effects. He acknowledges the legacy of recrimination and reprisals for the thirty-five years after the Civil War. In addition to this was an air of demoralization, perhaps leading to a complex of inferiority, and an undoubted perpetuation of out-worn hatreds. Allied to this is an instance of the motivation behind the rising, which has suffered at the hands of the clamour surrounding the role of Pearse and 'In the name of God and of the dead generations...' As a result of the broad support behind Redmond's statement which aimed to assure the English people at the outbreak of war that the Irish volunteers would protect Ireland, FitzGerald's father, Desmond, claims that:

> It was brought home to us that the very fever that had possessed us was due to a subconscious awareness that the final end of the Irish nation was at hand. For centuries England had held Ireland materially. But now it seemed that she held her in a new and utterly complete way. Our national identity was obliterated not only politically, but also in our own minds. The Irish people had recognised themselves as part of England.[52]

If nothing more were to be said in relation to the O'Brien counterfactual of 1916, perhaps it should be that in any such analysis we cannot arrogate all the good features of Ireland of the last half-century, with all the evil features automatically expunged.

While O'Brien does not exhaust the many possibilities, his counterfactual is more than one-dimensional. To this end it should be pointed out that he does not argue a 'violence achieves nothing' case. He feels that because of its introduction into the situation, it ensured further violence indefinitely. 'The new violence began immediately, with the Irish Civil War of 1922–3. It flared up again briefly at intervals, over the decades thereafter.'[53] In addition to this he also denies the validity of any historical parallels between the Anglo-Irish war and the IRA campaign from 1969. The fact that Sinn Féin was a representative authority is in utter contrast to the Provisional campaign. This, as already pointed out, has implications in terms of political morality. Finally O'Brien rejects the claim:

> That the state of whose government I am a member – the Republic of Ireland owes its existence to territorial terrorism, and to negotiation by the British government of that time with the terrorists. Basically our state owes its existence to the known and attested demand of a majority of its inhabitants for self-government and to the recognition by Britain and the rest of the world, of the legitimacy of that demand.[54]

At the beginning of this chapter mention was made of negative constructs and a new focus. This is most evident in the third and final area in O'Brien's interpretation of the legitimation of violence. An idea of this focus is given by O'Brien's portrayal of the intellectual environment to which he returned in the late 1960s.

> In the Republic of Ireland, where I lived, the people sincerely deplored the violence in the North, and also persisted in using language that legitimised that violence. Two of the three Dublin morning papers, one Sunday newspaper, and the solitary Dublin 'intellectual' periodical regularly published material tending to legitimise the existence and objective of the Provisionals never of course any specific tactic of theirs. Ireland's right to unity; the corresponding non-right of the Northern Ireland majority to have a state of their own; the deluded and ridiculous nature of that majority; the baseness of the British, the absurdity of their institutions and the brutality of their forces; the identification of Irish patriotism with anti-British feeling – these were the dominant assumptions of this press and of the vein of tribal self-righteousness which it fed, and on which it fed.[55]

Perhaps the most potent example of this aspect of O'Brien's analysis can be seen in his essay 'Shades of Republicans'. It arose out of a demand from *The Irish Times* to expand upon some ambiguous remarks made in the course of introducing his 1975 Broadcasting Authority (Amendment) Bill. In his Senate speech he referred to 'The lingering elusive doubts about the legitimacy of the state itself, to ambivalence to anti-democratic bodies which arrogate to themselves powers rightly belonging to the democratic state'.[56] He also spoke of people who 'speak and write as if the armed conspiracies known as the IRA have a legitimate or quasi-legitimate, though usually unspecified, role to play in our society'. Conceding that he pitched his speech for those whom it was intended to affect – journalists and broadcasters – he added that the prime responsibilities reside in the politicians' ambit. It is these responsibilities that he expanded upon in 'Shades of Republicans'.

The responsibilities of politicians are defined as 'a general amalgam of political attitudes in the Republic, inherited from the past and affording a kind of cover for IRA activities'.[57] Of these responsibilities, he 'had in mind primarily the relationship of Fianna Fáil ("the republican Party") to the rest of what is known as the republican movement'. This debate took place in 'the context of the Broadcasting Bill', which was an attempt to curb political spokespersons of armed groups from broadcasting. Fianna Fáil, according to O'Brien, is at the centre of this debate because its 'historical, psychological and rhetorical relationships to the post-Treaty IRA are incomparably closer than is the case with any other political grouping (Sinn Féin and Fianna Fáil republican splinters aside)'. He adds that he is not attempting to indict Fianna Fáil for its role in history as 'Edmund Burke knew of no way of indicting a nation, and it would not be much easier to indict such a significant part of a nation as has supported Fianna Fáil'.[58] That double-edged disclaimer put out, he proceeds to interrogate Ireland's history, and that certain dynamic that has characterized its relationship with Fianna Fáil.

He begins by quoting from the speech de Valera made in a secret session of the Dáil in 1921. Only published in 1972, de Valera likened the coercion of Ulster to 'making the same mistake as England had made with Ireland'. O'Brien also points out that de Valera 'would be in favour of allowing each county to vote itself out of the Republic if it so wishes'. O'Brien contrasts this with his speech in the Rotunda of 1925.

Spoken after the collapse of the Boundary Commission, it contains the lines, 'the sanction of our consent that partition can never have', and 'the right to win them back remains unimpaired for those to whom the future will bring the opportunity'. Of the 1921 and 1925 speeches, he comments:

> there can be few clearer indices of the damage done by the Civil War. Partition, then acknowledged as inevitable, and indeed legitimate in respect of any counties which would wish to 'opt out', was now rejected as utterly illegitimate, and anyone who might consent to it branded as base.[59]

Clearly there were ominous indications if this emotional appeal were to be acted upon. He subsequently quotes from Lemass's famous 'slightly constitutional party' of 1928, and de Valera's assertion in 1929 that the contemporary government did not come by their position legitimately: 'You brought off a *coup d'état* in the summer of 1922'. In the pre-election statement of 1932 there is no mention of the North. In 1933, de Valera enunciated the policy of securing 'in this part of Ireland such conditions as will make the people in the other part of Ireland wish to belong to this part'. This is adjudged to be 'a return in substance, though not *in form,* to the position of 1921'. For O'Brien, 'Articles 2 and 3 of *Bunreacht na hÉireann* served the purpose, I believe, not so much of "laying claim to the North" – though unfortunately they looked like that to the North – as of demonstrating the legitimacy of the state ruled over by Mr. de Valera ... who did not resume a crusading posture until he fell from office in 1948 and went on a world tour with Mr. Aiken to arouse the conscience of the world on the matter.'[60] Seán Lemass attempted a policy of rapprochement in the mid-1960s which might have worked were it not for the fact that in 1966 'the ghosts had to walk and the traditional rhetoric had to be heard again'.[61] Having outlined all this, he nonetheless concedes that in practice as distinct from sentiment, Fianna Fáil has proved, at critical moments in our history, the most effective enemy of the IRA.

On the basis of this admission and the inconclusiveness of his judicious extracts, how has Fianna Fáil been irresponsible in the execution of its 'political responsibilities' that gave rise to his 'lingering elusive doubts about the legitimacy of the State'? According to O'Brien it is to be found in the two great 'catches' which Fianna Fáil found itself in around the 1970s. The first is that their political stock-in-trade consisted of a certain *mystique* which is predicated on their original political contribution: 1916, the Anglo-Irish war, the civil war and the whole *coup d'état* ethos. The second catch is that the efficient, yet peaceful, harnessing of this *mystique* depended on the presence of a strong leader, such as de Valera or Lemass. O'Brien went on to say that the Fianna Fáil party of his generation contained no such leader. Even worse, their cadre was filled with those who were chosen on the grounds of their ability to follow. They were not chosen on their ability to discern the difference between what they had been saying, and acting upon what they had said. Thus,

> the new strain of the IRA which developed in 1969 was the product not just of the situation in the North – which could have and should have developed peacefully after 1969 – but *also* of that situation as envisaged and acted upon by that tradition in the Republic which spans Fianna Fáil and the rest of the republican movement, and which saw in that situation the opportunity prophesied by Mr. de Valera for a generation whose hour would be deemed to have struck.[62]

Once again this brings us back to the concern for democracy which was crucial to his writings in this period. In this case a very acute motivation was this fear for the democratic and law-abiding nature of Irish political institutions. For O'Brien this fear that he was living in 'the hour' when the events behind the Arms Trial gave rise to fears that there were elements within Irish society capable of carrying out a very real *coup d'état* and possibly leading to his 'malign scenario of a Greece of the colonels' taking place in Ireland.[63]

In common with many latter-day criticisms of the O'Brien critique, it has to be said that he provided little substance to his charge that there remain 'lingering elusive doubts about the legitimacy of the state itself'.[64] However, while his article 'Shades of Republicans' might fail to convict the Fianna Fáil party of its connection with the violence in the North, it does suggest that in terms of legitimacy and the *Herod* collection there are certain connections. It would seem to implicate (certainly the correct word by his lights) Fianna Fáil and the sizeable proportion of the population which supports them, of maintaining aspects of the republican tradition, that common culture, which they share with the Provisionals. This connection with Provisional IRA thought would be his focus in subsequent years. By linking general nationalist sentiment with Provisional IRA action, and by ceaselessly reiterating its immorality, he created a political reflex in the Republic that remains in the political arena to the present day.[65] Linked to this, he can imply a certain intentionality. When this is allied to the aspiration of unity, he can argue that it is sufficient grounds for unionist's fears.

To recap then, *Herod: Reflections on Political Violence* would seem to offer a flawed but useful interpretation of the situation in Northern Ireland. While the notion of legitimacy is a highly rewarding one, O'Brien's refusal to investigate the absence of legitimacy, his dismissal of institutionalized violence, and the inconsistencies in his account of the Northern Irish situation, greatly reduce its worth. In a sense he recoiled from the implications of translating his radical critique to Ireland. In terms of legitimacy itself, O'Brien would seem to present an unusual case. He argues in the stream of the liberal political philosophers. At the same time he presents criteria for the fulfilment of conditions whereby violence would be legitimate, which are almost Hobbesian in their stringency. While his role in the 1970s has attracted much comment, what seems to have been missed or ignored is that he also fleshed out three spheres within which the nebulous concept of legitimacy operates: institutionalized violence or more generally the conditions of society; the legitimacy of a society being based on history; and the use of the moral interpretation of history in order to de-legitimize a political tradition. This last point seems to be the basis of the revisionist debate. In the end I believe that this account of O'Brien's legitimacy argument not only firmly establishes his centrality to this debate, but also suggests how history came to have such an important role in Ireland's politics. Perhaps the main lesson to be drawn from O'Brien's *Herod* is that, like the majority of the population in the Republic, he was only interested in the North when it created problems down in the South. While this may appear overly flippant, it is the reality of his relationship with the North. The merit of O'Brien is that while he exploded our illusions about Northern Ireland, he, unlike his fellow countrymen, didn't fool himself with any imagined fondness for the place either. With the progress of time the warping effects of his brush with Irish nationalism would disfigure his entire intellectual cosmos. Even the non-Irish world which he had once commented on so luminously would now be twisted through the lens of O'Brien and Irish nationalism.

NOTES

1. Conor Cruise O'Brien, *Herod: Reflections on Political Violence* (London, 1978). The most important chapters are: the 'Introduction', 'A Global Letter', 'Liberty and Terror', 'American Aid to Freedom Fighters' and 'Shades of Republicans'.
2. *Salome and the Wildman* in O'Brien, *Herod* is an example of his flirtation with revolution.
3. He gives no date for its authorship but merely explains that it was 'a late product of the 1960s', *Herod*, p.7. In an interview with David Caute who worked closely with O'Brien at this time, Caute suggested that O'Brien became more radical than he actually was because of his closeness with his students. Author interview with David Caute, Institute for Historical Research, London, September 2005.
4. J.J. Lee, *Ireland: Politics and Society 1912–85* (Cambridge, 1989), pp.1383–4.
5. Tom Paulin, *Ireland and the English Crisis* (Newcastle upon Tyne, 1984), p.24. D.H. Akenson, *Conor: A Biography of Conor Cruise O'Brien* (Montreal, 1994).
6. F.S.L. Lyons, *Ireland since the Famine* (London, 1973); Lee, *Ireland: Politics and Society 1912–1985*; Roy Foster, *Modern Ireland 1600–1972* (London, 1972); Nicholas Mansergh, *The Irish Question 1840–1921* (London, 1965); Oliver MacDonagh, *The Union and its Aftermath* (London, 1977 edn); George Boyce, *Nationalism in Ireland* (London, 1985).
7. Lee, *Ireland: Politics and Society 1912–1985*, p.xiii.
8. Conor Cruise O'Brien, 'Reflections on Terrorism', *New York Review of Books*, 16 September 1976, pp.44–8.
9. Paul Wilkinson, *Terrorism and the Liberal State* (London, 1986), p.5.
10. Ibid., p.11.
11. O'Brien, *Herod*, p.11.
12. Ibid.
13. Ibid., p.10.
14. Ibid., p.12.
15. Ibid., p.11.
16. O'Brien's own term.
17. O'Brien, *Herod*, p.12.
18. Conor Cruise O'Brien, 'Liberty and Terror', The Cyril Foster Lecture delivered at University of Oxford, 6 May 1977.
19. Ibid., p.26.
20. Conor Cruise O'Brien, 'Holy War', *The New York Review of Books*, 6 November 1969. He also refers to a 'system of caste privilege'. His use of the term 'natives' was ironic.
21. Conor Cruise O'Brien, 'A Global Letter', *Forum*, February 1972, p.22.
22. Ibid.
23. O'Brien, *Herod*, p.12.
24. O'Brien, 'Holy War', p. 15.
25. See debate on 'The Legitimacy of Violence as a Political Act' between O'Brien, Noam Chomsky, Hannah Arendt, Robert Silvers and Susan Sontag. This took place in a forum known as the Theatre for Ideas. It was the first of many noted debates. The exchange is reprinted in Alexander Klein (ed.), *Dissent, Power and Confrontation* (New York, 1971).
26. O'Brien, 'Reflections on Terrorism', p.47.
27. O'Brien, 'A Global Letter', p.22.
28. Ibid.
29. Ibid.
30. O'Brien, *Herod*, p.10.
31. O'Brien, 'A Global Letter', p.23.
32. Ibid., p.18.
33. Ibid., p. 21. An explicit example of his growing disenchantment with his earlier radical colleagues is seen in the following: 'It is through such concepts as institutionalised violence that the more antique and atavistic parts of the repertoire of legitimation are themselves legitimised in the minds of, for example, students and ex-students, and of others who would be ashamed to think of themselves as obsessed with the past. And it is through such concepts, and through those who find comfort in them, that our forms of violence come to seem legitimate

internationally, and especially among the international left.'
34. Ibid., p.20.
35. Ibid., p.18.
36. R.G. Collingwood, *The Idea of History* (Oxford, 1993), p.10.
37. O'Brien, 'Reflections on Terrorism', p.43.
38. Ibid., p.44.
39. N. Mansergh, *The Irish Question 1840–1921* (London, 1965), pp.223–4. Mansergh is quoting from Gwynn's biography of Redmond, and offers the view that the bravado was specifically for Redmond's audience. Redmond, he assures us, would never act unconstitutionally. Perhaps not, but from our point of view, all that matters is that Redmond felt it necessary to say it to his audience.
40. D.G. Boyce, *Nationalism in Ireland* (London, 1992), p.289.
41. O'Brien, 'American Aid to Freedom Fighters?', in *Herod*, p.45.
42. Ibid, p.46.
43. Ibid.
44. Ibid., p.48.
45. Ibid., p.47.
46. Ibid.
47. Conor Cruise O'Brien, *States of Ireland* (London, 1972), p.303.
48. O'Brien, 'American Aid to Freedom Fighters?', in *Herod*, p.49.
49. G. FitzGerald, 'The Significance of 1916', *Studies*, 55 (Spring, 1966), p.33. See also Garret FitzGerald, 'Was 1916 Really Necessary?' *Irish Independent*, 22 and 23 February 1967. For a more recent take on a very similar counterfactual see Alvin Jackson, 'British Ireland: What if Home Rule had been Enacted in 1912?' in Niall Ferguson (ed.), Virtual History: Alternatives and Counter-factuals (London, 1997), pp.175–227.
50. O'Brien, 'American Aid to Freedom Fighters?', in *Herod*.
51. Ibid., p.50.
52. Garret Fitzgerald. *Towards a New Ireland* (Dublin, 1972), p.10.
53. O'Brien, 'American Aid to Freedom Fighters?', in *Herod*, p.50.
54. O'Brien, 'Liberty and Terror', in *Herod*, p.32.
55. O'Brien, *Herod*, p.10.
56. O'Brien, 'Senate Address' (Introduction to the Broadcasting Authority (Amendment) Bill, 27 March 1975, Seanad Éireann. Reprinted as 'Broadcasting and Terrorism', in *Herod*, pp.110–28.
57. O'Brien, 'Shades of Republicans', in *Herod*, p.128.
58. O'Brien, 'Senate Address'.
59. Ibid.
60. Ibid.
61. Ibid.
62. Ibid.
63. O'Brien, *States of Ireland*, pp.314–16.
64. O'Brien, 'Shades of Republicans', *The Irish Times*, 17 March 1975, reprinted in *Herod*, pp.128–40.
65. I accept that O'Brien might not actually have 'created' it. The immorality of violence had entered debate many times in the past in Ireland and elsewhere. In the context of the 1970s, O'Brien was the outstanding figure in not merely reintroducing it, but in remorselessly tarring all opponents with it.

12

O'Brien and Nationalism

If we think back to some of the seminal influences on O'Brien – Camus and his atavisms; distaste for O'Faoláin's 'delphic nationalism'; the radical lead of his cousin Owen; the self-satisfied Sheehy family's Catholic nationalism; his father's journeyman liberalism – we can see many heterogeneous elements. It is fair to say that all these complex and opposing parts of O'Brien don't meld together into one worldview. But they do seem to make him politically distinctive, as well as giving him a hard earned course in casting 'a cold eye'. As he said himself in another context:

> I don't, because of my training as a historian I can't, bring myself to believe in Utopias nor in Messianism of any kind.[1]

With regard to the latter part of this book's thematic approach to O'Brien, we can just as justifiably feel dubious as to the possibility of usefully combining all of the elements of O'Brien's thinking – the church and state, the North, the role of history in the South's body politic, and his historical perspective. Yet they are indicative of a political stance acquired through experience of a challenging chapter in Ireland's history. From the late 1970s onwards they solidified into a lasting view. This 'view', O'Brien's position on Ireland, while complex and partial, is nonetheless essential to fully understanding O'Brien. To attempt to forge the main currents in O'Brien's thought with an understanding of nationalism and politics would have to concern itself with four distinct yet connected areas. Firstly, we must attempt to put his view on nationalism into context with a whole series of other writers on this subject, and to ask whether his interpretation possesses validity when compared with these contributions to the study of nationalism. Secondly, we will quickly discover the centrality of religion in O'Brien's formulation of nationalism. While according religion its due space, it is fitting that we also inspect the implications of O'Brien's dismissal of other interpretations, which follows from this focus on religion. Thirdly, drawing on the image and tradition of Burke's political philosophy, and its increasing importance to O'Brien, the possibility of more apposite and logical parallels will be looked at. Finally, we will attempt to probe the very basis of his political conception. The problem of the interaction of an essentially rational manner of thinking, which is principally characterized by an antipathy towards romanticism and religion in an Irish context, will be sketched.

Before we can attempt to evaluate O'Brien's contribution to nationalism we must ensure that we are operating within a relevant and fair framework. It would make little sense to engage O'Brien at the theoretical level if he himself had no interest in this area. In this regard O'Brien seems a little unfortunate. From a certain point of view, the academic one, he will be judged against the backdrop of a wave of monographs which engulfed the subject of nationalism during the past two decades. Yet, the primary difficulty with measuring O'Brien against the increasingly theoretical bent of nationalism is that, to his credit, his work is firmly grounded in actual events. Between the gritty nascence of his reflections on nationalism and the theoretical forays of other more academic contributions on nationalism in recent years, lies a great deal of difference. This is perfectly illustrated by a review of *God Land: Reflections on Religion and Nationalism*,[2] his one purely theoretical contribution on nationalism. The review by one of the foremost thinkers on nationalism in recent times – Ernest Gellner – highlighted this very difficulty in an evaluation of O'Brien. Referring to the generic similarity between O'Brien and Elie Kedourie, 'they both seek the answer in the history of ideas',[3] Gellner reflects that:

> There is, alas, a touch of intellectual autism in O'Brien's thought. Kedourie's name does not appear in the index, and there is no reaction to his ideas. In fact, all participants in what might be called the LSE debate – Kedourie, Minogue, Anthony Smith, Percy Cohen, myself – are ignored. The same fate also befalls others who have made a contribution to this subject, such as Tom Nairn, Eric Hobsbawn, Michael Hechter, Peter Sugar, Benedict Anderson, Karl Deutsch, Walker Connor, Paul Brass, H. Kohn, J. Breuilly, J. Armstrong and others.

Gellner sums up by saying that, 'O'Brien evidently thinks he can crack the nut of nationalism almost unaided'.[4]

Another fundamental difference with these academics is that they are at odds with O'Brien on the question of when nationalism can be said to have been born. O'Brien's précis of *God Land* gives a clear idea that in his view, nationalism is an ancient phenomenon, not a modern one:

> *God Land* is about the mutual historical interactions of religion and nationalism, in the Judaeo-Christian culture especially in Europe and North America. Nationalism and Christianity have been interacting, and often converging, over many centuries, despite the uncompromising efforts of Jesus and the early Christians to separate religion from all attachment to territory.[5]

O'Brien seems happy to confound received academic opinion that nationalism is a distinctly modern phenomenon. The majority view would be that nationalism is a recent phenomenon – a post French Revolution phenomenon. The implications of this 'question' of nationalism's inception is only a partial explanation for O'Brien's 'autism'.

Another point that puts him at odds with the academics is that he uses nationalism in two senses: 'nationalism as doctrine or ideology; and nationalism as a collective emotional force'.[6] It is only towards the end of the historical narrative in *God Land* that O'Brien investigates the birth of what he admits to be 'nationalism as ideology'. 'What happened during the late eighteenth century was the separation of national feeling from religion, the emergence of secular nationalism.'[7] At the centre of this occasion he observes the thought of Rousseau, whose 'great achievement was to "fix" the emotional loyalties formerly associated with religion and now displaced. Rousseau diverted these loyalties toward the nation and exalted it into an absolute, in *The Social Contract*, through the concept of The General Will.'[8]

These views of O'Brien put him at odds with the received opinion in the study of nationalism. However, the academic perspective would do well to give due regard to O'Brien's writings, biased as they may be, if only for the reason that they were crafted at the coalface. Ultimately it is rewarding to look at how he pieced together his particular view on nationalism. If we return to the pivotal role of religion in O'Brien's other works, it will be remembered that there are two aspects to it. One is what could be termed the negative aspect: religion's role in preserving anachronistic attitudes, thereby providing the necessary 'tribal self-righteousness' for the conflict in Northern Ireland. The second aspect could be seen as an aspiration cherished by O'Brien: the removal of religion from politics, and with it the necessary conditions for the conflict. However, as a result of his exclusive focus on religion and the Northern Irish conflict, O'Brien dismissed several other interpretations put forward in an attempt to understand Northern Ireland, such as class-based or post-colonial perspectives. It is appropriate then to look at whether O'Brien has taken sufficient notice of these other interpretations and, if not, what was his reasoning behind their dismissal.

In *States of Ireland* the most significant interpretation, apart from religion, was class. Many of his writings from this time are devoted to refuting the view that class conflict was at the heart of the Troubles. By having to disassociate himself from class-based critiques, O'Brien is moving away from an earlier incarnation, the one that reflected his time spent in New York, where he increasingly was drawn toward a socialist position. Between his return home in 1969 and the publication of *States of Ireland* in 1972, his personal disassociation from socialism grows (ironically, considering he was representing the Labour party) and a strong case is put forward as to why the roots of conflict are not class-based. It should be stressed that this was formed against the backdrop of a zeitgeist that gave class far more credence than it now possesses, especially in student and academic circles. On one particular occasion O'Brien gave a lecture at Queen's College Belfast in the autumn of 1968. Most of the students in his audience saw religion and the existence of two separate communities of Protestants and Catholics as irrelevant. Religion was written off by one student as 'a red herring'. In O'Brien's view, it was a herring the size of a whale.

In attacking a class-based perception of the conflict, O'Brien relied on the findings of Richard Rose.[9] By using Rose's evidence O'Brien manages to show how the notion of class revolution was transformed into a sectarian one. In his view industrial solidarity alone – for him the only genuine aspect of class solidarity – can possibly lead to an improved society. And this will only occur when more favourable conditions exist: when religion and violence do not polarize Northern Irish society. Only when revolution, a supposedly class-based notion, yet in actual fact a sectarian appropriation, is removed can this solidarity occur. O'Brien instanced management and shop-stewards engineering confrontations between 'management and workers' in order to divert attention from the sectarian tensions. This for him demonstrates that in reality the 'false consciousness fabricated here was class consciousness'. Ultimately: 'in politics, in loyalty, in their reaction to different categories of violence, the Protestants of all social classes, react as one community; the Catholics, of all social classes, as another.'[10]

O'Brien's writings sometimes suffer because of the pressures of journalism. But we must also bear in mind that a corollary of this is that he is always trying to reach an audience. Just as his writings concerning legitimacy are largely for political effect in the Republic, so too with *States of Ireland*. It, too, has to be seen with this focus on the Republic as paramount. Conversely this stress on the role of the Republic means that he minimizes the role of England to the point where it could almost be described as incidental. So when he defines the conflict as a religious one he is moved, some might say bizarrely, to dismiss the idea that it is a national quarrel. 'To define it as a national question has arguments in its favour, but will not quite serve. What would the two nations be?'[11] This suggests a lack of sophistication in his appreciation of nationalism. It also highlights the relative youth of the debate on nationalism; when O'Brien began his critique there was only Mansergh's *The Irish Question*. However, even if we take into account the dearth of studies devoted to a formulation of nationalism in general, there can be little excuse for the presumption that it is a religious conflict at bottom and therefore is not a nationalist one. His formula laid out here is in direct contradiction with O'Brien's own latter day interpretations; namely that the conflict, past and present, both in Ireland and elsewhere, is a result of the fusion of religion and nationalism.

The other interpretation that is dismissed as a consequence of the focus on religion is the idea of the North as 'conflict between settlers and natives'.[12] According to O'Brien this is an important part of the truth, if only a part. While acknowledging the accepted part of land, that which they had fought over, he maintains that in its essentials it was a Reformation settlement in Counter-Reformation territory. What kept the conflict alive over the centuries was religion: 'The factor of religion, inseparably intertwined with political allegiance.' Ultimately, on the basis that he has previously described how allegiance is subordinate to religion – Ulster Protestants fought for a King because he was Protestant and to ensure a Protestant succession – we are brought back to 'the rather obvious fact of a conflict between groups defined by religion'.[13]

Before moving on perhaps we could observe the formulation behind what he labels 'settlers and natives'. This is to be found in the *States of Ireland* chapter dealing with colonialism: 'Colonists and Colonised'. O'Brien maintains that the root relation between Protestant and Catholic in Ireland is more complicated than a simple view of settler and native.

> Yet the vegetation sprung from these roots is complex and intertwined. Frantz Fanon's stark, dramatic Manichean contrasts between *le colon* and *le colonisé*, though suggestive, are too simple for the situation, and for most others ... it is relevant to distinguish not just two groups but six.[14]

One could say that if Fanon's contrasts, or dualism, of *le colon* and *le colonisé* are too simple for the various Irish situations, would it not be fair to suggest that his own dualism of 'besieger and besieged' is inadequate as well. We could also say about his 'post-colonial' critique that it is quite original. For instance the segregation of the island's populace into six distinct groupings: pre-colonials; country people of other areas, profoundly affected by Anglicization and modernization; urbanized, middle and lower middle-class; non-Unionist Protestants, Unionist Protestants; and finally the English; is a far more realistic portrayal than other views of the Irish (for example O'Faoláin's 'six branches' adumbrated in *The Irish*.)[15] In presenting this tableau of how Irish people actually viewed themselves, he was anticipating the four similar groups of F.S.L. Lyons in *Culture and Anarchy*.[16] While this is commendably original, it must be added that this insight barely troubled his primary view that Irish nationalism is 'a quarrel defined by religion'.[17] Ultimately he does not allow any insights afforded by the post-colonial critique, or of any other for that matter, to trouble his insistence that it is a religious conflict. It is a fact that outside of 'Ulster Protestants and Irish Catholics' there is no contribution. The 'significant' qualifications, of which he spoke of at the beginning, are mere obeisances to his original insight and formulation.

A further reason why we should be slow to endorse O'Brien's theory of nationalism lies in the manner in which it undergoes mutations.

These are in the nature of additions. Consequently as O'Brien's appreciation of nationalism becomes more sophisticated, more refined and formidable, one is left to wonder at the fact that there is little development. Throughout his subsequent writings nationalism is fuelled by religious passion. This is not just true of Irish nationalism, but, almost inconceivably, of all nationalisms. Thus, just as the Irish preserved their identity, their atavisms, and their rancour, there is a similar if not identical continuity in other nations over the centuries, right up to the present.

Observing, then, the steady refinement of this notion – 'it is a religious quarrel', or 'it is a quarrel defined by religion' – class and post-colonialism figure only as sub-plots, brief incidentals, confusing the participants, and obscuring an appreciation of the essentially religious nature of the quarrel. Other factors such as loyalty or allegiance are, unlike post-colonialism and class, a way of rephrasing the question of religion in terms of how the participants view it. More for negative reasons than positive, the nature of the quarrel is not a national question. It is important to see that political considerations determined this. His rejection of it as a national quarrel on the basis that he cannot isolate two nations seems to highlight the lack of sophistication in his earlier appreciation of nationalism. Unfortunately this was at the time when events were forging his original insight, and ultimately his lasting impression of the questions involved.

Even this refusal to entertain all possibilities without prejudice can to an extent be accepted. It could be maintained that there is no question as to the subjectivity and passionate involvement of his writings. Nor can it be denied that these were traumatic times, for him personally and for the entire island. Bloodshed and death were daily occurences; unkind names, abusive phone calls and intimidating letters were part and parcel of his life as a minister. Nonetheless it is strange that O'Brien feels it is necessary to assert that there is but one cause. Granted he does allow room for qualifications; yet the extent to which these broaden or affect his estimation is slight, and far from the postulated 'significant'. One could also argue against the restrictive categories put forward. In his dismissal of the quarrel as a national question, he asks: 'what would the two nations be?'[18] In response one could ask: Why two? Why, indeed, nations when the rigidity of 'nations' implies he is actually talking about states? Moreover why so clear-cut and categorical? On the basis that a 'factor' fails to supply an entire understanding it is discarded. Thus it is not a question of a quarrel between Ireland and England. While one may agree that this was not a factor around 1972, unquestionably it was previously. It would only seem reasonable to allow all the historical causes of which he was aware to come together and form a broad assessment of the conflict.

One begins to wonder at the disparity between the evinced subtlety of his probings elsewhere, and his procrustean insistences on this question; one with its pertinent nuances, the other apparently naive. When you read O'Brien's writings through the years, both public and private, you discover that he is entirely *au fait* with the full gamut of actual nationalism, recorded nationalism and interpreted nationalism: to take Tone for example – Tone's actions, his diaries, and his legatees. The same could be said for Parnell, Pearse, or de Valera. He realizes that nationalism is a contrary beast: he sees it as both the motive force that underwrote the actions of both Parnellism and the more 'Romantic' nationalism which proceeded from the fall of Parnell. In addition, O'Brien realizes that nationalism can have various manifestations.

Yet when we inspect the various indices of his many books, there is no entry for nationalism until we come to *God Land* in 1988. What does receive an entry in the index of *States of Ireland* is: 'Nationalist, nationalists, passim.'[19] This slant towards nationalists rather than nationalism is significant. What it seems to suggest is that O'Brien, like most of us, sees the world in a certain way. Furthermore this 'certain way' is, if not fundamentally opposed to, at least at variance with, an appreciation of ideology. To put it another way: he appreciates ideology, but will only understand it in human terms. What it seems to boil down to is that when he comes to think about nationalism there is no 'theory': nationalism consists of the deeds of nationalists.

If we turn our attention to his historical accounts, we see that history, and Irish history in particular, is generally about what the various actors did; frequently with the polarities of heroism and villainy. An important element of this is the interpretations of these actors by their heirs, with a surfeit of villainous misinterpretation. It is also interesting that his forays into fiction were all, from *Murderous Angels* to *King Herod Explains*, in drama. It is also instructive that

O'Brien quotes with great approbation the first words of Burke upon learning of the French Revolution: 'what players, what actors?' O'Brien is also fond of Burke's advice to 'Never wholly separate in your mind the merits of any Political question from the Men who are concerned in it'.[20] Burke himself is described as one who had a profound distrust for the abstract. It seems to suggest that at bottom, he found this whole 'nationalism as theory' debate, entirely uncongenial.

This bring us to the third question asked at the beginning: can we discover other interpreters of nationalism who resonate more fairly with O'Brien. There is a danger in ascribing too much influence to the impact of Burke upon the thought of O'Brien, especially as this is a very self-selecting identification. It is nonetheless evident that some harmonization with Burke was underway from the late 1960s. We can detect, in 1968, when O'Brien was just becoming familiar with Burke, areas where O'Brien made Burke's *Reflections* mirror his own situation.[21] This in itself is not terribly informative when we come to try to explain O'Brien's politics, especially as they related to nationalism. Another person who is very much within Burke's tradition, and yet who has the necessary positive political associations, would seem to be the historian Lord Acton. Pivotal in this comparison is the way in which Acton crafts an opinion of nationalism which O'Brien is clearly in accordance with.

The point of this comparison is to illustrate the political hierarchies of the two minds, and the subordinate place of nationalism in those hierarchies. Although Burke and Acton would have been in contradiction with O'Brien on the question of religion, Acton is to an extent the realization of the image of Burke which O'Brien most identifies with: liberal but counter-revolutionary.[22] Thus, if we are trying to place O'Brien, Acton offers an opportunity to do so. This is not to say that their opinions on nationalism are entirely similar. Nonetheless, on substantive issues they are in broad agreement. For instance, there is the fact that they both view nationalism as manifesting itself in the Old Testament. Would the Acton who said: 'In the ancient world idolatry and nationality went together, and the same term is applied in Scripture to both',[23] disagree with O'Brien's thesis in *God Land*?

If a comparison is made between Acton's seminal essay of 1862, 'Nationality', and a distillation of what is known of O'Brien's views on nationalism thus far, we find they are quite similar. For instance, both are written as responses to a particular context. For O'Brien's Northern Ireland, we have Acton's Italy. At another level they both tailor their writings to making sense of a particular context in their century. In short they both bear the stamp of the *journal de combat*, as well as clearly embodying the demands of contemporary history. As can be seen from *God Land*, there are for O'Brien two nationalisms: the emotional and the intellectual variety. Throughout his essay, Acton also refers to nationality as existing prior to what his essay attempts to explain: the innovation of the then 'modern theory of nationality'.[24] For Acton the 'modern theory of nationality' arises as a consequence of the more recent embodiment of a political collision. This is the contest between 'the existing order and the subversive theories that deny its legitimacy'. The impetus for this contest was the partition of Poland. The effect of this partition was to convert a dormant right into an aspiration, and a sentiment into a political claim. Significantly Acton's starting point, Poland, leads to his quoting the similar misgiving of Burke on the issue.

> The old despotic power which made the Poles its prey had two adversaries, the spirit of English liberty, and the doctrines of that revolution which destroyed the French monarchy with its own weapons; and these two contradicted in contrary ways the theory that nations have no collective rights ... The modern theory of nationality arose partly as a legitimate consequence, partly as a reaction against it. As the system which overlooked national division was opposed by liberalism in two forms, the French and the English, so the system which insists upon them proceeds from two distinct sources, and exhibits the character either of 1688 or 1789.

An explanation of 'the modern theory of nationality' follows with Acton explaining how national sentiment did not develop directly from the French Revolution, but first came to be exhibited in opposition to it: 'Napoleon called a new power into existence by attacking nationality in Russia, by delivering it in Italy, by governing in defiance of it in Germany and Spain.' The alliance which defeated Napoleon embodied two forces: absolutist restoration, and the liberals who 'cared for freedom in the shape of French institutions'. The former were perfectly willing to sacrifice the national ideal to the restoration of their dynastic rights. The latter were willing to subordinate the national ideal for the pursuit of French liberalism. Although he uses Mazzini to demonstrate the growth and subsequent strength of nationalism, for Acton, 'Metternich is, next to Napoleon, the chief promoter of this theory; for the anti-national character of the restoration was most distinct in Austria, and it is in opposition to the Austrian Government that nationality grew into a system.'

The object of this exegesis is not to demonstrate the theory itself, but rather to illustrate the compatibility of Acton's interpretation with O'Brien's. Initially it could be observed that they share a certain penchant for Manichean contrasts: 'The theory of nationality there-fore proceeds from both the principles which divide the political world, – from legitimacy, which ignores its claims, and from the revolution which assumes them; and for the same reason it is the chief weapon of the last against the first.' Acton then portrays the two variants of nationalism: in one, the primacy of unity, deriving from absolutism, and resembling the French system; in the other the primacy of national liberty, deriving from freedom, and resembling the English system. Crucially, 'they are connected in name only, and are in reality the opposite extremes of political thought'.

In the absolutist case the nation is seen as the ideal unit, overruling the rights and wishes of the inhabitants. It 'sacrifices their several inclinations and duties to the higher claim of nationality ... for the purpose of vindicating itself'. Acton's 'theory of freedom', can be distinguished from the nationalism of an absolutist character in its tendency towards diversity, and not towards uniformity; to harmony and not to unity; because it aims at careful respect for the existing laws of political life and not at arbitrary change. And finally, because – and this could be taken for Burke's sole theme – 'it obeys the results and laws of history, not the aspirations of an ideal future'. This could also be described as a pithy summation of the reasons for O'Brien's championing of the rationale behind Parnell's technique of power (parliamentary 'combinations': personality and historical 'residues' in the service of gradual change). In addition to this, what it illuminates quite starkly is the thinking behind O'Brien's total rejection of the 'republican tradition'. Dramatic shifts, inorganic political change, politics ruled by an ideology that scorches the earth of what has gone before, are all anathema to Acton's and O'Brien's idea of politics.

The compatibility of Acton and O'Brien is not accidental. This is demonstrated by their common appreciation of the manner in which nationality should operate, as it indicates their shared aspirations. Both would actively subordinate nationalism in their political hierarchies. The question: 'subordinate to what?', is answered by the following extract:

> The coexistence of several nations under the same state is a test, as well as the best security of its freedom. It is also one of the chief instruments of civilisation, and, as such, it is in the natural and providential order, and indicates a state of greater advancement than the national unity which is the ideal of modern liberalism. The combination of different nations in one state is as necessary a condition of civilised life as the combination of men in society.

To those who might ask what glamour there is in O'Brien's attraction to Parnell, if unconvinced by the Parnellian objective of 'peaceful coexistence of the two nations', or the goal of Ireland contributing to Imperial affairs (Parnell as a Cecil Rhodes), would do well to look at the philosophy which is revealed in the excerpt above. Firstly, there is the shared assumption concerning the notion of human progress. Acton's political conception would 'take the establishment of liberty for the realisation of moral duties to be the end of civil society'. With O'Brien we also have a fundamental concern with moral action, which uses, and appeals to, civil thought. One other intellectual thread which ties the two together is the fact that Acton was Gladstone's advisor.[25] The philosophy that O'Brien admired so much in Parnell's politics of the 1880s is inextricably linked to Acton.

Further substantiation can be gleaned from the similarity between his father's basic synopsis of the Irish question and O'Brien's own. In re-publishing Lecky's essay *Clerical Influences*, Francis Cruise O'Brien candidly endorsed the reasoning behind it. The essay maintained that, 'when public opinion is diseased, when there is no national life in a country, sectarianism which languishes when there is a public spirit to absorb it, flourishes unchecked'.[26] The extent to which the primacy of religion is asserted by both father and son is remarkable. What is even more compelling is the extent to which Francis Cruise O'Brien adheres to Lecky's 'spacious principles' that the existence of sectarianism in Ireland is the best recommendation for the establishment of a national government, of a particular character, in Ireland. As Francis Cruise O'Brien, in his joint editorship, put it:

> Instead of Protestant Unionists and Catholic Nationalists, the division of a diseased nation, we shall have the natural and healthy divisions of a nation which is no longer diseased. And in each of these divisions, Conservative and Liberal, Individualist and Socialist, or whatever they may be, we shall find members, not of one religion, but of all religions.[27]

This insistence on something higher, some greater goal, seems to reflect accurately the practical estimate in Acton's theory of nationality: 'The greatest adversary of the rights of nationality is the modern theory of nationality'.[28] It needs to be stated that for some minds the ideal of 'independence' did not represent the ultimate in political ambition. The Cruise O'Briens, even without the insistence on a secular order, appear to be of this genus. An example of this line of thought can be seen most strikingly in a contemporary of Francis Cruise O'Brien, George Bernard Shaw. Ireland, despite his paying it only sporadic interest, was much loved by him. In the second decade of the twentieth century he watched aghast, and with incomprehension, as his native country slid into war with his adopted land. At the time he attempted to get himself into the Irish Convention, and built up a sizeable correspondence with Plunkett on the platform of Federalism. However, in applying his internationalist and social democratic solutions to Ireland he ultimately had to admit that 'he had guessed ahead, and guessed wrongly, whilst stupider and more ignorant fellow-pilgrims guessed rightly'. Ultimately he concluded that: 'I find myself without real influence in Ireland because I am without provincial illusions.'[29] To somehow see the events of the Irish Revolution as 'provincial' brings Shaw and Cruise O'Brien into line with Acton who all share a supposedly higher ideal of Liberalism and secular values. O'Brien too seems to have found himself not fully in chime with his compatriots, not only in having political principles that belong to an older generation, but also in viewing nationalism as something faintly dangerous, and, to an extent, something which appeals only to baser, less evolved, instincts.

Perhaps this can be explained if we look at the role of reason in O'Brien's thinking. 'Reason is spirit when its certainty of being all reality has been raised to truth', is a pithy reflection of Hegel, which is relevant for looking at what is possibly the sole consistency of O'Brien's career.[30] For O'Brien it would appear that nationalism is a concept which is fundamentally irrational. O'Brien continually contrasts the perceived irrationality of nationalism with the character of Parnell's politics: 'his policy, in the time of his power, had been rational and unromantic'. For O'Brien the tragedy of Parnell was that in 'the end, Parnell acted not like the cool and rational leader of men he had been, but like the romantic hero he had been forced to seem'.[31]

Many years later the identical categories of the rational and the irrational re-appear in *States of Ireland*. He talks about a hoped-for future in Ireland where politicians avoid 'the heady wine of the Apocalypse: a politics in which both reason and compassion will be vital components'.[32] In his fears for the future he sees another scenario where Irish politics falls under the sway of 'the appeal of romantic nationalism and the cult of the dead'.[33] Or in another scenario, the country once more falls back on the hatred contained within nationalism: 'the general overtones of a mystic and irrational concept: an imprescriptible and inalienable quality, inherent in Irish nationhood'.[34]

What we might call his Parnellian vision seems to constitute his fundamental politics. It is a constant from both before and after 'the Troubles'. Furthermore, O'Brien's 'choice' – rational man over his irrational possibilities – seems to infuse all areas of interest. In the late 1950s, for example, he chose Tolstoy's common sense over Dostoyevsky's mysticism. While this in itself may be unremarkable, it is the extent to which he willingly maps utterly opposed ways of thinking onto the larger world that merits notice. He sees the mysticism of Dostoyevsky as a manifestation of his basically irrational manner of conceiving the world:

> the mystical chauvinism of Dostoyevsky, with its nonsense about territorial expansion, as part of 'the Christ-bearing mission of the Russian people.' Mystical chauvinism – extreme nationalism, combined with the inefficiency that flows from a superstitious contempt for reason – led logically to war, defeat in war, and the consequences of defeat: the Japanese war and the Revolution of 1905, the World War and the Revolution of 1917.[35]

Elsewhere, as if blame for both 'the World War and the Revolution of 1917' was insufficient, O'Brien opines: 'the Nuremberg rallies can, not less fairly, be traced back to the chauvinism and irrationalism of Dostoyevsky'.[36]

In exploring these absolute consistencies in O'Brien, I am not attempting to assert that rationalism is either good or bad, and irrationalism it's opposite. To be rational can of course be liberating, as in the case of, for example, Marcus Aurelius's *Meditations*, where a personally liberating philosophy is built up around rational man. There is another sense in which it can be restrictive. While this is mere opinion, there is possibly some truth in the notion that the splendour of various ideas cannot be grasped, as there is no imagination to intoxicate or behold it. Crucially, it is the irritation and incompatibility of 'one cure for many and special evils', Acton's speculation as to why nationalism attracts, which is distasteful to that mind which thrives on what is practicable, sequential and logical. And that certainly includes O'Brien's mind.

A profound antipathy to the irrational can be observed in O'Brien's reading of Sophocles's *Antigone*, which appeared in the *Listener* of November 1968; in addition a significant abstract was carried in *States of Ireland* some four years later. O'Brien's reading of *Antigone* reflects the coolly rational and unsentimental view of the North that separated him from his compatriots. 'The disabilities of Catholics in Northern Ireland are real, but not overwhelmingly oppressive: Is their removal really worth attaining at the risk of precipitating riots, explosions, pogroms, murder?'[37] It is in his dealing with Antigone, that the true importance of this excerpt is revealed. What is important here is that his view of *Antigone* formed the framework for his discussion of the Civil Rights Movement whose actions parallel Antigone's original behaviour. Antigone broke the law because she considered it contrary to a higher law. However for O'Brien Antigone's non-violent action either attracted or led to violence: Antigone's own death, the death of her betrothed, Haemon, and the suicide of Eurydice, Haemon's mother.

George Steiner, a colleague of O'Brien's in his Schweitzer programme in New York University, has given a highly resourceful interpretation of the meanings of *Antigone*. Steiner's 'Antigones' pursues the notion of variable interpretations, be they political, religious or emotional. Steiner asserts that the many differing readings of *Antigone* through the centuries demonstrates the centrality of each author's particular reading of *Antigone* to their own political core. For

Steiner, Hegel's reading of *Antigone*, to take one example, re-evaluates the role of Creon, and thereby the state. In adjudging neither wrong – Creon and Antigone are seen as 'the two highest moral powers'[38] – Hegel would seem to reveal his innate sympathy for the state. In addition, this reading reflects his famous theory of historical development, the dialectic. Kierkegaard's reading of *Antigone* highlights a sense of infinite sorrow, which reflects the primacy of this feeling within Kierkegaard himself. Or there is Anouilh's famous staging in wartime Paris, which reflects the contemporary equivocation of occupied France: pride and complicity. Brecht's *Antigone 48*, is possibly the best known of recent interpretations. It is certainly the most anti-fascist and unequivocally anti-capitalist of any interpretation, to the point where the distortions make it almost unrecognizable. Would anyone, however, suggest that its politics do not accurately reflect Brecht's own?

Steiner proceeds to suggest how the validity of all such readings (from one play!) can be reconciled. Just as people will continue to return to Sophocles to resolve the fundamental questions posed by him, *Antigone* shall continue to hold up its mirror to the foremost preoccupations of its readers. In O'Brien's case his adaptation of *Antigone* to the Northern Ireland of 1968 would, to put it simply, attempt to remove an aspect of our nature from the political mix:

> We should be safer without that troublemaker from Thebes. And that which would be lost, if she could be eliminated, is quite intangible: no more, perhaps, than a way of imagining and dramatising man's dignity. It is true that this way may express the essence of what man's dignity actually is. In losing it man may gain peace at the price of his soul.[39]

It should be stressed that this is not about the removal of a player from the stage, or a simple re-scripting of Sophocles. This is about the exorcism of what O'Brien, a few sentences previously, referred to as 'an element in our being'.[40] For O'Brien 'this way may express the essence of what man's dignity actually is. In losing it he may gain peace at the price of his soul.'

This would tend to suggest that he will be fundamentally at odds with the majority of his audience. Antigone's role has always proven the more attractive. The rebel who will not heed anyone has always proved more popular than Creon, the unglamorous and irascible hand at the helm of the state. For example, Hegel had to assert that Creon was not wrong, that he *too* was a moral power. If anything, this trait becomes stronger in O'Brien. His critique is hardened by the events which forced this 'choice' and by the fact that conditions not only continued, but worsened, throughout the 1970s. As the radius of effect from 'the Troubles' extended further south, moving closer to the foundations of the state which he represented, the obsession with justifiable action, moral onus, and thus legitimacy, asserts itself increasingly.

The Arms Trial and 'the Provisional offensive' violate what is central to O'Brien. All subsequent writings, content and objective, are definitely shaped by these events. We could then view O'Brien's critique of the Republic starting from the point when he wrote:

> It should not be forgotten that from the deployment of the troops in August 1969 up to June 1970 things were fairly quiet, at least on the surface, in and around the North. In May 1970 came the crisis in the Lynch cabinet and the dismissal or forced resignation of four of his ministers. In the following month, the most serious troubles since the previous August erupted, and the level of violence has risen fairly steadily since then.[41]

These events in particular invalidate previous interpretations. They are then taken as *the* cause. Consequently it is not just the political leadership of the Republic, but the nationalism which sustains it, that then becomes the subject of all his criticisms.

It has always been difficult to portray an accurate yet instructive parallel to O'Brien. The ones cited are partial, and those who embody certain aspects of O'Brien seem also to contain stunning contradictions. Strangely, *Antigone* again provides vital answers, for if O'Brien reflects anyone it is the figure of Haemon. As the rational politic son of Creon, he supports his father unquestioningly, to a point. In contrast to his father's increasingly tyrannical actions, Haemon's is the soothing voice of reason, educating and patiently illuminating as he argues. Beyond that point, however, he commits a volte-face, partially in anger, partially for love. Ultimately he falls on his own sword, having attempted to run his father through. In applying this parallel to O'Brien and Ireland, it is interesting that Haemon is initially motivated by duty, which is in a way fascinating when we think back to O'Brien's anti-partition activities of the 1950s. Much like O'Brien's own tightly buttoned nationalism, Haemon's passionate weeping upon the body of Antigone is the sole revelation of his love for her which had previously been hidden. *Antigone* would seem to suggest that O'Brien is one of those particular characters who can straddle the contradiction between Haemon's opening words:

> Father, I'm your son, ... you in your wisdom
> Set my bearings for me – I obey you.

and Haemon's final lines:

> Rage your heart out, rage with friends
> who can stand the sight of you.[42]

But to return to the original point, perhaps the implications of O'Brien's removal of Antigone – an element of our being – are not immediately clear. It is interesting to reflect on the various possibilities of what the play represents: what questions do the interaction of Antigone and Creon point to? The most salient consideration has to do with the rights of the private as opposed to the rights of the public. Here, then, we must resolve the demands of the state and its call for powers by which to protect itself, as against the integrity of the private imperative. As his Broadcasting Amendment Act of 1975 and the notorious Section 31 demonstrates, this is a clear implication of the choice to eliminate Antigone. But O'Brien's rationalization against Antigone also points to an impulse to subordinate the private conscience, albeit one publicly expressed. The drive to censor artistic and political expression in the mid to late 1970s (which O'Brien is synonymous with) can, as he argued at the time, be necessary to protect civil values. However, if it goes unchecked – if there is no Antigone to disobey Creon – it can also, as many people at the time feared, lead to a decline in civil society. O'Brien, as Christopher Hitchens pointed out in the 1980s,[43] began to think himself into Creon's position – and in doing so he became blind to the past charms and even the necessity of Antigone. We can see this in his earliest reading of *Antigone* in 1968 when he said very simply that, 'we should be safer without that troublemaker from Thebes'. This strong aversion to political upheaval was his initial instinct. Everything else – increasing conservatism, identification with Northern Protestants and an intemperate critique – fell into place with the worsening political conditions brought about by the initial spill over of the conflict into the South's political system.

O'Brien's reading of *Antigone* can also be seen as a struggle between young and old. As Steiner asks: what rights does Creon possess simply because he personifies authority; what rights does the purity of thought, symbolized in the virginal Antigone, possess? Perhaps more relevant in an Irish historical situation is the notion that *Antigone* poses basic and testing questions in regard to which generation O'Brien represents: the pre-1916 one or the post-1966 one? Certainly when forced to chose between 'the seventies will be socialist' and the reformist instincts of Acton, Lecky and his own father, one cannot help but think that O'Brien was right when he cried out in anguish as a young student that he was 'born too late'.

The final question mark hanging over him – this notion of a conversion – when seen through the lens of *Antigone* makes any charge that he travelled a short line from the left to the right more complex than it at first seems. Creon is self-evidently an anti-revolutionary force, and thus essentially conservative. O'Brien in removing Antigone would therefore seem to favour this tendency. But this decision took place in 1968 when he was still teaching in New York, scene of his anti-Vietnam and pro-Civil Rights agitation. However, when we analyze what Antigone actually represents, the left to right portrayal seems invalid. Is Antigone not the embodiment of tradition, familial rites and bonds; the striking assertion of ancestral piety, the primacy of ties of blood, and generational succession? These practices could be described as conservative. O'Brien, in removing her, would definitely establish his antipathy to them, the impulse they represent and the manner in which they asserted themselves in 1968 and after. This would seem to suggest a deeply rooted anti-conservatism. When we contrast his simultaneous support for divorce, contraception and greater secularization with his authorship of the inarguably illiberal Broadcasting Amendment Act, it would seem to render any categorization along this axis untenable. What it indicates is that this mess of contradictions can only be resolved if we keep the impulse to remove Antigone in focus. If we lose sight of this, the primacy of legitimacy, order and stability, we lose sight of O'Brien.

NOTES

1. 'Interview with CCOB'. J.S. O'Kelly, University of Kent, Summer, 1970.
2. O'Brien's main attempt to formulate a theory of nationalism, see *God Land. Reflections on Religion and Nationalism* (London, 1988).
3. E. Gellner, *Encounters with Nationalism* (Oxford, 1994), p.60.

4. Ibid., p.61.
5. Conor Cruise O'Brien, *Ancestral Voices* (Dublin, 1994), p.1.
6. O'Brien, *God Land*, p.1.
7. Ibid., p.50.
8. Ibid.
9. Richard Rose, *Governing Without Consensus: an Irish Perspective* (London, 1971).
10. Conor Cruise O'Brien, *States of Ireland* (London, 1972), p.307.
11. Ibid., p.305. It must also be said that this contradicts his 'Introducing Ireland', in Owen Dudley Edwards (ed.), *Conor Cruise O'Brien Introduces Ireland* (London, 1969).
12. O'Brien, *States of Ireland*, p.307.
13. Ibid.
14. Ibid., p.72.
15. S. O'Faoláin, *The Irish* (Harmondsworth, 1980).
16. F.S.L. Lyons, *Culture and Anarchy in Ireland, 1880–1939* (Oxford, 1980).
17. O'Brien, *States of Ireland*, p.307.
18. Ibid., p.305.
19. Ibid., p.333. Admittedly, this is after the fashion of indices of the time, and contrary to our present expectation of a concordance of sorts.
20. Quoted in Conor Cruise O'Brien, 'Introduction', in Edmund Burke, *Reflections on the Revolution in France* (Indianapolis, 1987), p.15.
21. Edmund Burke, *Reflections on the Revolution in France and on the proceedings in Certain Societies in London relative to the Event* (London, 1968). 'Introduction' and 'Edmund Burke: a Biographical Note', pp.7–81 by Conor Cruise O'Brien.
22. Phillipe Raynaud's 'A la fois liberale et contre-revolutionnaire' is, for O'Brien, 'the best succint definition of Burke's position on the French Revolution'. See Conor Cruise O'Brien, *The Great Melody* (London, 1992), p.596.
23. Lord Acton, 'Nationality', in W.H. McNeill (ed.), *Essays in the Liberal Interpretation of History* (Chicago, 1967) p.151. Subsequent references are from this same essay, pp.137–57.
24. This parallel apart, in terms of the details they are quite dissimilar. O'Brien glosses the various manifestations throughout the years, from both sides of the Judaeo-Hellenic tradition: Pericles, The Book of Genesis, St. Augustine, Dante, Machiavelli, The Crusades and the Puritans. Acton concerns himself with an elaborate causal theory, characterized by the persistent clash between Teuton and Latin.
25. Acton, 'Nationality', pp.156–7: 'The parliamentary system, ... in those countries in which different races dwell together, has not satisfied their desires ... It brings out more clearly than before the differences it does not recognise, and thus continues the work of the old absolutism in those countries, therefore, the power of the Imperial parliament must be limited as jealously as the power of the crown, and many of its functions must be discharged by provincial diets, and a descending series of local authorities.' Is there not some relevance here for the development of Home Rule?
26. Francis Cruise O'Brien, 'Introduction', in W. E.H. Lecky, *Clerical Influences: An Essay on Irish Sectarianism and English Government* (Dublin, 1911), p.6.
27. Ibid., p.12.
28. Acton, 'Nationality', p.157.
29. Quoted in G. Griffith, *Socialism and Superior Brains: the Political Thought of Bernard Shaw* (London, 1995), p.211. My emphasis.
30. Georg Wilhelm Friedrich Hegel, *Phenomenology of Spirit* (1998), p.438.
31. Conor Cruise O'Brien, *Parnell and his Party, 1880–90* (Oxford, 1957), p.351.
32. O'Brien, *States of Ireland*, p.325.
33. Ibid., p.324.
34. Ibid., p.319.
35. Conor Cruise O'Brien, *Writers and Politics* (London, 1965), p.148.
36. Ibid.
37. O'Brien, *States of Ireland*, p.158.
38. Sophocles, *Antigone*, in *The Three Theban Plays*, trans. by R. Fagles, edited by B. Knox (Harmondsworth, 1982), p.41.

39. O'Brien, *States of Ireland*, p.158.
40. Ibid.
41. In Conor Cruise O'Brien, 'Ireland: The Smell of Civil War', *The Observer*, 12 September 1971.
42. Sophocles, *Antigone*, p.93.
43. See Christopher Hitchens, 'Creon's Think Tank', in *Prepared for the Worst* (London, 1988).

13

Conclusion: 'Our Greatness with our Violence?'

When we attempt an estimate of O'Brien, we are likely to ask 'what is most important?' The fact that the man's life encompassed so many fields of thought raises a problem. Attempting to try to cover all of these facets of his wide personal experience can itself obscure a mind which might possess a natural simplicity. The riddle of O'Brien might be easily answered. That at least was the view of Isaiah Berlin when he wrote to O'Brien to tell him: 'though I may not be all that difficult to penetrate, I am not, I think, one of nature's more mysterious or complicated or unfathomable creatures, and don't terribly want to be – but neither, I am happy to say – are you.'[1] Locating that simplicity is the hard part.

We would first of all have to acknowledge that O'Brien's life does contain many complicated, even contradictory, aspects. If we recall the various influences on his life we see that there are areas of it that remain enigmatic. The influence of O'Brien's family demonstrates that regardless of the role of ideas, writers, historians and other intellectuals, he was irreducibly the son of Kathleen and Francis Cruise O'Brien – their perfect mélange. Most of what came after was just a way of sorting out the main concerns deriving from the legacy of his upbringing. It is important to understand with O'Brien that his views, his feelings and political inclinations did not suddenly come to the fore with *To Katanga and Back*. The moulding effect of the milieu he grew up in, allied to his evidently luminous intellectual gifts, his keen political interests and his wayward yet self-involved personality, all can be seen in his early articles and correspondence.[2] O'Brien, one way or another, introduced his own perspective and concerns either by conjecturing his thoughts onto his subjects, as in his essay on 'The parnellism of Seán O'Faoláin', or simply by exploring his family's past through the Trojan horse of his doctorate on Parnell. Likewise his volubility and his love of an argument can be seen in his column for *The Irish Times* as a student in Trinity, or most clearly in his first address to the Labour Party conference which was incendiary enough to ensure that he would not grace that particular stage for another thirty years.[3]

The influences upon the early O'Brien are themselves both complementary and contradictory. If we look at the influence of his father, we can determine the seeds of his aspirations for a secular society. We can also see a certain distance from ordinary thinking. O'Brien would always stand out from 'the plain people of Ireland' with his strange accent and diction, his education, love of theatre and poetry and exalted speech, as well as his comfort in the clubs, capitals and campuses of the world, even when they lay behind enemy lines. A classic example of this is when his own embassy was furiously trying to locate him in New York. When he was ultimately found it was in the bowels of a British embassy bash. That O'Brien could sup with the British, while excoriating their foreign policy in Africa, is what charms and infuriates fan and foe alike. What Countess Markievicz said of his own father – 'thought to be trying to be in with all sides in politics'[4] – could just as easily apply to O'Brien. Conversely the contrarian aspect of him is that he refused to fit in for too long and refused to lay down with any one party or tribe.

In the case of Owen Sheehy Skeffington's influence, there is no doubt his intellectual coding lies deep within O'Brien. Skeffington, as we saw, was raised to view 1916 and its republican promise as the 'revolution that missed'. Arising from this we can see where O'Brien derived his keenly felt views on foreign policy and specifically the independent stance at the UN which he was a key figure in designing and delivering. Another part of the Sheehy Skeffington heritage is the one he imbued from his Aunt Hanna, who was for a time a key contributor to *An Phoblacht*. If nothing else it explains the nationalist element in his genes and a facility for anti-partitionist propaganda that came all too easily to him. Paradoxically again, it led him into a keen perception of the fatuities of the State's aspirations, not to mention the yawning gap between its rhetoric and political reality. Maybe his awareness of this from an early age might have led to his early acceptance of partition which, as we can see from correspondence in the Department of External Affairs, O'Brien had come to accept by the mid-1950s.

When Francis Cruise O'Brien's and Owen Sheehy Skeffington's roles are commingled with the Sheehy inheritance – the prestige of a noted political clan that is tainted by the perceived betrayal of Parnell as well as the Irish Parliamentary Party's fall – an interesting tension arises. That the personal situation of his immediate family suffered in the new regime heightens the tension further. When that newly founded state distanced itself more from its republican ideals as well as remaining confessional (some would say increased its confessionalism), the tension mounts further. If it cannot be described as too much to bear, it certainly would be enough to deflect a man from a straightforward path.

Other intellectual influences deserve mention too. Burke is perhaps the most obvious 'mentor' in his political development, but because this influence arises so late, and because it contradicts earlier and more seminal influences, it is a role which should be approached warily. On the other hand O'Brien's dependence on Camus is clear. Without Camus, we would be dealing with an entirely different O'Brien. This makes the absence of any recent treatments of Camus by O'Brien more striking. Nonetheless a strong case could be made that it was O'Brien's discovery of Burke in 1967–68 which led to the 'more organic, more conservative' view of Camus.[5]

O'Brien's writings on the core subjects that he has focused on – what was important to him when he was most important – might be termed his practical philosophy. These contain three distinct yet competitive areas. When we reflect on *The Siege* we can see what was, for some, O'Brien's great service. To quote Seamus Heaney:

> It created some sort of clarity in Southerners' thinking about the Protestant community in the North. And it is not enough for people to simply say 'Ah they're all Irishmen', when some Northerners actually spit at the word Irishmen. There is in O'Brien a kind of obstinate insistence on facing up to this kind of reality, which I think is his contribution.[6]

As valuable as this contribution undoubtedly was, it also signalled the beginning of his unbalanced critique: a critique which looked at only one part of the situation, and which was antagonistic to Irish nationalism. Again it is well to reiterate that his writings are audience-centred. His criticisms of the North come to the fore when he was addressing lectures up there which could be every bit as critical of their ways and received wisdom as he famously was of Southern political mores. However, that should not deflect from the fact that he was primarily alarmed by what happened where he lived and grew up. To those who would chide him for being overly critical of his compatriots, he would doubtless respond that 'peace begins at home'.[7]

More so than trying to instil respect for Northern Protestant aspirations, legitimacy and a preoccupation with religion occupy his true political centre. There doesn't seem to be any difference in importance between the two, just in origin and audience. Religion seems to derive from others, and is more personally important. Legitimacy, on the other hand, was written for others. It is where we can see O'Brien at his civic-minded best. O'Brien's concern with legitimacy sought to deny the validity of violence, and in this respect it has perhaps had an even greater effect on the Irish *mentalité* than 'the siege'. The result has been historical revisionism. This in turn has led to a whole re-ordering of Irish political notions with regard to the Republic's political inheritance. Allied to this it has led to a change in the Republic's political action in the present. It has led to a restraint of expression that argues that the stability of the state and the pursuit of unity are inimical. By positing a nexus between the evil of violence and the nationalism of so many people in Ireland, it argues that the general population subscribe to a form of politics which is immoral.

The effect of his more personal feelings about religion is every bit as political as legitimacy. His position on religion and Ireland was present from the beginning. If we return to his first book, *Maria Cross*, we can see how enduring O'Brien's perception of Ireland is.

> In Mr. O'Faoláin's work we see the pattern again, showing its versatility in abstraction and elaboration. His heroes … are nailed to an ambiguous but definitely maternal cross. The characteristic divided feelings towards the dominant mother polarise in two unreliably distinct figures: Mother Church, who is to be for a time at least rejected, and Mother Ireland who is loved. It is, of course, Mother Ireland who catches the hero, when he turns to living women; the tragedy is that she, the elemental, the kind, the permissive, turns back into the other aspect of the mother, the stern and intransigent church. The characteristic result … is suicide … The escape was an illusion, the nails are the reality. The mother was the same mother all along.[8]

This one constant in his political imagination – the insight of the teenage O'Brien appears in all the works, from *Ancestral Voices* to *God Land*, through *Herod* and *States of Ireland*, *Maria Cross* and the earliest essay on Seán O'Faoláin – must surely raise doubts about his judgement. He possesses undoubted intellect and several lifetimes' experiences, and yet somehow we have an internal voice that says the same thing over and over again.

Maybe how he says *it* alerts us to a possible mask which obscures the real O'Brien. Throughout his writings there is a need to be distinctive. There is also the persistent strain where he can be seen to move on from the ground where he once was welcomed or found allies. He can be claimed by no one camp. In his attempts to carve out a space between two groups who are as happy to remain within as he must stay outside, he leads some commentators to view him as objective. This is misleading. Again it seems more of an extension of his temperament, a path-cutting exercise, which he has referred to on one occasion as 'the Freedom to Displease'.[9]

This ability to polarize opinion was never confined to Ireland. After his stint in Katanga he found that even though most were critical of his management of the affair, certain sections of the media looked upon him with favour. Since then he has had a nose for stances which, if they annoyed most, nonetheless, appealed to some. And it is a similar series of animosities and kinships which have been a feature of his career. Examples of this would be his Section 31 contribution and his subsequent post as Editor-in-Chief of *The Observer*, his Zionist writings, his breaking of the intellectual ban on South Africa, and his more recent offerings on Jefferson. It is generally concluded of O'Brien and his brush with Irish national pieties that it has been an education for the Irish nation. If his labours have been effective, we might wonder if this has been so because of his method of consistently 'upping' the dosage of his 'electric shocks' to the national psyche, or has O'Brien been effective primarily because of the nature of Ireland. Reflecting on his contribution to other countries, we might observe that 'God Land' still animates a good deal of American politics and the Israel-Palestine question still rages on.

Viewing the question of effectiveness through exacerbation, demonstrably the method of O'Brien in the last twenty years, we might ask whether this is a plan of his own creation, or whether it is an example of a writer who is a creature of his temperament? O'Brien could be correct in his conjecture that the greatest response to his writings would come if they included warnings which a reader could hardly avoid. Examples of this would be his tendency to mention apocalypses, holocausts, disasters and in general a doom-ridden prevision which coloured all his writings. This could be seen as a decision to provoke serious thought in his readers by reminding people of what they have to lose. It could be seen as the same rationale behind his focus on legitimacy: bring the consequences of the Northern conflict home to his readers in terms of their well-being, and the dangers to their civil order and security. That it is an example of his temperament more than an appreciation of the situation is hinted at by a rare example of O'Brien on O'Brien from his first book: 'Some things in the book surprised me when I re-read it. Did I really compare, however guardedly, Evelyn Waugh with Proust? And what are those apocalyptic passages doing here and there, those flashes of certainty about the future, those moments of elegant pessimism?'[10]

The 'apocalyptic passages', which were there from the beginning – even in his college diary – are scattered throughout almost all his other works. What could be labelled a general concern for the public is no such thing. This fearful prevision, regardless of the situation, be it Europe after the war, Ireland since the 1960s, or the world at the millennium, is another example of his temperament. This suggests that his judgement operates regardless of fact, situation or context, and therefore is not judgement at all.

Just as there are problems with what O'Brien is saying, there are many more with how he has been heard. There are many who admire O'Brien; there are many who do not. Most take issue with some aspects of his work, while many grant that he performed a valuable public service in the 1970s. Many are not prepared to follow him on the basis of his subsequent writings. Others would go along with most of what he has written. They would argue that there is nothing wrong with his writings, but that his political position is to an extent an eccentricity. Others perceive the fallacy of this last point of view. They realize that his position as a unionist is a consequence of his thought and writings. They are therefore unsure of where they themselves stand. If they accept his tenets they are left in a quandary. Do they follow? What holds them back? If they were as thorough as O'Brien, they should; but they don't. Why? Possibly more unsettling is the fact that having failed to proceed, to join him as it were, they have not retreated. Again why? The implications of O'Brien's conversion, or challenge, are shirked.

There is something right and something wrong in this situation. It is right because the thoughts which push O'Brien are personal, and derive from circumstances which he found himself in. They are the voices of his past which he chooses to heed. Others hear no such voices. Their personal histories are quite different. The circumstances of their lives are not filled with so complex a heritage. Nor have private voice and public deed lived in such splendidly vivid proximity, and nowhere is there more fidelity between their exchanges. Even if the perception of another's private voice is largely indeterminable, it would appear that there are many voices within O'Brien which beg for attention. Over the course of a life, some wax, some wane, and in his later years some come to the fore in a trenchant way to occlude others that were urgent and arresting in youth. This book can in retrospect be seen as an exercise in highlighting O'Brien's many voices.

Returning to the phenomenon of people who have different histories to O'Brien's endorsing his writings, it could be said that it is wrong because it speaks of a sheep-like mentality. It is indicative of something which O'Brien saw in the national psyche, and something which he abhorred. This mentality is the very same thing which he saw in the general acceptance of bilingual signposts and articles two and three, while refusing the logical requirements of what their aspirations demanded. It is what O'Brien decried in the population's criticisms of partition, the unionist community, and the Stormont executive. In short what he identified as 'the whole nationalist thinking'. The manner in which the O'Brien critique has been accepted is the same phenomenon as the flock's fidelity to the hierarchy's procrustean grasp and tutelage of Catholicism, which O'Brien castigated: 'In preferring authoritarian methods – "condemn", "excommunicate" – to open, rational, public discussion as a means of turning people away from violence.'[11] While many would point out that O'Brien has exercised his criticisms rationally and with civility and decorum, others would disagree. They would point to his view that, 'if you're not with me, you're against me'. More significantly, all those with opposing views – say those who want unity, or are republican in their outlook – are seen as aggressive to

Protestants, living in a violent past, or more generally, Provo sympathizers. It is a defeat for his own criticisms of the church when he himself operated in very much the same authoritarian manner as the Catholic Church.

The persistent reference in these pages to O'Brien's temperament might strike some as ill-considered. What, after all, are we accustomed to hearing both from and about O'Brien? Repeatedly it is stated that O'Brien is essentially a rational being. His critiques of Irish society are as logical as the complex of national feelings which he attacks is illogical. This study is no different. The previous chapter argued that the basic political conceptions with which he identified appealed to him because they were essentially rational: thus secularism, Parnellism, Legitimacy, Creon, and so forth. Why, then, this focus on temperament? Why does temperament appear at all when dealing with O'Brien?

The answer can be found if we revisit a typical O'Brien statement on Irish nationalism. Speaking of the effect of 1916 and Pearse's legacy, O'Brien points out that a rational person is at a disadvantage when dealing with the problems that history has bequeathed the Republic:

> The system I have described is inherently proof against reasoned argument, but its proponents can themselves effectively refute arguments which claim to derive from, or be consistent with, the non-rational assumptions from which the IRA itself derives its mystique and continuity.[12]

Here he is pointing to the problem that 1916 feeds both the legitimately constituted authority of the Republic and the IRA: a significant intellectual contribution on his behalf. The question that needs asking is: what is a 'non-rational assumption'? From a perusal of O'Brien's writings we could instance quite a few of what he would view as 'non-rational assumptions'. Mysticism, blood-sacrifice, atavisms, and chauvinism spring to mind. But what are these in themselves? Is mysticism not a form of religion? Is blood-sacrifice not a method? Are atavisms not shared history? Is chauvinism nothing but a perspective? Are these not aspects of nationalism? And is nationalism nothing but an ideology, or even a feeling, of how to best attain certain goals? One may disagree with this. It is nonetheless a rational question.

Now, let us ask ourselves another question: what are the rational assumptions of O'Brien? Secularism is one, as is agnosticism. Legitimacy would seem to be another. If we examine agnosticism or secularism, we might ask how he arrives at these? From what do they derive? They would seem to arise from his education. It could also be said that they derive from his father and his cousin, or indeed his entire upbringing. What are secularism and agnosticism in themselves? Are they inherently deducible from a condition of the world? Perhaps they are, but many would say they are not. What they do seem to be is a connected understanding of how to order things which are of this world, and an attitude for dealing with a very large part of that world: religion. But where do these come from? A short answer is that it is an outlook which is determined by an insistence on material phenomena, and a rejection of belief or faith. Yet these in themselves are nothing but a perspective and a stance. Of his agnosticism could we not say that this is merely a belief in non-belief? Furthermore, in that his agnosticism and secularism derive from the intellectual and emotional milieu of his upbringing, could we not say that his fidelity to the humanist tradition and his pride in his father's Burkean echo, is in many ways an atavism?

What of legitimacy? This is a rationale for the maintenance of social order. But would O'Brien always accept that the social order is legitimate if it were, say, confessional? And are O'Brien's writings on Ireland nothing but a challenge to the legitimacy of the *character* of the Irish Republic's order. And if these writings succeed in this, do they not undermine that state's legitimacy? Is it not reasonable to suggest that if legitimacy is the highest value, then it is irresponsible to demand it be upheld for one politics, and that it be altered for another?

What of O'Brien's Zionism? What is the rational assumption which underlies this? Is there something inherently rational about the Israeli state and its ideology, which is altogether lacking in the Palestinian or Arab world? What of O'Brien's unionism? Wherein lies the rational premise in this mentality, which is absent from any other nationalism. His writings tell of the fondness O'Brien has always had for minorities, which from his own upbringing arises from an identification with these groups. Fondness? Upbringing? Groups? Identification? How are these rational assumptions? They are not. Nonetheless they are normal, natural and necessary.

Leaving this, let us reflect on the decision to reject that which Antigone represents.

We should be safer without the troublemaker from Thebes. And that which would be lost, if she could be eliminated, is quite intangible: no more perhaps, than a way of imagining and dramatising man's dignity. It is true that this way may express the essence of what man's dignity actually is. In losing it, man may gain peace at the price of his soul.[13]

Is there not something inherently contradictory about this when we view it in relation to O'Brien's own associations? What are Israel and the Ulster Unionists without their rights, values and history? That which would be lost, if these could be eliminated, is more than a way of imagining and dramatizing their dignity. That which would be lost is even more than their understanding of how they came to be, and how to carry on their existence. It is the very reason for their existence as they conceive themselves. Is there not something unreal about this formulation? How else are we to establish human dignity if we remove what our whole experience tells us is dignified? Why should the nationalism of one group be defended, and the nationalism of another be denied?

This book, an inspection of O'Brien's life, his inheritance and associations confirms all of this. In the end it appears that it is not a question of rational and non-rational assumptions, but, as with all reason, a question of assumptions or premises. O'Brien's writings testify that in the case of the IRA he once saw them as 'brave, logical young men'.[14] The ultimate paradox is that with O'Brien and the IRA it seems we are dealing with essentially the same creatures. On the one hand you have the IRA's Pearsean premise, and on the other hand you have O'Brien's Parnellian premise. In the end both are taken to extremes. The result is what O'Brien aptly termed 'A mess of crazy premises'.[15]

To return to O'Brien and Ireland, we can conclude that this inherent tension between his personal belief and the public's belief seems to be the basis of the O'Brien critique. In the end it boils down to a question of premises. That is to say that neither are wrong, they are just antagonistic. O'Brien himself once saw this with utter clarity:

> What can we do? It is up to us to try to reverse some of the damage that we have done, or rather in most cases that our predecessors have done and which we have been hesitant about repairing. To try to undo that damage means questioning our resident myths, it means going a little against the grain of the particular tribe to which we are attached. It

means getting used to and trying to accredit the assumption that the other tribe is not actually either more wicked or more foolish than one's own.[16]

There remains only the question of what will O'Brien's legacy be. In the wake of one who was so certain and extreme, we might think of balancing all, while bringing all to mind. How we deal with O'Brien will determine the effect of that legacy. With the historical texts themselves we can only be wary. With the *impact* of this public intellectual the response is less certain. In the final analysis there is a lot to deal with. When we consider the reverberations of 'the siege' argument, we see a recognition of the unionist community's right to self-determination. If we look at the impact of his writings on legitimacy, we can see a re-evaluation of our history. We can also see a moral block on the unification of Ireland. Connected to this we can perceive a distancing of the two nationalist communities in Ireland. In the O'Brien reflex of disapproval of ambivalence, we can feel at first hand one of the tenets of the Republic's politics especially in the 1980s and 1990s. In the society of that Republic, we can experience the drift of his writings on religion in a more secular state. In all this O'Brien has had a signal influence. His legacy then in terms of his contribution to the Irish nation is that he has shaped twentieth-century Ireland like few others have. Paradoxically he is similar to other architects of our national intellect, Pearse and de Valera. Like them, his epitaph is the aftermath.

NOTES

1. Isaiah Berlin, letter to O'Brien, quoted in Conor Cruise O'Brien, *The Great Melody* (London, 1992), p.609.
2. Look at how the conclusions to both, *1880–90* (Oxford, 1957), and O'Brien's essay on Tim Healy, 'Timothy Michael Healy' in *The Shaping of Modern Ireland* (London, 1960), contain the expression 'as I do'. O'Brien's first ever publication was an article called 'Parnell and Tim Healy'. See *The Irish Times*, 8 January 1944.
3. For a report on this conference and the incendiary contribution of O'Brien, and the apoplectic response it drew, see *The Irish Times*, 7 April 1938; *Irish Press*, 7 April 1938; and *Irish Weekly Independent*, 9 April 1938. He went as the Trinity College delegate and denounced Franco and his 'fascist clique' which in Ireland of that day was a deeply unpopular view, especially for the rural Labour party TDs.
4. Francis Sheehy Skeffington to Hanna Sheehy Skeffington, 20 December 1913, SSP, NLI, MS 40,463/4.
5. Conor Cruise O'Brien, *Camus* (London, 1970), p.83.
6. 'Unhappy and at Home', interview by Seamus Deane in *Crane Bag* 1, 1 (1977), pp.62–4.
7. Statement on 'Church and State' by Dr Conor Cruise O'Brien TD, Minister for Posts and Telegraphs delivered to Irish Association of Civil Liberty, 28 February 1977. P82/327 (10).
8. Conor Cruise O'Brien, *Maria Cross* (London, 1953), p.235.
9. Conor Cruise O'Brien, 'Press Freedom and the Need to Please', in *Passion and Cunning* (London, 1988), p.324.

10. O'Brien, *Maria Cross*, p.vii.
11. Conor Cruise O'Brien, 'The Catholic Church and the IRA', in *Herod* (London, 1978), pp.99–103.
12. O'Brien, 'American Aid to Freedom Fighters', in *Herod*, p.48.
13. O'Brien, *States of Ireland* (London, 1972), p.158.
14. Conor Cruise O'Brien, 'The Embers of Easter 1916–1966', *The Irish Times*, 7 April 1966.
15. O'Brien, 'Shades of Republicans', in *Herod*, p.135.
16. 'Address by the Minister for Posts and Telegraphs, Dr Conor Cruise O'Brien at a meeting with Northern Ireland Journalists in Gresham Hotel, Dublin, 4th Dec 1975'. O'Brien papers, UCD, P82/312(3).

Select Bibliography

Archives

National Archives, Dublin
Department of Foreign Affairs
Confidential Reports Series
Council of Europe and UN Series
Embassy Series: Paris; Permanent Mission to the United Nations; Washington, DC
United Nations Series
Secretary's Series: P, PS, S Files

National Library of Ireland
Denis Devlin Papers
Leslie Daiken Papers
Eilís Dillon Papers
Frank Gallagher Papers
Rosamund Jacob Papers
Matthew O'Mahony Papers
Seán O'Mahony Papers
The Sheehy Skeffington Papers

UCD Archives
Conor Cruise O'Brien Papers
Frank Aiken Papers

Trinity Archives
Frederick H Boland Papers
Theo Moody Papers
Joseph Campbell Papers
Hubert Butler Papers

New York University
Albert Schweitzer Professor Papers

Personal Interviews

Dr Conor Cruise O'Brien
Mrs. Christine Hetherington
Mr. Justin Keating
Mr. James Kirwan
Dr Garret FitzGerald
Dr David Caute
Mr. David Sheehy
Justice Eugene Sheehy

Irish Government Publications

Dáil Éireann, Parliamentary Debates, 1969–77
Seanad Éireann, Parliamentary Debates, 1975–79
Éire-Ireland: The Bulletin of the Irish Department of External Affairs,
    Dublin 1948–61

Newspapers and Magazines
New York Times
TCD: A Miscellany
The Bell
The Cork Examiner
The Freeman's Journal
The Guardian
The Independent (London)
The Irish Independent
The Irish Press
The Irish Times
The Observer
The Times
Washington Post

Books by Conor Cruise O'Brien

[Donat O'Donnell], *Maria Cross: Imaginative Patterns in a Group of Modem Catholic Writers* (London, 1953). Second edition under Conor Cruise O'Brien (London, 1963).
Parnell and His Party, 1880–90 (Oxford, 1957).
(Editor) *The Shaping of Modern Ireland* (London, 1960).

To Katanga and Back: A U.N. Case History (London, 1962).
Writers and Politics (London, 1965).
Murderous Angels (Boston, 1968).
The United Nations: Sacred Drama (London, 1968).
(Edited with William Dean Vanich), *Power and Consciousness* (New York, 1969).
Camus (London, 1970).
(With Maire Cruise O'Brien), *A Concise History of Ireland* (London, 1972).
States of Ireland (London, 1972).
The Suspecting Glance (London, 1972).
Herod: Reflections on Political Violence (London, 1978).
Neighbours: The Ewart-Biggs Memorial Lectures, 1978–1979 (London, 1980).
The Siege: The Saga of Zionism (London, 1986).
God Land: Reflections on Religion and Nationalism (Cambridge, 1988).
Passion and Cunning: Essays on Nationalism, Terrorism and Revolution (London, 1988).
The Great Melody: A Thematic Biography and Commented Anthology of Edmund Burke (London, 1992).
Ancestral Voices (Dublin, 1994).
On the Eve of the Millennium: the Future of Democracy through an Age of Unreason (New York, 1996).
The Long Affair: Thomas Jefferson and the French Revolution 1785–1800 (Chicago, 1996).
Memoir: My Life and Themes (Dublin, 1998).

Articles and Essays by Conor Cruise O'Brien

'Parnell and Tim Healy', *The Irish Times*, 8 January 1944.
[Donat O'Donnell], 'The Fourth Estate: The Irish Independent', *The Bell* (February 1945), pp.386–94.
[Donat O'Donnell], 'The Catholic Press: A Study in Theopolitics', *The Bell*, (April 1945), pp.30–40.
[Donat O'Donnell], 'A Rider to the Verdict', *The Bell* (May 1945), pp.164–7.
[Donat O'Donnell], 'Parnell's Monument', *The Bell* (October 1945), pp.566–73.
[Donat O'Donnell], 'Horizon', *The Bell* (March 1946), pp.1030–8.

[Donat O'Donnell], 'Raffles, Stalin, and George Orwell', *The Bell* (May 1946), pp.167–71.

[Donat O'Donnell], 'The Pieties of Evelyn Waugh', *The Bell* (December 1946), pp.38–49.

[Donat O'Donnell], 'The Unfallen', *Envoy*, I (December 1949), pp.44–50.

[Donat O'Donnell], 'Review of The Irish by Seán O'Faoláin', *Envoy*, I (February 1950), pp.89–90.

[Donat O'Donnell], 'L'Unité de l'Irlande et les Irlandais d'Amerique', *Revue Generale Belge*, 57 (July 1950), pp.1–9.

[Donat O'Donnell], 'Liberty in Ireland', *Spectator* (30 July 1954), pp.152–3.

'My Case', *The Observer*, 10 December, 17 December 1961.

'Passion and Cunning: An Essay on the Politics of WB Yeats', in A.N. Jeffares and K.G.W. Cross (eds), *In Excited Reverie* (London, 1965).

'Michelet Today', in *Writers and Politics* (London, 1965).

'The Embers of Easter 1916–1966', *The Irish Times*, 7 April 1966.

'Ireland, the United Nations and Southern Africa: A Public Lecture Delivered in Dublin, July 20th, 1967'.

'Two-Faced Cathleen', *New York Review of Books*, 29 June 1967, pp.19–21.

'In Quest of Uncle Tom', *New York Review of Books*, 14 September 1967, pp.10–11.

'Inside Biafra', *The Observer*, 8 October 1967.

'Contemporary Forms of Imperialism' (Nashville, 1968).

'Foreword', in John Gerassi, *North Vietnam: a Documentary History* (London, 1968).

'The Irish Question – 1969', *The Irish Times*, 21 January 1969.

'Student Unrest', *The Irish Times*, 10 March 1969.

'What More Must Biafrans Do?', *The Observer*, 11 May 1969.

'Introducing Ireland', in Owen Dudley Edwards (ed.), *Conor Cruise O'Brien Introduces Ireland* (London, 1969).

'Ireland and International Affairs', in Owen D. Edwards (ed.), *Conor Cruise O'Brien Introduces Ireland* (London, 1969).

'Biafra Revisited', *New York Review of Books*, 22 May 1969, pp.15–27.

'Holy War', *New York Review of Books*, 6 November 1969, pp.9–16.

'Imagination and Order: Machiavelli', *Times Literary Supplement*, 13 November 1969.

'What Exhortation?', *Irish University Review*, I (1970), pp.48–61.

'Vulnerable Ireland', *Listener*, 84 (27 August 1970).

'The Gentle Nietzscheans', *New York Review of Books*, 5 November 1970, pp.12–16.

'The Irish Troubles: The Boys in the Back Room', *New York Review of Books*, 8 April 1971, pp.35–9.

'Ballot Box or the Bullet in Northern Ireland', *The Times*, 14 August 1971.

'Ireland: The Smell of Civil War', *The Observer*, 12 September 1971.

'Violence in Ireland: Another Algeria?', *New York Review of Books*, 23 September 1971, pp.17–19.

'Little Hope Now of Help from Dublin', *The Observer*, 28 November 1971.

'The Green Card and Mr. Wilson', *The Observer*, 28 November 1971.

'Celebrating Patriotic Violence', *The Observer*, 12 December 1971.

'Thoughts on Commitment', *Listener*, 86 (16 December 1971), pp.834–6.

'A Global Letter', *Forum*, February 1972, p.22.

'Different Roads to the Cemetery', *The Observer*, 6 February 1972.

'Northern Ireland, its Past and its Future', *Race*, 14 (1972), pp.11–20.

'Ireland: Dying for Bones', *New York Review of Books*, 25 January 1973, pp.36–9.

'Shades of Republicans', *The Irish Times*, 27 March 1975.

'Politics and the Poet', *The Irish Times*, 21 and 22 August 1975.

'Eradicating the Tragic Heroic Mode', *The Irish Times*, 22 August 1975, p.10.

'A Slow North-east Wind', *Listener* 94 (25 September 1975), pp.404–5.

Address to Historical Society, Portora Royal School, Enniskillen, 8 December 1975. O'Brien Papers, UCD, P82/314.

'Reflections on Terrorism', *New York Review of Books*, 16 September 1976, pp.44–8.

'Nationalism and the Reconquest of Ireland', *Crane Bag* I, 2 (1977), pp.8–13.

'Liberty and Terror', The Cyril Foster Lecture delivered at University of Oxford, 6 May 1977.

'The Anti-Politics of Simone Weil', *New York Review of Books*, 12 May 1977, pp.23–8.

'What the Irish Voters Didn't Want to Know', *The Observer*, 26 June 1977.

'Liberalism in Ireland', *Sunday Press* (25 September 1977), p.2.

'Two Edmund Burkes?', *New York Review of Books*, 29 September 1977, pp.3–7.

'Nationalism and the Reconquest of Ireland', *The Crane Bag*, 1, 2 (1977), pp.8–13.

'American Aid to Freedom Fighters?', in *Herod: Reflections on Political Violence* (London, 1978).

'Liberty and Terror', in *Herod: Reflections on Political Violence* (London, 1978).

'Decade of Violence', *The Sunday Times*, 19 and 26 Augusts 1979.

'Hands Off', *Foreign Policy* 37 (Winter 1979–80), pp.32–4.

The Press and the World: the Haldane Memorial Lecture (London, 1980).

Why Did the Irish Want Home Rule? [video recording; Sussex video] (London, 1981).

'The Protestant Minority: Within and Without', *The Crane Bag* 5 (1982), pp.46–9.

'Parnell and his Party, Reconsidered', *University Publishing* (Spring 1981), p.7.

'Blueshirts and Quislings', *Magill*, 4 (June 1981), pp.15–16.

'Ireland: the Shirt of Nessus', *New York Review of Books*, 29 April 1982, pp.30–3.

'*Religion and Politics*: 10th Annual Convocation Lecture', 9 May 1983 (NUU, 1983).

'The Nationalist Trend', *Times Literary Supplement*, 1 November 1985, pp.1230–1.

'Ireland: The Mirage of Peace, *New York Review of Books* (21 April 1986).

'Danger in Indignation', *Times Literary Supplement*, 28 April 1986, p.447.

'The Intellectual in Power' (discussion with John Lukacs), *Salmagundi*, 69 (Summer 1986).

'The Intellectual in the Post-Colonial World: Response and Discussion' with Edward W. Said and John Lukacs, *Salmagundi*, 70–71 (Winter 1986).

'Coping with Terrorism: a Case for International Law', *Center Magazine*, 20, 2 (March 1987).

'Sandinismo: the Nationalist Faith of Nicaragua', *Center Magazine*, 20, 4 (July 1987).

'Nationalism and the French Revolution', in Geoffrey Best (ed.), *The Permanent Revolution: The French Revolution and its Legacy, 1789–1989* (London, 1988).

'An Exalted Nationalism', *The Times*, 28 January 1989.

'The Decline and Fall of The French Revolution', *New York Review of Books*, 15 February 1990, pp.46–51.

'Nationalists and Democrats', *New York Review of Books*, 15 August 1991, pp.31–6.

'Memorial Address', *Cork Review* (1991), pp.95–6.

'Foreword', in André Malraux, *The Walnut Trees of Altenburg*, translated by W. Fielding (Chicago, 1991).

'Foreword', in Andree Sheehy Skeffington, *Skeff: The Life of Owen Sheehy Skeffington, 1909–1970* (Dublin, 1991).

'Foreword', in Frank Callnan, *The Parnell Split 1890–1891* (Cork, 1992).

'Foreword', in Susan Dunn, *The Death of Louis XVI* (Princeton, 1994).

Memoir: My Life and Themes (Dublin, 1998).

'My Time at Trinity College', *The Recorder: Journal of the Irish-American Historical Society* (Spring 2000).

Secondary Sources - Writings on O'Brien

Akenson, D.H., *Conor: A Biography of Conor Cruise O'Brien.* 2 Vols: Biography and Anthology (Montreal, 1994).

Avis, Patricia, *Playing the Harlot* (London, 1996).

Bailyn, Bernard, 'Sally and her Master: the Evolving Views of Thomas Jefferson on Slavery, Race and the French Revolution', *Times Literary Supplement* (14 November 1996), pp.3–4.

Barnard, Toby, 'An Abrasive Palesman: Conor Cruise O'Brien and Modern Ireland', *Times Literary Supplement*, 16 December 1994.

Barratt, Michael, 'Jokes and Peace – Conor Cruise O'Brien in Conversation with Michael Barratt', *Listener*, 79 (30 May 1968).

Browne, Terence, *Ireland: A Social and Cultural History 1922–2002* (London, 2004).

Cosgrave, Patrick, 'Yeats, Fascism and Conor O'Brien', *London Magazine*, 7 (July 1967).

Crick, Bernard, 'Great Rogue Elephant', *New Statesman and Society*, 8 (31 March 1995).

Deutsch, Richard and Vivien MacGowan, *Northern Ireland 1968–1973: A Chronology of Events* (Belfast, 1973).

Dunne, Tom, 'Unchained Melody', *The Irish Review*, 13 (Winter 1992/93) pp.165–9.

Eagleton, Terry, 'The Last Jewish Intellectual', *New Statesman*, 133 (29 March 2004).

English, Richard and Joseph Morrison Skelly (eds), *Ideas Matter: Essays in Honour of Conor Cruise O'Brien* (Dublin, 1998).

Fennell, Desmond, *Heresy: The Battle of Ideas in Modern Ireland* (Belfast, 1993).

Garvin, Tom, 'Imaginary Cassandra?:Conor Cruise O'Brien as public intellectual in Ireland', *Irish University Review: a Journal of Irish Studies*, 37, 2 (Autumn/Winter 2007).

Gellner, Ernest, 'The Sacred and the National', in *Encounters with Nationalism* (Oxford, 1994), pp.59–73.

Gordenker, Leon, 'Conor Cruise O'Brien and the Truth about the United Nations', *International Organization*, 23, 4 (Autumn 1969), pp.897–913.

Hickey, Des and Gus Smith (eds), *A Paler Shade of Green* 'Cruise O'Brien: The Playwright Politician' (London, 1972).

Hitchens, Christopher, 'Creon's Think-tank', in *Prepared for the Worst* (London, 1989), pp.40–54.

Holland, Mary, 'Conor Cruise O'Brien and the Church', *New Statesman* (30 April 1976), pp.559–60.

Jordan, Anthony, *To Laugh or to Weep: a Biography of Conor Cruise O'Brien* (Dublin, 1994).

'An Interview with Conor Cruise O'Brien', *20th Century Studies: Ireland* (November 1970), pp.94–101.

Kenny, Mary, 'Honouring the GLI', *The Spectator* (8 November 1997), p.19.

Kiberd, Declan, *Inventing Ireland* (London, 1995).

Kidd, Colin, 'Sing Tantara', *London Review of Books*, 19, 20 (30 October 1997).

Laqueur, Walter, 'An Irish Statesman and Writer', *Partisan Review*, LXVIII, 2 (2001).

Lloyd, J., 'Alone with his Views and Mind', *Financial Times*, 10 April 1999.

Lysaght, D.R., *End of a Liberal: The Literary Politics of Conor Cruise O'Brien* (Dublin, 1976).

Madigan, Timothy J, 'A Founding Father's Feet of Clay: Interview with Conor Cruise O'Brien', *Free inquiry*, 18, 2 (Spring 1998).

McCormack, W.J., 'The Mystery of the Clarity of Conor Cruise O'Brien', in *The Battle of the Books: Two Decades of Irish Cultural Debate* (Dublin, 1986).

McCormack, W.J., 'The Historian as Writer or Critic? Conor Cruise O'Brien and his Biographers', *Irish Historical Studies*, 30, 117 (1996), pp.111–19.

McNally, Mark, 'Conor Cruise O'Brien's Conservative Anti-Nationalism: Retrieving the Postwar European Connection', *European Journal of Political Theory*, 7 (2008), pp.308–30.

Morgan, David Gwynn, 'Nationalisms and O'Brien', *The Irish Review*, 6 (Spring 1989), pp.128–30.

Murphy, John A., 'Further Reflections on Irish Nationalism', *The Crane Bag*, 1 & 2 (1978), pp.304–11.

Murphy, Richard, *The Kick* (London, 2002).

O'Connor Lysaght, D.R., *End of a Liberal: The Literary Politics of Conor Cruise O'Brien* (Dublin, 1978).

O'Glaisne, Risteard, *Conor Cruise O'Brien agus an liobralachas* (Dublin, 1974).

O'Hagan, A., 'Heavy Cruiser, Loose Cannon', *The Guardian*, 28 November 1998.

O'Toole, Fintan, 'The Life and Times of Conor Cruise O'Brien', *Magill*, 9 (April, May and June 1986).

Pyle, Fergus, 'Profile' [interview], *The Irish Times* (Weekend), 12 September 1992.

Sampson, Denis, 'Passion and Suspicion: an Approach to the Writings of Conor Cruise O'Brien', *Éire-Ireland: the Canadian Journal of Irish Studies*, 2, (December 1976).

Thompson, E.P., 'Review of *The Great Melody*', *Times Literary Supplement*, 4 December 1992, pp.3–4.

Walsh, Maurice, 'A Talent to Offend', *New Statesman* (1 January 1999), pp.45.

Wheatcroft, Geoffrey, 'Terror, Law and Press Freedom: an Interview with Conor Cruise O'Brien', *Spectator*, 4 December 1976.

Wheatcroft, Geoffrey, 'The Most Hated Man in Ireland', *Spectator*, 7 January 1995.

Wheatcroft, Geoffrey, 'Ethnic Cleansing in the Free State', *New Statesman*, 11 (10 July 1998).

Wheatcroft, Geoffrey, 'The Press and the Swinish Multitude', *New Statesman*, 15 (21 January 2002).

Young-Breuhl, Elisabeth, Robert Hogan and Joanne L. Henderson, *Conor Cruise O'Brien: An Appraisal and a Checklist* (Newark, DE, 1974).

Secondary Sources – General

Acton, Lord, *Essays in The Liberal Interpretation of History,* edited by W.H. McNeill (Chicago, 1967).

Alter, Peter, 'Symbols of Irish Nationalism', in Alan O' Day (ed.), *Reactions to Irish Nationalism* (London, 1987).

Alter, Peter, *Nationalism* (London, 1989).

Anderson, Benedict, *Imagined Communities: Reflections on the Origin and Spread of Nationalism* (London, 1983).

Arnold, Bruce, *Haughey: His Life and Unlucky Deeds* (London, 1993).

Aurelius, Marcus, *Meditations,* trans. George Long (Buffalo, 1991).

Bardon, Jonathan, *History of Ulster* (Belfast, 1992).

Barnard, F.M., *Self Direction and Political Legitimacy: Rousseau and Herder* (Oxford, 1988).

Beckett, J.C., *The Making of Modern Ireland* (London, 1966).

Beetham, David, *Issues in Political Theory: The Legitimation of Power* (Basingstoke, 1991).

Berlin, Isaiah, *Against The Current: Essays in the History of Ideas,* ed. and with a bibliography by Henry Hardy (London, 1979).

Berlin, Isaiah, *The Crooked Timber of Humanity: Essays in the History of Ideas* (London, 1990).

Berresford Ellis, Peter, *A History of the Irish Working Class* (London, 1996).

Bew, Paul, *Conflict and Concilliation in Ireland, 1890-1910: Parnellites and Radical Agrarians* (Oxford, 1987).

Bew, Paul, *Ideology and the Irish Question: Ulster Unionism and Irish Nationalism 1912–1916* (Oxford, 1994).

Blanshard, Paul, *The Irish and Catholic Power: an American Interpretation* (London, 1954).

Bowyer Bell, J, *The Secret Army: A History of the IRA, 1916–1979* (Dublin, 1980).

Boyce, George, *Nationalism in Ireland* (London, 1992, rev. edn).

Brady, Ciaran (ed.), *Interpreting Irish History: The Debate on Historical Revisionism* (Dublin, 1994).

Burke, Edmund, *Reflections on the Revolution in France.* Edited with an introduction and notes by J.G.A Pocock (Indianapolis, 1987).

Cairns, David and Shaun Richards, *Writing Ireland, Colonialism, Nationalism and Culture* (Manchester, 1988).

Callnan, Frank, *The Parnell Split 1890–91* (Cork, 1992).

Chatterjee, Partha, *Nationalist Thought and the Colonial World: A Derivative Discourse* (Minneapolis, 1993).

Chomsky, Noam, *American Power and the New Mandarins* (New York, 1969), pp.23–4, 28.

Coffey, Diarmuid and Francis Cruise O'Brien, *Proposals for an Irish Settlement. Being a Draft Bill for the Government of Ireland* (Dublin, 1917).

Cole, Robert, *A.J.P. Taylor: The Traitor Within the Gates* (London, 1993).

Collingwood, R.G., *The Idea of History* (Oxford, 1993).

Collini, Stefan, *Public Moralists Political Thought and Intellectual Life in Britain* (Oxford, 1991).

Corish, Patrick, *The Irish Catholic Experience: A Historical Survey* (Dublin, 1985).

Cruise O'Brien Sheehy, Kathleen, *Luathscríbinn Gregg, [le] Caitlín níc Shíothaigh. Gregg Shorthand Adapted to Irish* , with a Foreword by John F. Burke (London, 1928).

Cullingford, Elizabeth Butler, *Yeats, Ireland and Fascism* (London, 1981).

Darby, John, *Conflict in Northern Ireland: The Development of a Polarised Community* (Dublin, 1976).

Devlin, Denis, *The Complete Poems of Denis Devlin*, edited and with an Introduction by J.C.C. Mays (Dublin, 1989).

Dickson, D., D. Keogh and K. Whelan (eds), *The United Irishmen* (Dublin, 1993).

Edwards, O.D. (ed.), *Conor Cruise O'Brien Introduces Ireland* (London, 1969).

Edwards, O.D. *The Sins of Our Fathers* (Dublin, 1970).

Edwards, O.D. and F. Pyle (eds), *1916: The Easter Rising* (London, 1968).

Edwards, Ruth Dudley, *Patrick Pearse: the Triumph of Failure* (London, 1977).

Eliot, T.S., *Notes Towards a Definition of Culture* (London, 1948).

English, Richard, *Ernie O'Malley: IRA Intellectual* (Oxford, 1998).

English, Richard, *Armed Struggle: a History of the IRA* (London, 2003).

English, Richard, *Irish Freedom: the History of Nationalism in Ireland*

(London, 2006).

Fanning, Ronan, '"The Rule of Order": Eamon de Valera and the IRA 1923–1940', in J.P. O'Carroll and J.A. Murphy (eds), *De Valera and his Times* (Cork, 1983).

FitzGerald, Garret, 'The Significance of 1916', *Studies*, 55 (1966).

FitzGerald, Garret, *Towards A New Ireland* (Dublin, 1972).

Fennell, Desmond, *The Revision of Irish Nationalism* (Dublin, 1989).

Foster, R.F., *Paddy and Mr. Punch: Connections in Irish and English History* (London, 1993).

Garvin, Tom, *The Evolution of Irish Nationalist Politics* (Dublin, 1981).

Goldring, Maurice, *Faith of our Fathers: The Formation of Irish Nationalist Ideology 1890–1920* (Dublin, 1982).

Goldring, Maurice, *Pleasant the Scholars Life: Irish Intellectuals and the Construction of the Irish Nation-State* (London, 1993).

Griffith, Gareth, *Socialism and Superior Brains: The Political Thought of Bernard Shaw* (London, 1995).

Harkness, D.W., *Northern Ireland Since 1920* (Dublin, 1983).

Hathman, Richard.E., 'Legitimacy', in Robert. E. Godin, and P. Pettit (eds), *A Companion to Political Philosophy* (Oxford, 1993).

Himmelfarb, Gertrude, *Victorian Minds* (London, 1968).

Horgan, John, *Irish Media: a Critical History since 1922* (London, 2001).

Horgan, John, *Broadcasting and Public Life: RTÉ News and Current Affairs 1925–1997* (Dublin, 2004).

Huizinga, Johan, *Homo Ludens: A Study of the Play-element in Culture* (Boston, 1955).

Hutchinson, John and Anthony Smith, *Nationalism* (Oxford, 1994).

Jackson, Alvin, *Home Rule: An Irish History* (Oxford, 2003).

Jordan, Anthony, *To Laugh or To Weep* (Dublin, 1994).

Keane, Elizabeth, *Seán MacBride* (Dublin, 2007).

Kedourie, Elie, *Nationalism* (London, 1985 edn).

Kee, Robert, *The Green Flag* (London, 1972).

Kettle, Tom, *The Day's Burden* (Dublin, 1910).

Kiberd, Declan, *Anglo-Irish Attitudes* [Field Day Pamphlets, No. 6] (Derry: Field Day 1984).

Kiberd, Declan, *Inventing Ireland* (London: Jonathan Cape 1995), pp.558–61.

Klein, Alexander (ed.), *Dissent, Power and Confrontation* (New York, 1971).

Larkin, Emmet, *The Roman Catholic Church in Ireland and the Fall of Parnell 1888–91* (Liverpool, 1975).

Lawrence, R.J., *The Government of Northern Ireland: Public Finance and Public Services 1921–64* (Oxford, 1965).

Lecky, W.E.H., *Clerical Influences: An Essay on Irish Sectarianism and English Government*, edited and with an Introduction by W.E.G. Lloyd and F. Cruise O'Brien (Dublin, 1911).

Lee, J.J., *Ireland 1912–1985: Politics and Society* (Cambridge, 1989).

Lee, J.J., *The Modernisation of Irish Society 1848–1918* (Dublin, 1973).

Levenson, Leah, *With Wooden Sword: A Portrait of Francis Sheehy-Skeffington, Militant Pacifist* (Dublin, 1983).

Lyons, F.S.L., *Culture and Anarchy in Ireland 1880–1939* (Oxford, 1980).Lyons, F.S.L., *Ireland since the Famine* (London, 1971).

MacDonagh, Oliver, *The Union and its Aftermath* (London, 1979 edn).

MacDonagh, Oliver, *States of Mind* (London, 1983).

MacDonagh, Oliver, W.F. Mandle and PauricTravers (eds), *Irish Culture and Nationalism, 1750–1950* (London, 1983).

MacDonagh, Oliver, 'Ambiguity in Nationalism: The Case of Ireland', in Ciaran Brady (ed.), *Interpreting Irish History: The Debate on Irish Revisionism* (Dublin, 1994).

MacManus, F. (ed.), *The Years of the Great Test, 1926–1939* (Cork, 1967).

MacPherson, C.B., *Burke* (Oxford, 1980).

Mansergh, Nicholas, *The Irish Question 1840–1921* (London, 1965).

McCann, Eamon, *War and an Irish Town* (London, 1974).

McGarry, Fearghal (ed.), *Republicanism in Modern Ireland* (Dublin, 2003).

Miller, D.W. *Church, State and Nation in Ireland 1898–1921* (Dublin, 1973).

Moody, T.W., *The Ulster Question 1603–1973* (Dublin, 1974).

Moran, D.P., *The Philosophy of Irish Ireland* (Dublin, 1907).

Murphy, John A., 'Further Reflections on Irish Nationalism', *The Crane Bag* 2 (1978).

Nabokov, Vladimir, *The Gift* (London, 1963).

Ni Dhonnchadha, and Theo Dorgan (eds), *Revising the Rising* (Derry, 1991).

O'Brien, Francis, *Co-operation in Ireland* (Manchester, 1921).

O'Brien, Francis, *Co-operative Mills and Bakeries* (Dublin, 1915).

O'Brien, Francis, with Lionel Smith-Gordon *Starvation in Dublin*

(Dublin, 1917).

O'Brien, Francis, *Co-operation in Many Lands*. Vol. 1 (Manchester, 1919).

O'Connor Lysaght, D.R., *The Lace Curtain: A Magazine of Poetry and Criticism* (1969).

O'Faoláin, Seán, *The Great O'Neill: A Biography of Hugh O'Neill, Earl of Tyrone,1550–1616* (London, 1942).

O'Faoláin, Seán, *King of the Beggars: A Life of Daniel O'Connell* (Dublin, 1980).

O'Faoláin, Seán, *The Collected Stories of Seán O'Faoláin* (London, 1980).

O'Faoláin, Seán, *The Irish* (Harmondsworth, 1980).

Oakeshott, Michael, *Rationalism in Politics and Other Essays* (London, 1967).

O'Day, Alan, *Reactions to Irish Nationalism 1865–1914* (London, 1987).

Paulin, Tom, *Ireland and the English Crisis* (Newcastle upon Tyne, 1984).

Pearse, P., *Political Writings and Speeches* (Dublin, 1966 edn).

Puirséil, Niamh, *The Irish Labour Party: 1922–1973* (Dublin, 2007).

Said, Edward, *Culture and Imperialism* (London, 1993).

Sheehy Skeffington, Andree, *Skeff: The Life of Owen Sheehy Skeffington 1909–1970* (Dublin, 1991).

Shaw, Revd. F., 'The Canon of Irish History: a Challenge', *Studies*, LXI (1972), pp.113–53.

Skelly, Joseph Morrison, *Irish Diplomacy at the United Nations 1945–1965: National Interests and the International Order* (Dublin, 1997).

Skinner, Quentin, *The Foundations of Modern Political Thought,* 2 Vols (Cambridge, 1978).

Sophocles, *The Three Theban Plays,* trans. by R. Fagles, edited by B. Knox (Harmondsworth, 1982).

Stewart, A.T.Q., *The Narrow Ground: Aspects of Ulster 1603–1969* (London, 1969).

Sunday Times Insight Team, *Ulster* (Harmondsworth, 1972).

Steiner, George, *Antigones* (Williton, 1979).

Thompson, W.I., *The Imagination of an Insurrection: Dublin, Easter 1916: A Study of an Ideological Movement* (London, 1967).

Ward, Margaret, *Hanna Sheehy Skeffington: A Life* (Cork, 1997).

White, Hayden, *Metahistory: The Historical Imagination in the 19th Century* (Baltimore and London, 1990 edn).

Whyte, J.H., *Church and State in Modern Ireland 1923–1970* (Dublin, 1971).

Wilkinson, Paul, *Terrorism and the Liberal State* (London, 1986).

Williams, T.D. (ed.), *The Irish Struggle 1916–1926* (London, 1966).

Wilson, Edmund, *To the Finland Station: A Study in the Writing and Acting of History* (Harmondsworth, 1972).

Wylie, Paula, *Ireland and the Cold War* (Dublin, 2006).

Yeats, W.B., *Yeats's Poems* (Dublin, 1989).

Index

1798 Rising, 90
Abbey Theatre (Dublin), 24, 25, 27, 32
Acton, Lord, 123, 160–4, 165, 166, 170
Adams, Gerry, 6
Æ (George Russell), 27
agnosticism, 5, 13, 17, 33, 36, 37–8, 47, 49, 181
of CCOB, 37–8, 49, 55, 96, 97, 180–1
Aiken, Frank, 53, 147
Akenson, D.H., 35, 38, 59, 84, 110, 129
Algeria, 68, 69, 70, 71, 72, 75
alienation and dispossession, 5, 6, 7, 60, 166
'American Aid to Freedom Fighters' (Conor Cruise O'Brien essay), 143
Ancestral Voices (Conor Cruise O'Brien, 1994), 4, 5, 110–11, 112, 177
Ancient Order of Hibernians, 22
Anglo-Irish Agreement (1985), viii–ix
Anglo-Irish War, 8, 26, 72, 92, 145, 148
Anouilh, Jean, 167
Antigone (Sophocles), 166–71, 180, 181–2
anti-Semitism, 5
Arendt, Hannah, 82
Arms Trial (1970), 7, 75, 148, 168
Aurelius, Marcus, 166
Avis, Patricia, xi

Beckett, Samuel, 50
The Bell (journal), 57, 58–9, 64
Berlin, Isiah, 173
Biafran crisis, 82
Bird Alone (Seán O'Faoláin, 1936), 60–1
Blanshard, Paul, 99
Boer War (1899–1902), 90–1
Boundary Commission, 92, 144, 147
Bowen-Colthurst, John, 49
Brecht, Bertolt, 167
Broadcasting Amendment Act (1975), 112, 146, 169, 171
Browne, Noel, 102
Burke, Edmund, xii, 4, 75, 82, 85, 120, 146, 153, 160, 161, 162, 175

Camus (Conor Cruise O'Brien, 1970), xiv, 67–8, 73, 120
Camus, Albert, xii, 65, 67–76, 85, 143, 152, 175
Carson, Sir Edward, 118, 119
caste system, institutionalized, concept of, 83, 132, 133, 135, 136
Cathleen ni Houlihan (W. B. Yeats play, 1902), 112–14, 121, 126
Catholicism, 61, 65, 81, 103–4, 179, 180, 181
Fenian and clerical sections, 104–5
Irish state and, xvi, 5, 28, 37, 82, 88, 92, 96–107, 126, 175
in Northern Ireland, 88, 92, 103, 132, 134–6, 156, 166
Kathleen Cruise O'Brien and, 12, 33–4, 36–7, 38, 42, 43, 45, 47

Seán O'Faoláin and, 61, 62, 64
Sheehy family and, 12, 36
'siege' metaphor and, 87–94, 103
violence and, 141
Ceannt, Ronán, 50
censorship, 28, 97, 101, 169–70
Chomsky, Noam, 82
Church and State in Modern Ireland (John Whyte, 1971), 99, 100
'The Church of the People' (Conor Cruise O'Brien essay, 1956 and 1966), 97
La Chute (Albert Camus, 1956), 68, 69, 70–1
civil rights movement, 82, 83, 92, 96, 114, 129, 132, 135–7, 138, 167
Civil War, Irish (1922-3), 5, 8, 27, 92, 144, 145, 147, 148
Clerical Influences (W.E.H. Lecky, 1911 edition), 21, 164
Cold War, 69, 71–2, 73
Collingwood, R.G., 139
colonialism, 68–72, 82, 83–4, 156–7
Come Back to Erin (Seán O'Faoláin, 1940), 61
communism, 5, 58, 69, 72, 73–4, 75
A Concise History of Ireland (Conor Cruise O'Brien and Maire Cruise O'Brien, 1972), 73, 120
Conditions of Employment Act (1934), 11
Congo, vii, xii, 81, 83, 112, 177
Connolly, James, xiii, 19, 51, 52, 53
Conor: A Biography of Conor Cruise O'Brien (D.H. Akenson, 1994), 35
conservatism, 71, 75, 84, 170
contraception, 97, 101, 102, 105, 171
'conversion' of CCOB (early 1970s), viii, xv, 72–3, 75, 83, 84, 96, 107, 110–15, 128, 179
Antigone and, 166–71, 181–2
death of Owen Sheehy Skeffington (1970) and, 54
legitimacy and, 129, 133, 135–6
Conway, Cardinal, 97, 105
Co-operative movement, 25, 26
Corish, Brendan, ix
Corkery, Daniel, 59
Cosgrave, Liam, ix
counterfactuals, 121–2, 143–5
Culhane, Frank, 44
Culhane, Gary, 18
Culture and Anarchy (F.S.L. Lyons, 1980), 157
Cumann na nGaedheal, 92, 101

de Valera, Eamon, ix, 10, 49, 50, 51–2, 101, 146–7, 148, 159, 183
democracy, 4, 7, 91, 98, 101, 130, 134, 148
Derry, siege of (1689), 87
dispossession and alienation, 5, 6, 7, 60, 116
divorce issue, 28, 100–1, 105, 171
Dominion status argument, 22, 26, 38
Dostoyevsky, Fyodor, 63, 165–6
Drennan, William, 93

Easter Rising (1916), 25, 44, 52–4, 61, 91, 111, 115, 117, 119, 121, 143–5, 148
  legitimacy and, 130, 139
  Patrick Pearse and, 111, 118, 119, 141–2, 180
  Sheehy family and, 8, 10, 12, 25
  Sheehy Skeffington family and, 49, 174
  W.B. Yeats and, 113–14, 126
ecumenical movement, 97
education, 48, 50, 51, 105
Ellmann, Richard, 32
'The Embers of Easter 1916-1966' (Conor Cruise O'Brien essay, 1966), 52–5, 64, 83, 115, 144
Encounter magazine, 84
Enlightenment culture, 38, 48, 55
L'Étranger (Albert Camus, 1942), 68
European outlook, 4, 38, 48, 55, 65
External Affairs, Department of, xiii, 11, 53, 54, 57, 58, 81, 110, 116, 174

The Fall of Parnell (F.S.L. Lyons, 1960), 116
Fallon, Brian, vii
Famine, Great, 90
Fanon, Frantz, 157
fascism, 5, 58, 75
Fenianism, 60, 61, 75, 104–5, 140, 141, 143
Fennell, Desmond, 54
Fianna Fáil, 11, 49, 50, 92, 102, 146–9
First World War, 5, 10, 23–4, 25–6, 35, 38, 111, 144, 166
Fisher, Desmond, xiv
Fitzgerald, Desmond, 144
Fitzgerald, Garret, xiv, 144
Flynn, Ed, 110
Foster, Christine (ex-wife of CCOB), 27, 33
Foster, Roy, vii, 130
France, 4, 31, 62–3, 65, 69–70, 81, 121–4, 125, 161–2
Freeman's Journal, 26–7
The French Revolution (Jules Michelet, 1847–53), 122
Front de Libération Nationale (FLN), 70

Gaelic Athletic Association (GAA), 117, 118
Gaelic League, 58, 117, 118–19
Gaelic revival, 32
Gellner, Ernest, 153–4
General Election (1918), 10, 11, 91
Ghana, 82
Gladstone, William, 90, 119, 163
'A Global Letter' (Conor Cruise O'Brien essay, 1972), 136, 137
God Land: Reflections on Religion and Nationalism (Conor Cruise O'Brien, 1988), 82, 153, 154, 159, 161, 177
'GodLand' theme, 5, 177
  see also religion: nationalism and
Gonne, Maud, 44
Government of Ireland Act (1920), 92
'The Great Day' (W.B. Yeats, 1938), 73–4
The Great Melody: A Thematic Biography and Commented Anthology of Edmund Burke (Conor Cruise O'Brien, 1992), xiv, 4
The Great O'Neill: A Biography of Hugh O'Neill, Earl of Tyrone, 1550–1616 (Seán O'Faolain, 1942), 62
Greece of the colonels, 6, 148
Gregg shorthand primer for Irish, 32, 41
Griffith, Arthur, 10, 20, 117

Halligan, Brendan, ix
Haughey, Charles, 7, 82, 107, 129
Healy, Tim, 10, 115–16
Heaney, Seamus, 175

Hegel, Georg Wilhelm Friedrich, 165, 167, 168
Herod: Reflections on Political Violence (Conor Cruise O'Brien, 1978), 128, 129–30, 131, 133, 136, 148, 149, 177
historians, Irish, 8, 28
historical approaches and interpretations, 21–2, 76, 107, 109–26, 138, 139–40, 145–9, 160
  1891–1916 period, 115–21, 140–1
  counterfactuals, 121–2, 143–5
  French tradition, 121–4
  Irish tradition, 124
  Jules Michelet and, 121–3, 124, 125
  nationalism and, 110–20, 125–6, 140–5, 154, 159–65
  personal history of CCOB and, 5, 6, 7–10, 11, 12
  'siege' metaphor, 88–92, 93, 101, 103, 175, 183
  use of evidence and, 112–21, 125, 140
  writing style and, 107, 118, 120–6
  see also legitimacy
Hitchens, Christopher, 170
Hobbes, Thomas, xii, 131
Holland, Mary, xiii, 104, 105–6, 107
Holmes, Erskine, 98
Home Rule Act (1914), 22, 144
Home Rule movement, 11, 14, 20–1, 22, 89, 91, 99, 110–11, 116
L'Homme Revolté (The Rebel, Albert Camus, 1951), 69, 73–5
Horgan, John, xiii–xiv
Hughes, Tommy, 50
Hume, John, 6, 86–7, 93
Hungarian Rising (1956), 69, 70

Indo-China, 69
institutionalized violence theory, 137–9, 149
Ireland, pre-independence, 5, 6, 8, 10–11, 25–6, 115
  1798 Rising, 90
  1891-1916 period, 115–21, 140–1
  Dominion status argument, 22, 26, 38
  Fenianism, 60, 61, 75, 104–5, 140, 141, 143
  First World War and, 5, 10, 23–4, 25–6, 35, 38, 111, 144
  General Election (1918), 10, 11, 91
  Home Rule movement, 11, 14, 20–1, 22, 89, 91, 99, 110–11, 116
  labour unrest, 19, 20, 117
  'siege' metaphor and, 87–91
  see also Easter Rising (1916); Irish Parliamentary Party; Parnell, Charles Stewart
The Irish (Seán O'Faoláin, 1980), 59, 157
Irish Association of Civil Liberties, 94–5
Irish Convention (1917-18), 25–6, 164
Irish Dominion Party, 26, 38
Irish Free State *see* Irish state
Irish Independent, 26–7
Irish language, 17, 32, 35–6, 38–9, 41, 51, 52–3, 179
Irish News Agency, 81
Irish Parliamentary Party, 20, 91, 111, 115–16, 119, 143
  Sheehy family and, 4, 8, 9, 10, 11, 17, 18, 119, 175
The Irish Question: 1840-1921 (Nicholas Mansergh, 1965), 156
Irish Republican Army (IRA), xv, 73, 75, 96, 114, 180, 182
  Fianna Fáil and, 146, 147, 148–9
  Irish state and, 143, 145–9
  legitimation of violence and, 114, 132, 136, 139–40, 142, 143, 145–9
  religion and, 98, 104
  Owen Sheehy Skeffington and, 48, 50, 53, 54
Irish Republican Brotherhood (IRB), 141, 142, 143
Irish state, 27–8, 50–5, 115, 152, 156, 176, 182–3

Arms Trial (1970), 7, 75, 148, 168
Catholicism and religion, xvi, 5, 28, 37, 82, 88, 92,
     96–107, 115, 126, 175, 176–7
  CCOB's criticism of, 28, 52–3, 72, 73, 74, 75, 92, 112,
     114, 133, 168, 175
  Civil War, 5, 8, 27, 92, 144, 145, 147, 148
  Constitution (1922), 53, 99
  Constitution (1937), 92, 128, 147, 179
  IRA and, 143, 145–9
  legitimacy and, 132, 139–49, 156, 180
  Mother and Child crisis (1951), 102
  Labour Party
  Protestants in, 21, 43, 100–1
  'siege' metaphor and, 92–5, 103
  the Troubles and, 75, 114, 133, 145–9, 168
  violence and, 114, 132, 139–46
  see also partition
The Irish Statesman, 25, 26, 32
Irish Times, xiv, 4, 7, 11, 14, 49, 86, 144, 146, 174
Irish Transport and General Workers' Union (ITGWU), 19
Irish Volunteers, 24, 111, 144
Israel, vii, xvi, 84, 177, 181, 182

Jacob, Rosamund, 37
Journal of Modern History, 8
journalism, 4, 82, 107, 156, 174, 177
Joyce, James, 9, 12–13, 32, 117
Les Justes (Albert Camus, 1949), 74
justice, 70, 71, 72–3, 75–6

Katanga (Congo), 81, 83, 112, 177
Kearney, Richard, xiv, 47
Kedourie, Elie, 153
Kettle, Andrew, 13
Kettle, Mary (Mary Sheehy), 4, 8, 9, 13, 18, 25, 31, 40
Kettle, Tom, 4, 5, 9–11, 12, 13–14, 18, 23, 24, 44, 116
Kierkegaard, Soren, 167
King Herod Explains (Conor Cruise O'Brien play), 129,
     160
King of the Beggars: A Life of Daniel O'Connell (Seán
     O'Faoláin, 1938), 62
Kirk, Percy, 87

labour disputes, 19, 20, 117, 156
Labour Party, viii, ix, xiii, xiv, 81, 82, 96, 128–9, 155,
     174
Land League, 118
The Leader, 17
Lecky, W.E.H., 20–1, 22, 164, 170
Lee, J.J., 130
legitimacy, xvi–xvii, 74, 85, 129–32, 162, 176, 178,
     180–1, 183
  institutionalized violence theory, 137–9, 149
  Ireland and, 132, 139–49, 156
  Northern Ireland and, 130, 132–9, 145, 147, 148, 149
  violence and, 114, 131, 132–49
Lemass, Seán, 11, 147, 148
Lenin, 121
Leviathan (Thomas Hobbes), 131
liberalism, 4, 82, 152, 165
'Liberty and Terror' (Conor Cruise O'Brien lecture,
     1977), 134, 137
Lynch, Jack, 87, 139, 168
Lyons, F.S.L., 116, 130, 157

MacBride, John, 44
MacEntee, Máire (wife of CCOB), 8, 82
MacEntee, Seán, 8
MacHaughey, Seán, 50
Machiavelli, Niccolo, 89, 90

Macmillan, Harold, vii
Manning, Cardinal, 105
Mansergh, Nicholas, 130, 156
*Maria Cross: Imaginative Patterns in a Group of Modern
     Catholic Writers* (Conor Cruise O'Brien, 1953), 57–8,
     60–4, 176, 177
Markievicz, Countess, 19, 20, 44, 113, 174
Marxism, 133
Masaryk, Jan, 51
Mauriac, Francois, 57, 62–3
McTier, Mrs., 93
'Meditations in Time of Civil War' (W.B. Yeats, 1928), x
Memmi, Albert, 72
Memoir: My Life and Themes (Conor Cruise O'Brien,
     1998), 3, 36, 37, 40, 84
Mercier, Vivian, 58–9
Michelet, Jules, xii, 121–3, 124, 125
'Michelet Today' (Conor Cruise O'Brien article, 1950s),
     121–3, 124
Monteagle, Lord, 39, 43
Moran, D.P., 119
'The Most Hated Man in Ireland' (Geoffrey Wheatcroft
     essay, 1995), 3
Mother and Child crisis (1951), 102
Murderous Angels (Conor Cruise O'Brien play, 1968),
     160
Murphy, Richard, xi
mysticism, 165–6, 180

Nabokov, Vladimir, 5–6
Napoleon Bonaparte, 162
nationalism, 59–65, 72–3, 85, 152–71, 176
  1891–1916 period, 115–21, 140–1
  academic perspectives, 153–4
  Lord Acton and, 160–4, 165, 166, 170
  Antigone, interpretations of, 166–71, 180, 181–2
  CCOB's opposition to, xv, 55, 83, 89, 96, 107,
     110–11, 149–50, 175, 179, 180, 182
  CCOB's support for, 55, 73, 83, 110, 111, 125, 182
  class-based perspectives, 155–6, 158
  as emotional force, 62, 142, 154, 159, 161, 180
  historical approaches and interpretations, 110–20,
     125–6, 140–5, 154, 159–65
  as ideology, 154, 159, 160, 161, 180
  irrationality and, 142, 165–6, 180
  origins of, 154
  post-colonial perspectives, 83, 155, 156–8
  religion and, 5, 61, 62, 64–5, 98, 101, 107, 110,
     152–3, 154–9, 160–1, 164
  romanticism and, 153, 159, 165
  Sheehy family and, 11, 12, 38, 47, 119
  siege metaphor and, 87, 89
  see also Parnell, Charles Stewart
Nazism, 5, 58
*Neighbours: The Ewart-Biggs Memorial Lectures, 1978–
     1979* (Conor Cruise O'Brien, 1980), 135
neo-conservatism, 84
A Nest of Simple Folk (Seán O'Faoláin, 1933), 60, 61
New York Review of Books, 130, 135
New York University, 82, 128, 129, 132, 137, 155, 167,
     170, 174
Newman, Bishop Jeremiah, 82, 106
Nkrumah, Kwame, 82
Northern Ireland, 72–3, 81, 83, 149–50, 155–6, 175–6
  Algerian parallel, 72, 75
  Catholics in, 88, 92, 103, 132, 134–6, 156, 166
  deployment of British troops (1969), 132, 134–5, 168
  institutionalized caste system concept, 83, 132, 133,
     135, 136
  legitimacy and, 130, 132–9, 145, 147, 148, 149

Protestantism *see* Protestantism, Ulster
'siege' metaphor and, 86–94, 103
see also partition; Troubles, the

O'Brien, Conor, 39
O'Brien, Conor Cruise (CCOB)
  academic career, 82, 128, 129, 132, 137, 155, 167, 170, 174
  agnosticism, 37–8, 49, 55, 96, 97, 180–1
  anti-partitionist activities (1950s), viii, 54–5, 72, 81, 109, 110, 111, 112, 169, 174
  childhood and upbringing, 33–45, 47–8
  consequences and, 85
  'conversion' (early 1970s) *see* 'conversion' of CCOB (early 1970s)
  dispossession and alienation, 5, 6, 7, 60, 116
  Enlightenment culture and, 38, 48, 55
  European outlook, 4, 38, 48, 55, 65
  family, 4–14, 17–28, 116, 119, 173, 174, 175, 181
  fiction and poetry, vii, 57, 160
  as historian, xiv, xvi, 8–9, 107, 124–5, 152
  see also historical approaches and interpretations
  journalism, 4, 82, 107, 156, 174, 177
  mugging of at Apprentice Boys march (1970), 112
  nationalism, opposition to, 55, 83, 89, 96, 107, 110–11, 149–50, 175, 179, 180, 182
  nationalism, support for, 55, 73, 83, 110, 111, 125, 182
  Parnell, doctorate and scholarship on, 8–9, 57, 81, 101, 116, 126, 174
  personality and temperament, ix, x–xii, xiii, 22, 59, 177–8, 179–80
  political career *see* political career of CCOB
  public fact and personal memory, 3–5, 116, 119, 120–1, 179
  republican idealism, 49, 52, 54–5, 83
  secularism, xvi, 23, 48–9, 55, 97, 105–6, 165, 171, 174, 180–1
  unionism of, viii, xv, 83, 85, 86, 110, 112, 178–9, 181, 182, 183
  writing talent and style, x, 33, 107, 118, 120–6, 178
O'Brien, Darcy, xi
O'Brien, Francis Cruise (father of CCOB), 13, 14, 17–28, 33, 36, 164, 170, 173, 174, 175
  agnosticism, 5, 17, 33, 36, 37, 38, 47, 49, 181
  death of (1927), 28, 33, 34, 36, 39–42, 44
  debt and extravagance, 19, 20, 27
  Irish language and, 38–9
  literary works, 24–5, 27
  parallels with Conor Cruise O'Brien, 21–3, 24
  political views, 19, 20–1, 38
O'Brien, Kate Cruise (daughter of CCOB), 5
O'Brien, Kathleen Cruise (Kathleen Sheehy, mother of CCOB), 12, 13, 17–19, 20, 28, 31–6, 39–45, 173
  Catholicism, 12, 33–4, 36–7, 38, 42, 43, 45, 47
  death of (1938), 37
  debt and extravagance, 19, 20, 34–5, 41
  Irish language and, 32, 35–6, 38–9, 41
  literary works, 25, 32–3
  teaching career, 32, 41, 42
O'Brien, William, 141
The Observer, 4, 82, 107, 177
O'Casey, Sean, 9
O'Connell, Daniel, 21, 62, 140
O'Connor, D.R. Lysaght, 19
O'Connor, Frank, 58
O'Donnell, Peadar, 50
O'Faoláin, Seán, xii, 7, 49, 57–65, 152, 157, 176, 177
O'Hegarty, P.S., 113
O'Leary, Olivia, xv

O'Moráin, Micheál, 102
Orange Order, 90, 92

pacifism, 13, 23, 49, 50
Parnell, Charles Stewart, 117, 119, 141, 159, 162–4, 165, 180, 182
  CCOB's doctorate and scholarship on, 8–9, 57, 81, 101, 116, 126, 174
  fall of, 9, 90, 101, 115, 120–1, 159
  religion and, 60, 99, 100–1
  Seán O'Faolain and, 60, 61
  Sheehy family and, 9, 11, 13, 175
  siege metaphor and, 88–9, 90
Parnell and His Party, 1880–1890 (Conor Cruise O'Brien, 1957), xiv, xvi, 8–9, 101, 116, 120
'The parnellism of Seán O'Faolain' (Conor Cruise O'Brien essay, 1948), 7, 9, 60–4, 115, 173
partition, 52, 91–2, 110–11, 143, 144, 147, 174, 179
  CCOB and viii, 54–5, 72, 81, 109, 110, 111, 112, 169, 174
Passion and Cunning: Essays on Nationalism, Terrorism and Revolution (Conor Cruise O'Brien essays, 1988), 84, 85
Paulin, Tom, 129
Pearse, Patrick, 51, 52, 75, 111, 141–2, 159, 182, 183
  blood sacrifice and, 53, 74, 121, 141, 142, 180
  Easter Rising (1916) and, 111, 118, 119, 141–2, 144, 180
Peguy, Charles, 57, 63
Penal Laws, 89
Peoples Democracy, 136, 137
La Peste (Albert Camus, 1947), 68–9, 71, 143
Phoenix magazine, xii
Plunkett, Sir Horace, 24, 25–6, 118, 164
Poland, partition of, 161
political career of CCOB, vii, xiii, xiv, 81, 133, 158, 174
  Charles Haughey and, 7, 82, 129
  parliament and, xii, 49, 82, 96, 107, 128–9, 146
Poolbeg Press, 5
post-colonial perspectives, 83, 155, 156–8
Powell, Enoch, viii–ix
Protestantism, Ulster, 94, 99, 101–2, 103–4, 110–11, 114, 156, 170, 175, 176, 180
  'siege' metaphor and, 86–94, 101, 103
  violence and, 92, 132, 138
Protestantism in Irish state, 21, 43, 100–1
A Purse of Coppers (Seán O'Faoláin, 1937), 61

Rathmines Technical Institute, 32, 41
rationalism, 153, 165–6, 180, 181–2
Redmond, John, 10, 23, 51, 118, 141, 143, 144
Reflections on the Revolution in France (Edmund Burke, 1790), 120, 160
religion
  Charles Stewart Parnell and, 60, 99, 100–1
  IRA and, 98, 104
  Irish state and, xvi, 5, 28, 37, 82, 88, 92, 96–107, 115, 126, 175, 176–7
  Irish state, Protestants in, 21, 43, 100–1
  nationalism and, 5, 61, 62, 64–5, 98, 101, 107, 110, 152–3, 154–9, 160–1, 164
  the Troubles and, 97–8, 103–4, 130, 155
  see also Catholicism; Protestantism, Ulster
Republic of Ireland *see* Irish state
Republican Congress (1935-7), 50
republicanism, xv, 6, 12, 48, 49, 50, 51–5, 83, 140, 141–2, 163
  see also Irish Republican Army (IRA); Sinn Féin
'A Rider to the Verdict' (Conor Cruise O'Brien article, 1945), 58–9

Robinson, Lennox, 27
romanticism, 119, 153, 159, 165
Rose, Richard, 155
Rousseau, Jean Jacques, 154
RTÉ, xiii–xiv
Russia, 5–6, 165–6
Ryan, Frank, 50

Sacred Drama (Conor Cruise O'Brien, 1968), 120
Salome and the Wildman (Conor Cruise O'Brien play),
    129
Sandford Park School, 36–7, 42, 49, 81
Sartre, Jean Paul, 69, 71, 73
Schlesinger Jr., Arthur, 84
Schweitzer, Albert, viii
Second World War, 3–4, 6, 58, 68
sectarianism, 21–2, 105–6
secularism, 22–3, 48–9, 55, 155, 165
    of CCOB, xvi, 23, 48–9, 55, 97, 105–6, 165, 171,
      174, 180–1
sexual issues, 60–1, 97, 101, 102, 105, 171
'Shades of Republicans' (Conor Cruise O'Brien essay,
    1975), 146, 148
The Shaping of Modern Ireland (ed. Conor Cruise
    O'Brien, 1960), 9, 116–20
Shaw, George Bernard, 164–5
Sheehy, Bessie, 10, 13
Sheehy, David, 4, 10, 11, 12–13, 14, 17, 18, 25
Sheehy, Eugene, 11, 12, 18, 23, 38
Sheehy, Margaret, 13, 18, 25
Sheehy family, xii, 4, 6, 9–14, 23, 25, 27, 31, 44, 47
    Catholicism and, 12, 36, 152
    Easter Rising (1916) and, 8, 10, 12, 25
    'fall' of, 4, 6, 10–11, 12, 119
    French connection, 65
    Irish Parliamentary Party and, 4, 8, 9, 10, 11, 17, 18,
      119, 175
    nationalism and, 11, 12, 38, 47, 119, 152
    Parnell and, 9, 11, 13, 175
    Kathleen Sheehy marriage and, 13, 14, 17–18, 28
    see also O'Brien, Kathleen Cruise (Kathleen Sheehy,
      mother of CCOB)
Sheehy Skeffington, Andrée, 50
Sheehy Skeffington, Frank, 13, 14, 17–18, 19, 20, 21, 23,
    24, 28
    death of (1916), 44, 49
Sheehy Skeffington, Hanna, 18, 23, 24, 27, 31, 41, 47,
    48, 51
    republicanism and, 4, 11–12, 13, 25, 49, 50, 174
Sheehy Skeffington, Owen, 31, 37–8, 41, 45, 47–55, 81,
    152, 174, 175
'siege' metaphor, xv, 87–94, 101, 103, 175, 183
The Siege: The Saga of Israel and Zionism (Conor Cruise
    O'Brien, 1986), xvi, 3, 82, 87, 175
Sinn Féin, 4, 11, 12, 25, 26, 27, 91, 92, 116, 119
    1921–1970s 'parallels', 134, 145
social class, 8, 10, 13, 35, 38, 100, 117–18, 155–6, 158
Social Democratic and Labour Party (SDLP), 86
socialism, xiii, 13, 48, 51, 55, 81, 82, 155
Sophocles, 166–71, 180, 181–2
South Africa, 177
Soviet Union, 5
States of Ireland (Conor Cruise O'Brien, 1972), xiv, 6, 8,
    65, 72, 86–7, 120, 128, 132, 136, 166, 177
    Camus' influence on, 68, 73, 143
    nationalism and, xv, 85, 89, 155, 157, 159, 165
    religion and, 87–94, 98–107, 155, 156
    siege metaphor, xv, 87–94
Steiner, George, 167, 170
Stephen Hero (James Joyce, 1944), 13

'The Story of Ireland' (Conor Cruise O'Brien 'lost
    book'), viii, 110, 111, 112
Suez crisis (1956), 69, 70
suffragism, 13, 14, 38

Thornley, David, 6
'Timothy Michael Healey' (Conor Cruise O'Brien essay,
    1955), 115–16
To Katanga and Back: A U.N. Case History (Conor
    Cruise O'Brien, 1962), ix, 120, 124, 173
Tone, Wolfe, 75, 89, 140, 141, 159
trade unionism, 19
Trinity College Dublin (TCD), 38, 48, 49, 81, 116, 174
Troubles, the, xii–xiv, xv, 49, 73, 82, 93, 96, 114, 130,
    178
    institutionalized violence theory, 138
    Irish state and, xiii, 75, 114, 133, 145–9, 168
    religion and, 97–8, 103–4, 130, 155

Ulster, 22, 118, 139
    de Valera and, 146–7
    Protestantism *see* Protestantism, Ulster
    'siege' metaphor and, 86–94, 103
    see also Northern Ireland; partition
Ulster Volunteers, 139
Ulysses (James Joyce, 1922), 117
unionism, xv, 86–7, 92, 182, 183
    of CCOB, viii, xv, 83, 85, 86, 110, 112, 178–9, 181,
      182, 183
    see also Protestantism, Ulster
Unionist Party, 92, 134, 182
United Arts Club, 27
United Irish League, 14, 18, 20–1, 23
United Irishmen, 93
United Kingdom Unionist Party (UKUP), vii, 82, 83, 112
The United Nations: Sacred Drama (Conor Cruise
    O'Brien, 1968), 120
United Nations (UN), ix, xiii, 11, 53, 54–5, 81, 83, 120,
    174
United States of America (USA), 82, 128, 129, 132, 137,
    155, 167, 170, 174, 177
University College Dublin (UCD), x–xi, 48, 97

Vietnam War, 82, 129, 132, 170
violence, 74–5, 96, 105, 114, 176
    Camus and, 69–70, 73–5
    institutionalized violence theory, 137–9, 149
    IRA and legitimation of, 114, 132, 136, 139–40, 142,
      143, 145–9
    Ireland and, 114, 139–46
    legitimacy and, 114, 131, 132–49

Walsh, Archbishop, 118
War of Independence, Irish, 8, 26, 72, 92, 145, 148
Weber, Max, 130, 131
West Britons, 119
Wexford Free Press, 19
Wheatcroft, Geoffrey, 3
Whyte, John, 99, 100
Writers and Politics (Conor Cruise O'Brien, 1965), 48,
    71, 75, 83

Yeats, W.B., vii, x, 9, 27, 52, 63, 73–4, 85, 112–14, 117,
    120–1, 126
Young Ireland branch, United Irish League, 14, 18, 20–1

Zionism, 82, 87, 177, 181, 182